Itineraries of Power

Harvard East Asian Monographs 395

Itineraries of Power

Texts and Traversals in Heian and Medieval Japan

Terry Kawashima

Published by the Harvard University Asia Center
Distributed by Harvard University Press
Cambridge (Massachusetts) and London 2016

Printed in the United States of America

The Harvard University Asia Center publishes a monograph series and, in coordination with the Fairbank Center for Chinese Studies, the Korea Institute, the Reischauer Institute of Japanese Studies, and other faculties and institutes, administers research projects designed to further scholarly understanding of China, Japan, Vietnam, Korea, and other Asian countries. The Center also sponsors projects addressing multidisciplinary and regional issues in Asia.

Library of Congress Cataloging-in-Publication Data

Kawashima, Terry, author.
Itineraries of power : texts and traversals in Heian and medieval Japan / Terry Kawashima.
Harvard East Asian monographs ; 395.
Cambridge, Massachusetts : Published by the Harvard University Asia Center, 2016. |
Series: Harvard East Asian monographs ; 395 |
Includes bibliographical references and index.
LCCN 2016001295 | ISBN 978-0-674-97052-6 (hardcover : alk. paper)
Japanese literature—Heian period, 794–1185—History and criticism. | Japanese literature—To 1600—History and criticism. | Power (Social sciences) in literature.
LCC PL726.2 .K394 2016 | DDC 895.609/0014--dc23
LC record available at http://lccn.loc.gov/2016001295

Index by Anne Holmes

♾ Printed on acid-free paper

Last figure below indicates year of this printing
20 19 18 17 16

For Sandy and Kai

Contents

List of Maps

Acknowledgments

The seeds of this book were planted when I was working on my first book, *Writing Margins.* I found that I was repeatedly encountering texts that rendered states of wandering as a marginalizing feature for figures such as late Heian professional female entertainers, even when other texts suggested that such women may not have wandered much at all. This ascribed identity between marginality and movement led me to think about the ways in which motion should be understood less as a descriptive state of being than as an explicit, purposeful trope.

I have many people to thank for their support, input, and advice concerning this project. To begin, I would like to remember H. Richard Okada. His work formed the foundational stance of my scholarship; the combination of rigorous analysis informed by contemporary critical theories, together with his level of deep and virtuosic understanding of premodern texts, is what I strive for but will never attain. I am deeply saddened by his passing and by the loss of a thinker of his caliber.

I feel extremely fortunate to continue receiving advice and encouragement from Edwin A. Cranston, who has been most kind in providing insight into the manuscript, particularly concerning the poetry sections. He also tirelessly combed through my translations and gave me suggestions on how to improve them, although my results continue to be far less elegant than his; I am very grateful for his input.

Many others have helped shape this book, in contexts ranging from conference and presentation venues to less formal conversations. In particular, I would like to extend my gratitude to Sonja Artnzen, Janice Brown, Wiebke Denecke, Charo D'Etcheverry, Matthew Fraleigh, Reginald Jackson, Rebecca Jennison, Edward Kamens, Elizabeth Oyler, Brian Ruppert, Vyjayanthi Selinger, Haruko Wakabayashi, and Tomiko

Yoda. I am especially thankful for the friendship and kind advice provided by Melissa McCormick, who generously located the beautiful cover image. This book benefited greatly from a Japan Foundation Research Fellowship and a Visiting Faculty Fellowship at the Associated Kyoto Program, which together funded my research time in Japan. Closer to home, the Reischauer Institute for Japanese Studies has provided essential library access as well as venues to exchange fresh ideas with colleagues near and far. I would also like to express my heartfelt thanks to the anonymous reviewers of the manuscript; their suggestions were extremely helpful in sharpening the arguments in this book.

I am deeply indebted to the wonderful and tireless editors at the Harvard University Asia Center Publications Program, Bob Graham and Deborah Del Gais. They indulged my many questions and quirky translation habits and were vital in bringing the manuscript to fruition. I would also like to express special thanks to Scott Walker, the digital cartography specialist at the Harvard College Library, who created the terrific maps for this book. He was incredibly patient with and responsive to the many peculiar minutiae I queried. I also owe many thanks to Anthony Lee for the gorgeous cover design, to Maura High for copyediting the manuscript, and to Anne Holmes and Rob Rudnick for indexing the book.

My colleagues at the University of Massachusetts Boston, particularly those in the Departments of Modern Languages, Literatures, and Cultures and Asian Studies, have provided me with much inspiration and moral support, for which I thank them. The offices of the Provost and the Dean of the College of Liberal Arts have consistently encouraged me in my research. I would also like to thank my colleagues at Wesleyan University, in the former Department of Asian Languages and Literatures and the East Asian Studies Program. I learned a great deal from my interactions with them for over a decade. I owe a particular debt to Ellen Widmer, now at Wellesley College, whose mentorship has been crucial in my development as an academic.

Through the many years it has taken to complete this book my family's support has been unwavering. My parents, Sue Atsuko and Toshikuni, have taught me the importance of perseverance and the quest for precision, which were hallmarks of one of my ancestors, Ōtsuki Fumihiko. I also wish to thank my in-laws, Roger, Jessie, Dan, Alexa, and Maia, for their constant cheer and kindness. This book is dedicated to Alexander

Des Forges and Kai Deshima; in their own ways, each has inspired critical thinking and has never failed to remind me of the joys of curiosity. Last but not least, I end these acknowledgments with a second remembrance: of Alison Liebhafsky Des Forges, who for me will forever be a model of intellect, dedication, and compassion.

Note to the Reader

I have chosen to translate *waka* poems by maintaining their *kaminoku* (first verse)–*shimonoku* (second verse) format, instead of dividing them into five separate lines, as is more commonly done. This approach parallels my tendency toward literal translation and my use of slashes to indicate multiple possible meanings in a single original line; I hope these choices, despite the annoyances they may pose the reader, will inspire future analyses and different translations of these texts.

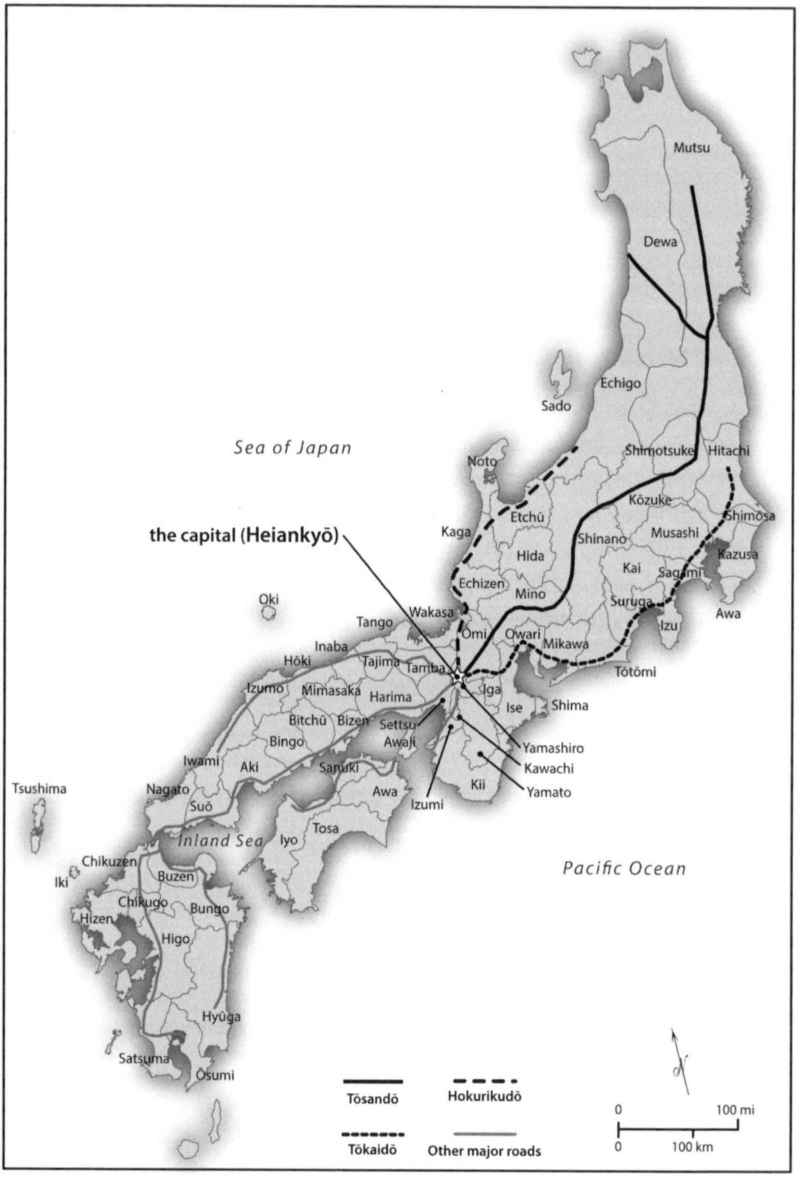

Map 1 Heian and medieval Japan.

INTRODUCTION

Heian and medieval Japan was full of movement: courtiers ventured forth on nocturnal amorous adventures and on imperial outings; official messengers and warriors were dispatched to missions afar; merchants transported their wares between provinces; and religious pilgrims, wandering poets, and traveling performers journeyed across a landscape bustling with traversings from place to place. Movement was not, however, restricted to the physical comings-and-goings of individuals from one geographic point to another. There was also motion at a more symbolic, abstract level, as texts from this period attest; such figures of literary motion include sudden transfers between textual registers and genres within a single piece of writing, and narrative trajectories that shift at a dizzying pace.

This book argues that tropes of movement are crucial in understanding how texts imagine structures of power. Reading through the lens of movement—from gender and political relations at the highest levels of society to the distribution of religious charisma—allows us to focus upon how texts construct complex and multilayered visions of struggle between individuals and groups. Each of the two types of movement I invoke above—that is, depictions of characters going from one place to another, and the mechanics of textual shifts and transfers—offers significant moments for reflection concerning the workings of power. However, when *both* types of movement coexist in a text, such tropic nodes are particularly potent as springboards for the exploration of what those movements might mean, and what they in turn give meaning to. Be it the geopolitical significance of the points of departure and arrival, or a reconceptualization of exact methods through which power is constructed and disseminated across time, space, and stories, textual moments that feature the double presence of literal and literary movements say something particularly important about how a text articulates, promotes, or critiques specific paradigms through which authority is constructed, maintained, and distributed.

Scholars have studied tropes of movement from various angles for decades, if not centuries. In the field of critical theory, attention to figures such as exile, diaspora, and transnational migration in addition to tropes of travel, tourism, and the circulation of goods and people in a globalized economy has produced lively and engaging dialogues. Particularly since the 1990s, theorists have explored various rubrics of movement as moments that can destabilize and hybridize categories such as identity, nation, and imperialism; they have used these rubrics to highlight contestations and negotiations that occur in the process of subject formation under modern global conditions.[1]

My approach in examining movement in premodern Japan is certainly influenced by this body of scholarship, as the chapters to follow should show. What distinguishes this project from much of the work in the categories mentioned above is twofold: first, I am as interested in movements across borders that are metaphorical (such as ones that differentiate between literary genres, or between levels of political power) as I am in those that are physical (characters said to be moving through bounded

1. See, for example, Homi Bhabha's *The Location of Culture*, as well as his introduction to Naficy, *Home, Exile, Homeland*; Edward Said's *Culture and Imperialism*, especially the chapter "Movements and Migrations"; Arjun Appadurai's *Modernity at Large*; and James C. Scott, *The Art of Not Being Governed*, specifically, the idea of Zomia as a space that renders possible movements of peoples between the "hills" and dynastic centers that cross modern national boundaries. With reference to East Asia, Rey Chow's numerous writings, such as the classic *Writing Diaspora*, rigorously theorize diaspora and the construct of "modern China"; Masao Miyoshi interrogates terminologies such as "globalization" and "transnationalism" in works such as "A Borderless World?: From Colonialism to Transnationalism and the Decline of the Nation-State" (reprinted in Cadzyn, *Trespasses*, 127–50); Aihwa Ong's *Flexible Citizenship* pursues the relationship between transnational capitalism, migration, and logics of culture; more recently, Shih Shu-mei argues for a focus on the "scattering of capitalism" that allows for explorations—beyond the global-local dichotomy—of how visual images travel between places and differently signify (*Visuality and Identity*).

spaces); this book's examination of movement as a literary technique adds a further dimension to the study of motion articulated in works that analyze movements of a range of material beings, from humans to inanimate objects. Second, when figures move across geographic spaces in the texts I am about to examine, the demarcations are not bound by the rules of and identities associated with modern nation-states.

Indeed, what I hope to explore is the workings of movement that are not limited to questions such as ethnicity and citizenship that we find in the modern period. Units of governance are a complex topic in premodern Japan: the Heian and medieval term *kuni* denotes both "country" and "province"; the line between hierarchies of rulership is thus linguistically blurred from the beginning. Take, for example, a fourteenth-century text I explore in detail in the fourth chapter of this book. In this narrative, entitled "Suwa engi" (The origins of Suwa), the term *kuni* is repeatedly attached to both Nihon ("Japan," the larger unit of governance) and names of provinces (smaller units into which Nihon is divided). Furthermore, the protagonist finds himself traveling in a mysterious underground world, which is divided into many *kuni*; the peoples and practices of these underground *kuni* are consistently contrasted with those of Nihon, rather than opposed to particular provinces within Nihon—suggesting that at certain times, there is a strategic awareness of difference between the various types of *kuni.* Definitions of nationhood, divisions of governance, and community identities, therefore, are here slippery and relational. I would argue that such slipperiness is not necessarily an inalienable feature of a "premodern condition" that is radically different from a modern one (consider, for example, the complex relationships between states, territories, Native American nations, and the federal government in the contemporary American context); rather, the case of premodern Japan presents an opportunity to consider how tropes of movement symptomatically alert readers to various modes of power formation, regardless of how such powers are specifically configured and bounded at particular times.

Among scholars of premodern Japan, tropes of movement have received significant attention for many years. Scholars have developed ways to categorize and theorize types of movement, particularly in the field of *minzokugaku* ("folk" studies); two especially notable examples are *kishu ryūritan* and *hyōhaku.* The former term, coined by Orikuchi

Shinobu (1887–1953), refers to narratives that feature nobility in exile: famous cases include Ariwara no Narihira (825–80), whose trip eastward as related in *Ise monogatari* (Tales of Ise; dates and author unknown, ca. 9th–10th century) set a poetic precedent for centuries to follow, as I note in more detail in the third chapter of this book; the fictional Prince Genji of *Genji monogatari* (The tale of Genji; Murasaki Shikibu, ca. early 1000s), who wandered through Suma and Akashi before returning to the capital to climb his way back to prosperity; and mythical imperial ancestors such as Susano'o and Ōkuninushi, who suffered expulsion from divine realms according to texts such as *Kojiki* (Records of ancient matters, ca. 712) and *Nihon shoki* (Chronicles of Japan, ca. 720). The significance of such journeying nobles has been the topic of reflection for decades; Orikuchi was interested in potential resonances between the narrative contents of *kishu ryūritan* and the supposed lifestyles of wandering performers who popularized some of these tales.[2] Others, meanwhile, focused on the narrative of trials and tribulations, understanding *kishu ryūritan* as mostly temporary banishments and explaining the travels in economic terms, as repentant payments for past wrongdoings and/or the acquisition of greater charisma through suffering.[3]

Hyōhaku, on the other hand, tends to refer to more extended or even permanent states of motion on the part of less aristocratic members of society; examples range from traveling poets such as Saigyō (1118–90) and Bashō (1644–94) to groups and categories of peoples who are perceived as leading nomadic lifestyles, such as the wandering performers in Orikuchi's theories. The subjects of the *hyōhaku* paradigm tend to be romanticized for their mobility: literary-minded wanderers have been heralded as jour-

2. Orikuchi sought to render analogous the fates of tragic exiles with those of wandering performers who may have had a role in propagating narratives about these figures. See Takahashi Tōru, "Kishu ryūritan no kōzō." For further detailed discussions of Orikuchi's notion of *kishu ryūritan*, see Stockdale, *Imagining Exile in Heian Japan*, chap. 1. Similarly, Hasegawa Masaharu reads Ariwara no Narihira's eastward journey as a sign of the protagonists' liminal state, belonging neither to the capital nor to the east (*Kyōkai kara no hassō*).

3. A classic example of this theory can be found in Mitani Eiichi's *Monogatari shi no kenkyū*, 82–88 and 394–403. The trials-and-tribulations paradigm remains popular; for example, the most prevalent reading of the "Suwa engi," the topic of the fourth chapter of this book, is that the hero undergoes extensive and difficult travels in order to qualify for divinity (see, for example, Henmi, "Kōga no Saburō no hyōhaku," 452–55).

neymen in search of some goal, either philosophical or artistic,[4] while traveling performers and other wanderers are often celebrated for their subversive possibilities due to their apparent social ostracization and/or divine associations.[5]

All of these scholarly examinations suggest the extent to which specific types of motion have been recognized as significant features of the premodern literary landscape: when a person or people are in motion, we should pay attention to what such motion may mean. What I wish to do in this book is to show that movement is, in fact, a vital trope in an even wider sense, beyond what the specific paradigms of *kishu ryūritan* or *hyōhaku* imply. When we expand the definition of movement beyond mere varieties of travel—whether temporary or permanent, noble or base—to include more abstract forms of motion, particularly those pertaining to changes in literary techniques and shifting narrative arcs, we find evocative examples of movement in both expected and unexpected textual places. In fact, I will suggest that tropes of movement that belong to this broader category invariably point to struggles for authority and legitimacy beyond the most apparent; tropes of movement are signposts that invite investigations and reconsiderations of how power functioned during the periods in which the texts were produced.

Recent scholarship on Japan has seriously questioned the undisputed supremacy of the capital, which was established in the location of present-day Kyoto in 794 at the beginning of the Heian period (and thus called the Heiankyō) and remained there until the late nineteenth century; scholars have also reconsidered the effectiveness of centralized governance throughout the history of Japan. Amino Yoshihiko, one of the pioneering critics of the discourse of a unified premodern Japan under the

4. See, for example, Mezaki Tokue's *Hyōhaku*, which positions the state of *hyōhaku* as something neither religious nor political, but "purely literary/artistic"; he argues that this artistic pursuit is a search for the "meaning of life" (24).

5. As noted above, Orikuchi's work is the locus classicus for this stance. More recent examples include *Hyōhaku to teichaku* (vol. 6 of *Nihon minzoku bunka taikei*), which is edited by Amino Yoshihiko and contains numerous essays on transportation and other peoples who travel; Yamaori Tetsuo and Miyata Noboru's edited volume, *Hyōhaku no minzoku bunka* (vol. 8 of *Nihon rekishi minzoku ronshū*), which emphasizes the connection between assignations of divinity and *hyōhaku*; and Akasaka Norio, *Hyōhaku no seishinshi: Yanagita Kunio no hassei*, which critically traces Yanagita's Meiji-era explorations of the relationship between *hyōhaku* and otherness, leading up to the modern-day *burakumin*.

imperial court, has been instrumental in pointing out the extent to which various groups existed, interacted, and competed for power in and out of the Japanese archipelago according to norms and boundaries that are different from those traditionally conceived.[6] In English-language scholarship, center-periphery relations have been a major focus in the past two decades: important studies, such as those by Bruce Batten, David Bialock, and the edited volume *Heian Japan: Centers and Peripheries* have effectively problematized past assumptions about the relative significance of centralized sources of authority and those that were considered politically, socially, economically, or religiously peripheral for one reason or another.[7] Such timely reexaminations are part of a body of scholarship that has sought to dismantle the myth of a coherent entity called "Japan," governed by a singular lineage of rulers since the dawn of time; by problematizing the premodern as always already contested and complex, these studies contribute to the broader project of imploding modern nationalist discourses that found their claims upon a unified vision of history.

This book seeks to participate in and augment this body of scholarship that reconsiders the ways in which "Japan" has been interpreted and understood in the past. Tropes of movement, I will argue, are vital in showing the extent to which stability—both geographic and conceptual—is at once contingent and a manufactured effect; these tropes offer an angle of analysis that complements but is distinct from approaches that are grounded on a center-periphery paradigm. This binary, even in its critique of monolithic discourses, can itself create equivalences within each category (e.g., liminal spaces of the capital and traveling performers both become part of an undifferentiated "peripheral"). In reconsidering the implications of the center-periphery mode of analysis, Gayatri Spivak's discussion of Marx's "Asiatic Mode of Production" is useful by analogy. Spivak notes that Marx's term is "the name and imaginary fleshing out of a difference in terms that are consonant with the development of capitalism and the resistance appropriate to it as 'the same'"—that is, the Asiatic Mode of Production is an "other" that functions *within* the narrative of a dialectic transformation of capitalism into communism in

6. Amino's prolific output includes seminal works such as *Muen, kugai, raku*, *Umi to rettō no chūsei*, and the above-mentioned *Hyōhaku to teichaku*, which he edited.

7. Batten, *To the Ends of Japan*; Bialock, *Eccentric Spaces, Hidden Histories*; Adolphson, Kamens, and Matsumoto, *Heian Japan*.

Marx's worldview.[8] Similarly, a problematization of power that begins with a center-periphery paradigm can remain tied to those fundamental terms and their relationships to each other, despite subsequent attempts to add nuance to that binary.

Tropes of movement offer an analytical point of entry that diminishes the effects of the potent center-periphery discourse by allowing us to focus on specific instances in which relations of power are established, without always assuming a preexisting set of power configurations that are only later subjected to scrutiny and critique. I treat movement not as a *category of being*—that is, as a mode of existence with a set of associated properties vis-à-vis authority—but rather as a tropic, *textual marker* that summons our analytic attention; as such, tropes of movement allow us to step away from predetermined structures of identities and equations (such as "those who move = necessarily subversive").

Indeed, the studies of modern global traversals cited above have shown that movement is a multivalent trope that evades simple categorization or uniform theorization. Focusing on movements across boundaries calls our attention to different perceptions of how power is derived and maintained; for instance, governments in exile or migrant labor suggest that stationary states of being tend to be cast as desirable, empowered conditions, whereas in contrast, movement in the form of leisure sightseeing is enabled precisely because the tourist possesses at least some degree of economic and social advantage. Thus since movement can point to a range of conditions and relations of power, what is in order is less a single, blanket theory of movement than sustained examinations of *how* and *what*—in all of their varieties—individual instances of movement-as-trope signify.

It is from this standpoint that I identify specific nodes of motion in the texts that are explored in this book. These nodes range widely in concern and scope: from a poetic strategy based on movement as a premise that advances particular courtly agendas by masking internal conflict among elite groups vying for authority, to an envisioning of a national network of power based not on centralization but on notions of ubiquity and clout ascribed to presences that are from elsewhere, each case of tropic traversings can be approached productively by examining

8. Spivak, *A Critique of Postcolonial Reason*, 79.

in detail its particular significances and implications. Thus, moments of literary and physical movements in texts share vectors toward relations of power, even as the expressions of such vectors differ significantly from text to text.

The chapters of this book are arranged in broadly chronological fashion. The texts under discussion date to a span of over five centuries, beginning in the middle of the Heian period (794–1192), an era typically cast as the "golden age" of court rulership and court culture. The end of this period is marked by a large-scale civil war, and the usual story of the medieval period (late twelfth through sixteenth centuries) is dominated by warriors. The Kamakura period (1192–1333) begins with the establishment of a separate military government in the eastern part of Japan; this government eventually falls, followed by a period of divided imperial rule and the establishment of a new warrior dynasty in the Muromachi period (1336–1573). Against this sweeping, generalized narrative of history, the specific studies of this book seek to add nuance, provoke thought, and challenge conventional understandings. Many of the texts narrate events from previous generations, and the ways in which they imagine such events through tropes of movement are crucial in thinking about how and why the texts invoke networks of power both past and contemporary.

Chapter 1 examines *Yamato monogatari* (Tales of Yamato), a tenth-century collection of courtly tales, likely penned by a woman who served at the imperial court. These short narratives each focus on specific poems in the genre of *waka* (or *tanka*); *waka* usually consist of thirty-one syllables, and were commonly composed, recited, and appreciated among courtly circles. The *Yamato* stories provide contextual accounts for *waka* poems, such as how they came to be composed or what sort of impact they had upon specific individuals. *Yamato* is a text that clearly prioritizes court culture, with named aristocratic characters populating the major portion of its tales, and its obvious interest in the courtly poetic form of *waka*. However, *Yamato*'s narratives also render complex the exact nature of the culture that is being privileged. Tropes of movement are abundant in this work; they range from recently abdicated emperors wandering in desolation to multiple-register narratives that surf in and out of storylines and genres. Yet we also find female court attendants who appear to embrace ensconcement as a positive and powerful state of being. By turning our attention to such tropes, we can begin to see how the figure of movement highlights the struggles and uncertainties that are involved in the attainment and attempted maintenance of power. Furthermore, I will argue that these tropes challenge some of the most enduring conceptualizations of gender relations in this era.

One of the more familiar characteristics attributed to aristocratic women in the Heian period is restricted physical mobility. The long-haired, multi-robed upper-class woman who is confined to her quarters while she waits for sporadic visits by her suitor is a canonical figure in texts from this period; even when employed at court as an attendant, her relative lack of mobility compared to her male counterparts is assumed to be obvious. We, as modern readers and scholars, tend to ascribe a negative quality to this static condition, and in contrast regard the less restricted movements of male aristocrats as a positive aspect of their daily lives. Indeed, it seems like common sense to understand the physical stasis of these women as a straightforward product of patriarchal oppression, and the lack of hindrance to men's ability to roam freely as a performative proof of their gender's privileged status. *Yamato*, however, dismantles these expectations by envisioning a radically alternative interpretation of this gender configuration: the narratives in this collection instead imagine male mobility as an undesirable state of instability, in which defeated aristocrats wander despondent, and emperors abdicate after brief reigns. In contrast, female stasis—both literal and figurative—is situated as a potentially powerful positionality from which one can critically observe and even ultimately triumph over the comings and goings of less fortunate male counterparts; that positionality becomes a metaphorical, metanarrative space from which the women can consider and often critique the geopolitical ambitions of men in power, which were crucial to the project of nation building at this time.

The second chapter, too, is concerned with complex, fraught relations among those who vied for power within the central government. This time, the protagonist is a courtier named Fujiwara no Sanekata (958–98), who was born into one of the most powerful families in the capital but was suddenly sent away to serve at a surprisingly low-prestige post: the provincial governorship of the most remote northeastern province, Mutsu (also called Ōshū). Three years after arriving at his post, he passed away. It is not difficult to imagine that Sanekata's life came to be woven into textual tellings and retellings, given its curious contours; from his own poetry collection to prose works in later centuries, his figure becomes the subject of many interpretations, most of them casting him as a tragic noble who was forcibly sent away to wander in distant lands.

There is more to Sanekata, however, than this sad tale of misfortune: I will argue that his figure, too, represents a series of textual moments that involve double-layered tropes of movement. I begin with an examination of *waka* poems by Sanekata that are featured in the poetry collection *Sanekatashū* (Poetry collection of Sanekata), compiled during and after his lifetime. These poems appear to insist on solidifying the supremacy of courtly culture; one prime technique for this project is the poems' abundant use of *utamakura*, or "poem pillows." A literary flourish found across genres of court literature throughout the premodern era, *utamakura* are words—and consequently, imagery and emotions that come to be associated with these words—that are tropically tied to specific place-names. Such places are scattered across the country, and a large number of them are located a good distance away from the capital, including many in the northeastern region to which Sanekata was dispatched. In the context of this book, I choose to understand *utamakura* as a trope of movement: for courtly poets who dwell in the capital, *utamakura* allows them to bring imagined, faraway places into the playing field of aristocratic aesthetics. *Utamakura* is thus a strategy that transports visions of distant locales into the comfort of the courtiers' residences and official spaces without the annoyances of travel; it is an effective, if illusory, method for integrating territories into the regime of *waka* signification. The poems of *Sanekatashū* take matters a step further in the project of *utamakura*, in that the tropic places are actual geographical locations that exist materially in front of his eyes, since he is sent away to those very lands. Sanekata's poems faithfully replicate the wordplay and imagistic associations rendered familiar within the context of courtly aesthetics, appearing to prove the discursive veracity of the *utamakura* and reinforce the privileged status of court culture.

Here, I locate Sanekata as an exilic figure—that is, a character for whom travel symbolizes exclusion and a downturn in fortunes, regardless of the exact reasons for that fall. I situate this particular exilic figure, as portrayed in texts dominated by courtly aesthetics, as an important agent in the dynamics of the central government's efforts at domination over the northeastern territories through the power of courtly cultural practices; in the narrative of *Sanekatashū*, this domination is a seamless and uncontested venture. However, other texts from and about the mid-Heian period portray rather different visions of the relationship between various areas of premodern Japan. What we find in these texts are narratives about raging battles between forces dispatched by the central government and the locals who attempt to resist the conquerors; stories about inept governors, of which Sanekata is said to be one; intense military conflicts between local strongmen; and rivalry among those representing the central government. It is within the context of this embattled landscape that we can resituate poetry by and about Sanekata; I will suggest that the poems are discursive strategies designed to highlight the primacy of a textual/cultural means of asserting power over a fraught region. That is, the poems are not simply dreamy denials of resistance from the subjugated residents of the northeast; rather, they represent an insistence on the power of *court culture* as the one and only necessary tool for territorial governance. What is denied, then, is less the fraught relationship between "center" and "periphery" than the power struggle *between* groups at the center: civilian courtiers and the rising military families. The mid-Heian period marked the beginning of the increase in power among those who were militarily capable; the northeastern theater was one major arena in which the civilian court officials clashed with newly powerful military commanders. *Sanekatashū*'s blatant disavowal of force and struggle in the northeast—that is, the complete suppression of any reference to armed expeditions—read together with the collection's intense rhetoric of the supremacy of court culture, can be understood as a championing of elite aesthetics as the ultimate and most important weapon in the subjugation of a frontier territory. The legacy of the northeast as a symbolic venue in which conflicts between those who seek dominance within the national government are performed continues into the medieval period, albeit in different guises; the chapter closes with an examination of a medieval prose narrative in which the figure of Sanekata, pictured as a haughty aristocrat-in-exile, is pitted in conflict against a deity in Mutsu who is also an exile from the capital.

Chapter 3 examines a narrative of forced travel found in a particular version of *Heike monogatari* (The tale of Heike), the lengthy epic dating from the fourteenth century about the civil wars that took place two centuries earlier. As one of the most famous texts of premodern Japan, *Heike* contains many renowned passages of intrigue, valor, and tragedy that have become legendary. One of the lesser-known moments, however, is the story of Taira no Shigehira (1157–85), a son of the supposedly nefarious Kiyomori, who is said to be responsible for both the rise and fall of his entire clan. Known as an elegant courtier and a skilled general, Shigehira nevertheless suffers capture in the hands of his enemy, the Minamoto; thus begins the tale of movement for this prisoner of war, who is first taken to the capital from the battlegrounds, then marched hundreds of miles eastward to Kamakura, the newly established center for warrior governance, in order to be questioned by Yoritomo, the leader of the Minamoto.

Shigehira's journey as narrated in *Heike* is, again, a case of motion both physical and abstract. His figure is literally in motion as he is made to travel from place to place, uncertain about his destiny or the duration of his remaining days. At the same time, his story is cast into two distinct textual modes; the narrative makes a sudden leap from one to the other midway through. First, his trip from the capital to Kamakura is told along the familiar lines of a journey eastward as related in a Heian-era locus classicus: Shigehira is said to have composed *waka* poetry and made poetic allusions in a manner that echoes those of numerous others before him who undertook the same route. Once he reaches Kamakura, however, we are abruptly transported to a space in which all literary references are measured against the world of *kanshibun*, or Chinese poetry and prose.

This jump from one literary genre to another in the telling of Shigehira's voyage, I will argue, is far from incidental or accidental. The two genres of *waka* and *kanshibun* represent the main pillars of courtly literature, and thus cover the range of textual genres that elites routinely commanded. It is thus striking that the story of Shigehira, an ideal of the courtier-warrior of the late twelfth century, is related in each of these genres in a manner that radically undercuts his powers. On his way east, the prisoner coerced into motion appears to pay proper tribute to the centuries of accumulated *waka* tropes associated with this itinerary—yet, when we examine that performance more closely, it turns out that the texts he produces are ones that continuously subvert and render awry the very tradition of courtliness. When he arrives in Kamakura, we suddenly enter the world of *kanshibun* allusions, which once again work to disempower Shigehira's figure: the captive in the story interprets famous *kanshibun* passages in ways that figuratively imprison him by encouraging him to accept his doomed fate.

Thus Shigehira is portrayed as virtually texting himself to death—that is, the narrative casts him as invoking past texts and understanding them in ways that seem to convince him of the inevitability of his own demise. The reason for the appearance of this striking twelfth-century figure in the best-known version of the *Heike*, I will argue, may lie in the late fourteenth-century context of the text. Produced in an era of upheaval in which the division within the imperial house remained unresolved, and a new shogunal dynasty was busily establishing itself, Shigehira's acquiescence to his own destruction becomes proof of the obsolescence of the courtier-warrior ideal of the late Heian era. Being versed in and invoking past literary traditions, it seems, is not only inadequate for survival in the brave new medieval world, but potentially downright harmful; texts are powerful, and can directly affect the details of an elite aristocrat's life, and catastrophically so, if the wrong interpretive and compositional buttons are pushed. Shigehira's negative example thus serves as a call for the newly powerful to pay attention to the maintenance, propagation, and interpretation of texts as an important tool for the new rulers of the nation.

The final chapter turns to a text that perhaps best exemplifies the subject of this book. A series of three stories about the Suwa Shrine, a religious complex located in the middle of the present-day prefecture of Nagano, is included in *Shintōshū* (A Shinto collection), a compilation of narratives that purport to explain the origins of various shrines across Japan. Like the version of the *Heike* discussed in chapter 3, this collection was likely compiled in the fourteenth century; the origin tales are thought to have been told orally for advertisement and proselytizing purposes. The most striking feature of the three Suwa narratives is their extreme display of tropes of movement, which permeate each story throughout. The prominence of motion both at the diegetic level (that is, characters moving through identities, spaces, and time) and in the realm of narrative method (for example, seemingly random shifts in plot and setting that suggest a disregard for conventions of narrative focus; travels over great distances that are told and retold multiple times in different textual registers) makes the Suwa stories rather puzzling and difficult to read; I argue, however, that it is precisely this seeming opacity that is the key to understanding how the text envisions a new order for the dissemination of power.

Through tropes of movement, the Suwa narratives together paint a dynamic landscape both positive and negative. Emperors and those in the upper ranks of government become doubles of human rebels and disobedient demons, who are all in motion; identity turns out to be always fluid, frequently unexpected, and often subversive. At the pinnacle of movement in the Suwa stories is the tale of a man who travels through country after country in the underground world in search of his abducted wife. Perhaps this voyage sounds familiar, as it bears a certain similarity to other adventures such as the deity Izanagi's travels to the netherworld in early Japanese mythology, or those of Orpheus in the Greek tradition. However, the most crucial and distinguishing feature of Suwa's version is the incessant and insistent repetitiveness with which the hero's journey is told: not only does he cover a vast amount of distance through his travels, but his trip is related over and over in various guises by different individuals. I will argue that the sheer number of times the travel is recounted is not a sign of confused storytelling, but rather a means to an effect: the hero achieves a kind of omnipresence in multiple spaces at once by passing through each space again, and again, and again.

The Suwa narratives together represent a blueprint for a new order of power that is delineated through striking tropes of movement. It is a paradigm that focuses not on a central authority that manages the regions, but rather on an even, ambient influence present in many places simultaneously; it is also a specific situating of a type of otherness—which I call "elsewhere" in the chapter—that assists in the implementation of this power derived from ambient ubiquity. If, as I will argue in the earlier chapters of this book, the very idea of a central government whose various arms operated in harmony with each other was, in many ways, anachronistic fiction that fit the vision of "history" in later generations, then the tremendous movements of the Suwa narratives provide an alternative mode for the operation of power that is less hierarchical and seemingly more organic, perhaps vaguely botanical. A new vision of governance and influence is, of course, nonetheless still a claim to power that is reorganized, reconsolidated, and repackaged into a different guise. In the final analysis, the Suwa narratives participate in their own consolidationist project analogous to a unified vision of national authority.

Through the meditations on these four case studies, I attempt not only to reframe discourses of power in Heian and medieval Japan, but also to reenvision the nature of power in a broader sense, as I will argue in the epilogue. This book is in no way a comprehensive examination of premodern Japanese textual examples of movement; given the abundance of instances in which tropes of movement play an important role in texts, it is simply not possible to be exhaustive. Thus I have chosen four distinct textual moments from a range of eras that I believe are particularly concerned with discourses of movement and power as case studies in the exploration of this trope. These moments represent instances in which the two types of movement outlined at the beginning of this introduction—the physical movement of characters from place to place, and shifts and changes at the level of genre and literary technique—are both crucial to the narratives and their implications. In this sense, the chosen texts are not necessarily representative of their respective genres, but rather, denote marked examples in which the serendipitous coexistence of movements points particularly strongly to discourses of power; my concern lies less in a generic overview based on potential typicality than in the study of tropes of movement as a potential tool for analysis. It is my hope that these studies might inspire future investigations of this trope in other texts as well—premodern or modern, Japanese or otherwise.

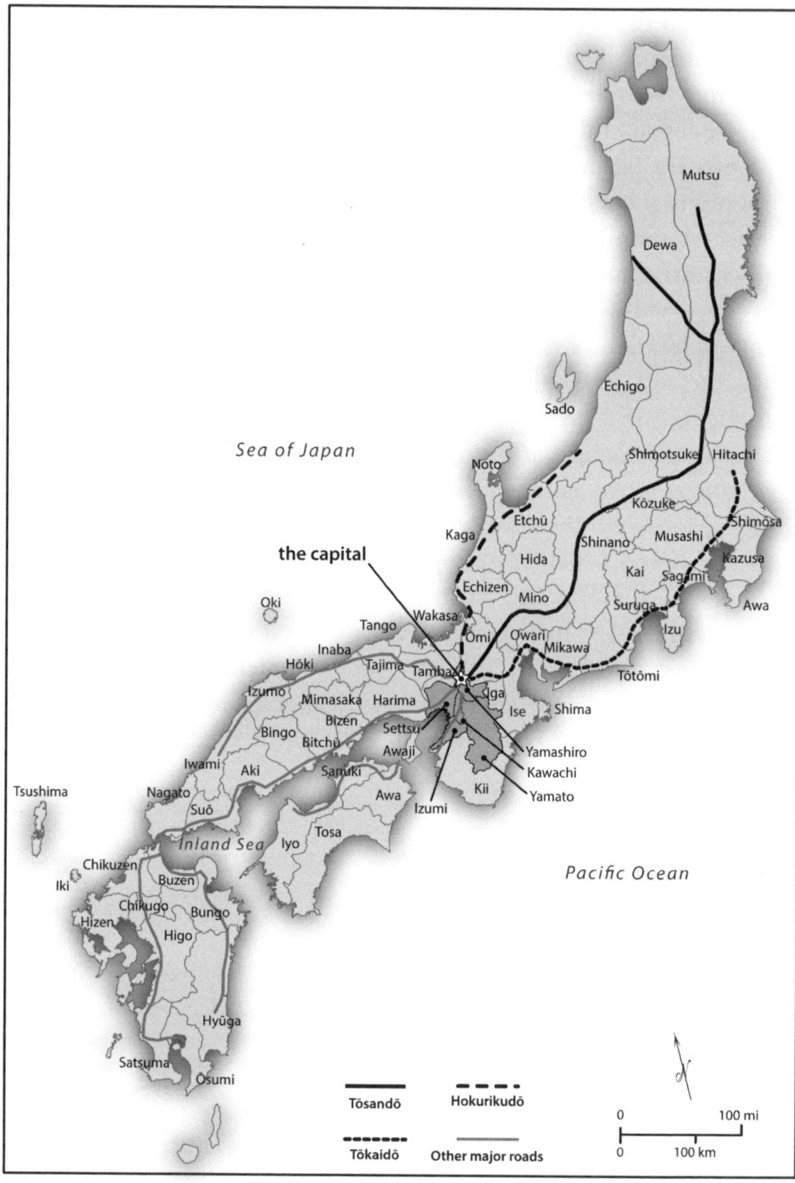

Map 2 Heian and medieval Japan: the shaded area represents the Kinai Provinces (Yamato, Yamashiro, Kawachi, Settsu, and Izumi).

ONE

Yamato monogatari

Movement, Gender, and Nation

There are certain tropes of the mid-Heian period that are so prevalent as to constitute the era as a recognizable cultural product. The iconic figure of the aristocratic woman who must await the visits of her suitors arguably represents the epitome of such a trope. Indeed, there seems to be ample textual evidence from this period that supports this tropic imagery, from the protagonist who resentfully waits for the erratic visits of her spouse in *Kagerō nikki* (Kagero diary, ca. 974) to the many heroines of *Genji monogatari* who are placed in similar situations. Thus we as readers and scholars are accustomed to understanding the relationship between gender and mobility according to conditions that seem to arise naturally out of uxorilocal marriages that were the standard for the upper classes at the time.

This chapter, however, reexamines the ways in which we understand movement to be a defining feature of gender relations in the Heian period. In modern analytical discourses, the freedom of the male subject to move about at whim tends to be contrasted with the comparatively cloistered fates of female subjects who are unable to venture out whenever they wish; movement thus becomes a symbol of empowerment, whereas its restriction is attributed to oppressive social structures and the resulting position of weakness.[1] While this paradigm obviously provides

1. See, for instance, Richard Bowring's classic introductory handbook to *The Tale of Genji*, which states: "The testimony we have from the literature of the period . . . draws a picture of women subject to the usual depredations of their menfolk, prey to torments of jealousy, and condemned to live most of their sedentary lives hidden behind a wall of

a significant and useful strategy for the critique of gender relations in this era, it is equally important to consider which other interpretations become obfuscated when empowered subjectivity is unquestioningly equated with movement.

Below I will explore an alternative approach to the ascription of movement—or its lack—to individuals along gender lines. A mid-Heian collection of short stories, *Yamato monogatari* features narratives that center on gendered figures in motion; what is most striking about these figures is that they provide opportunities for unexpected readings of the ways in which movement, power, and gender work. These texts may appear to replicate the norm: men are portrayed as being able to move about, whereas women, for the most part, remain stationary. However, the *values* associated with these states of being differ radically from the usual uxorilocal model: *Yamato* narratives situate the lack of mobility on the part of female figures as something positive, in contrast to male mobility, which is cast as being undesirable and disempowering. I will argue that this specific configuration of gender dynamics informs the text's critique of male-dominated sociopolitical agendas; what *Yamato* instead promotes is a particular, static female positionality that is privileged as a place from which such critiques are possible. This text, therefore, not only permits analyses that problematize past notions about the workings of gender in the Heian period but also points to the critical possibilities of movement as a textual figure.

The authorship of *Yamato* has long been debated, and still today it remains in the realm of speculation. It may have been written by a

---

screens and curtains" (*Murasaki Shikibu*, 3). Even Thomas Lamarre's ground-breaking study *Uncovering Heian Japan* concludes that "the case of Heian Japan, with its insistence on hobbling noble women with layers of robes and dresses, shows clearly how conventions contributed to a sexed dimorphism of movement and patterns of locomotion. . . . [F]eminine [calligraphic] styles lower the center of gravity and raise the center of motion to such an extent that movement produces a wobbling, toppling, swaying, or swooning effect." Even as he deftly deconstructs the so-called feminine hand as a calligraphic style rather than an essentialized mode of gendered writing, Lamarre writes that "there arose real differences with respect to the mobility of court women. Overall, the ability to move between styles and places belonged to male courtiers and coincided with a decrease in women's mobility and visibility. It is important to keep in mind that the authority of women depended on the aura of the feminine hand . . . yet the feminine hand also exceeded them and thus 'subjected' them" (110–13).

woman attendant at court, perhaps one who had been in the service of Emperor Uda (867–931). The text is thought to have been first completed around 951, with further editing touches added in subsequent years by other individuals, possibly reaching the forms of the various extant versions by around 1000.[2] *Yamato* is most famous as a text of the *uta monogatari* genre, which involves prose narrations concerned with the production of *waka* poetry. These narratives range from anecdotes about a poem's compositional circumstances to its impact and efficacy. It is a collection of relatively brief, discrete tales; though the number varies among versions, the standard text contains 173 short stories, each of which features one or more *waka* surrounded by prose. Previous scholarship on *Yamato monogatari* has tended to focus on questions of authorship, genre, and the biographies of named individuals who appear in the text—that is, scholars have often treated this collection as a source of information about well-known personages or have highlighted it as one moment in the flow of generic development.[3] My focus, however, lies elsewhere: I am interested in exploring the ways in which gender and movement as featured in this text intersect in unexpected ways that allow for multivalent discourses on matters ranging from imperial secession to literary genres to territorial conquests.

2. My translations are based on Imai, *Yamato monogatari hyōshaku*, vols. 1 and 2, and informed by two other editions, Kakimoto, *Yamato monogatari no chūshaku to kenkyū*, and Katagiri et al., *Taketori monogatari, Ise monogatari, Yamato monogatari, Heichū monogatari*.

3. For example, Okayama Miki explores the genre of *utagatari* (storytelling based on *waka*) and *uta monogatari* in *Yamato monogatari no kenkyū*; Seno'o Yoshinobu investigates authorship possibilities in *Heianchō uta monogatari no kenkyū*; biographies of named individuals in the text are the focus of Morimoto Shigeru's *Yamato monogatari no kōshōteki kenkyū* and Yamashita Michiyo's *Utagatari no jidai*; more general, comprehensive studies include Yanagita Yoshinori's *Yamato monogatari no kenkyū*, which includes a detailed annotated bibliography of past scholarship, and Abe Toshiko's *Kōhon Yamato monogatari to sono kenkyū*. In English-language scholarship, Mildred Tahara provides a broad introduction to this text along the biography and social customs lines in both her article with selected translations ("Yamato Monogatari") and her book of complete translations, *Tales of Yamato*.

Ensconced Women, Men Adrift

The aristocratic woman represents the mid-Heian period to the modern readerly imagination. We tend to envision her as burdened with the metaphorical and literal weight of gendered expectations: laden with layers of robes and cascading hair, she is ordinarily confined to her residence, having no choice but to wait for visits by suitors; consequently, she lives in a state of constant anxiety about the loyalty and dependability of her male partners who, at any moment, might decide to stop calling and to withdraw their social and financial support. As an attendant in the imperial palace, she would have more freedom to socialize with both genders and to go on more frequent outings, but even then her mobility is quite limited compared to that of male aristocrats, who are far less hindered in their movements and can come and go as they please. True, such men faced constraints as well: political considerations governed their actions, including their movements from place to place, and directional taboos applied to both men and women when considering auspicious travel routes. However, when compared to the fates of upper-class women, the men seemed to enjoy far more freedom.

If this vision represents the dominant tropic understanding of the upper-class woman in this period, we may need to rethink some of the assumptions at its foundation: the status of the quality of mobility for the ruling class. The figures of the tragically ensconced aristocratic woman and the freely moving male courtier are constructed upon the notion that being able to move about is, by default, a positive thing, whereas being stationary is, generally speaking, an unfortunate state of existence. Staying put in one place comes to be equated with an uncertain and precarious condition: the pining woman must patiently wait for visits by her whimsical man, whose emotional and financial reliability is hardly guaranteed. In contrast, mobility is ascribed to the freely choosing subject, who displays his power through his unhindered ability to go from one place to another. The act of movement, therefore, comes to be strongly gendered in this process; the values placed upon movement or its lack, moreover, stem from systems of thought that prioritize individuals who exercise their supposedly free wills through acts that prove their unfettered agencies. *Yamato*, however, encourages us to reconsider these highly familiar tropes and assumptions; this text presents its audience with understandings of gender and mobility that differ significantly from what we are accustomed to expect in the Heian period.

Right from the beginning, *Yamato* directs the attention of its audience to the question of gendered movement. The text opens with a poetic exchange between the renowned female poet Ise (dates unknown)—who was an attendant to and lover of Emperor Uda—and that emperor himself:

wakaruredo *ai mo woshimanu* *momoshiki wo*
mizaran koto no *nani ka kanashiki*

The palace: though I depart, it will not miss me in return;
to see it no longer: why does that sadden me so?

—Ise

mi hitotsu ni *aranu bakari wo* *oshinabete*
yuki megurite mo *nado ka mizaran*

Not to me alone— go and serve them, one by one
as the years pass on by; then, why should you not return to see the palace again?

—Emperor Uda[4]

We are told that Uda is about to abdicate the throne and leave the imperial palace; Ise, grieving the end of his reign and her service at court, writes the first poem on the wall in the Kokiden quarters. The narrator states that upon seeing this poem, Uda inscribed his own poem next to Ise's as a reply. This is a fascinating exchange: Uda, in sarcasm or in earnest, points out that although he, the emperor, must leave the palace after his reign is over, a woman attendant at court can continue to stay at the palace or return after a hiatus in order to serve different emperors, "one by one," if she so chooses.[5] What could this imply—that is, how might we read

4. Imai, *Yamato monogatari hyōshaku*, 1: 3.

5. Another possible interpretation of the first half of the poem is "Things are different for me [the emperor] only," which further emphasizes the uniqueness of Uda's inability to return to the palace, contrasted with the possibility of the likes of Ise and other women attendants to remain at the palace. See ibid., as well as Yamazaki, "*Yamato monogatari* shodan no shijitsuteki waka kaishaku," 25–41.

the positioning of a woman attendant's role at court as being potentially more continuous, stable, and comparatively more permanent than even that of the emperor himself?

Before coming to an answer, let us proceed to examine story 2, which immediately follows the above exchange:

> The emperor abdicated the throne, and in the autumn of the following year, shaved off his hair [to take the Buddhist tonsure] and walked from this mountain to that mountain as an ascetic practice. There was someone named Tachibana no Yoshitoshi who had been a secretary of Bizen Province; he served the emperor at the palace as an official during his reign, and when the emperor shaved off his hair, Yoshitoshi also did the same. Though the emperor journeyed without letting people know about his whereabouts, Yoshitoshi did not fail to catch up with him and to serve him. "It is a terrible thing for the emperor to walk around like this," it was said, and the palace ordered a dispatch, saying, "Minor Captain, Middle Captain, and so on, go serve [retired emperor Uda]"; however, the emperor walked on, avoiding these dispatched people. When he reached Izumi Province, there was a night he spent at a place called Hine. Yoshitoshi felt saddened, thinking how very lonely the retired emperor looked. At that point, [Uda] said, "Compose a poem about Hine"; thus the august monk Yoshitoshi composed:
>
> *furusato no* *tabine no yume ni* *mietsuru wa*
> *uramiyasuran* *mata to towaneba*
>
> On the road at Hine I have dreamed of my old home;
> could it be that people resent me because I have not sent word?
>
> Everyone present shed tears, and no one was able to compose poetry. Yoshitoshi's Buddhist name is Kanren, and he served the retired emperor for many years afterward.[6]

In contrast to the woman attendant in story 1, who is positioned as potentially able to remain stationary at the palace over the span of many imperial reigns, continuing to function within the busy life of the palace, the retired emperor is here portrayed as a lonesome wanderer, maintaining only the bare minimum (male) entourage. The desolation is tangible:

6. Imai, *Yamato monogatari hyōshaku*, 1: 9.

although Uda is depicted as strongly desiring to be left alone, most likely because he chose to adhere to Buddhist ascetic customs that required the renunciation of worldly pleasures, he still suffers in his solitude and is brought to tears, like everyone else who accompanied him, by thoughts of the life he left behind.

The forlorn portrayal of the retired Uda is found elsewhere in *Yamato* as well. Story 35 entangles this former sovereign's figure even more explicitly with the question of place and power. The narrator notes that when Middle Counselor Fujiwara no Kanesuke (877–933) visited the abdicated sovereign at his residence on Mt. Ōuchi (present-day Mimuro, in the western part of the capital), he "felt very moved that [Uda] appeared lonesome." Kanesuke thus composes the following poem:

shirakumo no kokonoe ni tatsu mine nareba
ōuchiyama to iu nizo arikeru

The white clouds rise in nine layers upon this peak,
thus "Mt. Ōuchi" is what the mountain is called.[7]

The term *kokonoe,* or "nine layers," is a poetic reference to the imperial palace, as is the term *ōuchi.*[8] What is striking is the contrast between these seemingly august references to the locational base of imperial power, and the portrayal of Uda's forlorn condition. As an abdicated sovereign, Uda is no longer a resident of the "real" palace in which the reigning emperor is situated; the retired emperor's abode might still be called a palace, but it is not the same as *the* imperial palace that he has left behind. Furthermore, it is in this displaced space that Kanesuke composes his poem; in fact, this passage likely represents one of the earliest instances of the use of Mt. Ōuchi as a reference to the palace.[9] If so, it would mean that an originary moment for a literary term that poetically symbolizes the imperial

7. Ibid., 1: 123.

8. It was said that in China, the imperial palace had nine-layered gates. As for *ōuchi*, the characters that are usually read as *dairi* (palace) could also be pronounced *ōuchi*, and thus Mt. Ōuchi became a convenient pun.

9. Later commentators have debated about the first use of ōuchiyama; many claim that *Yamato* marks its first appearance, while some others propose that its use in *Genji monogatari* is a more elaborate and thus representative first case. See Kakimoto, *Yamato monogatari no chūshaku to kenkyū*, 99.

palace is, in fact, fundamentally marked by its absence: composed at a location away from the actual palace grounds in an attempt to comfort a desolate former emperor now denied the possibility of reigning again at the palace, the term *ōuchi* embodies the fraught complexity of claims to imperial power, even as it becomes a linguistic referent for the emperor's residence.

We now return to the question, what can we make of the *Yamato* passages that juxtapose the positionality of female court attendants, who are rhetorically situated as being able to maintain a stable place for themselves at the palace over the span of multiple imperial reigns if they so desire, with that of the emperor, who is positioned as one who either wanders in desolation after abdication, or leads a lonesome life at his retirement residence? I suggest that the author(s) sought to highlight the instability of the emperor's position as a way to bolster, in contrast, the strength of the social, literary, and even potentially political space from which women attendants could observe and speak. The passages in *Yamato* I have outlined so far suggest that female immobility is prioritized over male mobility in this text; as opposed to the uxorilocal trope of the waiting woman and the suitor who flits about at whim, the static position of the woman attendant at court can outlast and outshine imperial instability. The wandering, lonesome portrait of Uda has the effect of privileging, by contrast, the positionality of women—specifically, the positionality of the woman attendant at court, who is here said to not necessarily have to subject herself to the ebb and tide of a single emperor's fate.

Let us contextualize matters more specifically. We know that although the emperor stands (supposedly) as the single pinnacle of power, he reigns for a limited number of years. Imperial succession was fraught for centuries before the time of *Yamato,* and the ninth century was no exception; in the second half of that century, the turnover was quite rapid. The infamous Yōzei (868–949; r. 876–84), whose sanity was questioned after he committed murder in the palace, was deposed and replaced by his great-uncle Kōkō, who reigned only for three years (830–87; r. 884–87); and Kōkō's son Uda, whom the author of *Yamato* is thought to have served, did not reign for particularly long (r. 887–97). Matters changed with the reign of Daigo, who followed (885–930; r. 897–930), of course; however, before 951, when *Yamato* is first thought to have been completed, we see two more emperors take the throne: Suzaku (923–52; r. 930–46) and Murakami (926–67; r. 946–67). It is therefore possible that the author or authors of *Yamato* experienced the reign of up to six emperors in her or his lifetime before the text came into being. Moreover, among the six, half of the emperors abdicated instead of seeing their reign come to an end due to natural causes; emperorship was far from being a guaranteed lifelong employment. Precarious mobility in status, therefore, existed at the very core of the imperial system of rule.

Among the numerous emperors that could have come and gone in this period, Uda is a particularly interesting choice for *Yamato*, which otherwise mentions only a few other emperors and very briefly when it does.[10] Uda was the seventh prince to his father, Emperor Kōkō, and had been granted the surname of Minamoto in order to be released from imperial status so that he might serve at court as an aristocrat. He was returned to imperial status at his father's deathbed and named the next emperor, whereupon he got off to a rocky start by engaging in a conflict with Fujiwara no Mototsune (836–91), the prime minister. What came to be called the Akō Incident (887), a dispute over the wording of an imperial decree concerning Mototsune's official position, was resolved through an imperial admission of fault and the marriage of Mototsune's daughter, Onshi, to Uda; it would be difficult to call the incident a resounding triumph for the newly enthroned sovereign. Uda was also known as a supporter of the courtier Sugawara no Michizane (845–903), famous for his *kanshi* (Chinese poetry) and his rivalry with the Fujiwara family;

10. Uda is featured in twenty stories in *Yamato*; of course, if the author had been in Uda's service and had particularly deep ties with him, it would make sense that he would be featured most prominently. However, the details of Uda's portrayal in this text remain of interest: there seems to be little in the way of purposeful flattery or a vision of imperial might. Aside from the stories discussed in this chapter (1, 2, 35, 172), Uda appears either as a neutral secondary figure (3, 12, 48, 61, 77, 98, 99, 103, 145, 146), or a partner in poetic exchanges (48, 49, 51, 52). One interesting group of narratives revolve around grievances addressed to Uda by courtiers who did not receive the promotion they thought they deserved (30, 32, 33); these stories add to the contested atmosphere of court politics. In addition to Uda, emperors who appear in *Yamato* are as follows: Yōzei: stories 14 and 15; Saga (786–842; r. 809–23), story 153; Seiwa (850–80; r. 858–76), stories 38 and 165; Daigo, stories 24, 45, 95, 100, 101, 131, 132, 133, 134, 139; Nara no mikado, unidentified, possibly referring to an emperor during the Nara period, stories 150, 151, and 152; Heizei (774–824; r. 806–9), story 153; Ninmyō (810–50; r. 833–50), story 168.

through his alliance with Michizane, Uda was able to command influence at court. Matters went awry, however, when Michizane was permanently chased out of the capital to Dazaifu in 901 due to the machinations of his aristocratic rivals, thus causing a painful blow to his supporter. Uda's life trajectory is thus one that was far from a smooth narrative of unchanging or uncontested authority. Uda may have been the first emperor to appear in *Yamato* because of his proximity to the possible author(s), but the rough terrain of his reign, together with the featured event of the first story (his abdication) and the manner of its presentation, all suggest that this emperor's textual presence points to the instability of male power at the pinnacle of society.

Uda was, however, not a powerless emperor—in fact, other texts suggest quite the opposite. It seems that although he faced a number of adverse conditions, he achieved significant authority, particularly after his abdication and after the death of Fujiwara no Mototsune and his son, Tokihira (871–909). Indeed, this emperor is famous as one who fostered the development of the poetic arts, sponsoring a number of poetry contests that became well known.[11] Scholars argue that Uda's years as emperor and retired emperor were, in fact, quite lavish and full of activity, with banquets, excursions, and arts patronage as well as political innovations within the court system.[12] How much the more striking, then, the figure of Uda as it is presented in *Yamato*: by choosing to focus on the less stable aspects of his reign and retirement while suppressing his accomplishments, the text makes a powerful impression in contrasting his fate with that of the woman attendant at court.[13]

11. Lamarre, *Uncovering Heian Japan*, 72; Gustav Heldt also deftly elaborates on how Uda, faced with political competition, chose the arena of such contests as a means to assert and exhibit his authority (see *The Pursuit of Harmony*).

12. Kudō, *Heianchō ritsuryō shakai no bungaku*, 172–96; Sakaue, *Ritsuryō kokka no tenkan to "Nihon,"* 235–43.

13. Indeed, there is one narrative in *Yamato* that differs significantly from the figure of Uda I have analyzed so far. Story 172 addresses the retired emperor's frequent pilgrimages to Ishiyama Temple in Ōmi Province. The provincial governor expresses grief that hosting imperial entourages so many times was placing a heavy burden on the provincial budget and its people; Uda, hearing this, instructs other provinces to provide some relief. The governor is greatly embarrassed that his complaint had reached the retired emperor's ears, and cannot bear to face him. He leaves the famed poet Ōtomo no Kuronushi (dates unknown) to entertain Uda with a poem; Kuronushi comes through with an apt compo-

Similarly, there is a discrepancy between the portrayal of individual male aristocrats in *Yamato*, and how modern-day readers might tend to understand their status as a class. The established scholarly view is that aristocratic power increased overall in the late ninth into the tenth century, culminating in the "golden age" of Fujiwara rule in the late tenth century.[14] Positions such as *sesshō* and *kanpaku* (both translated as regent, or chief advisor to the emperor) came into being during this period; such duties clearly indicate the close relationship between the emperor and his "advisors."[15]

---

sition and rewards are distributed. In this story, the figure of the retired emperor fulfills one's expectations for someone in this position: devoutly religious as a monk, yet benevolent to his subjects, and powerful enough to command the movement of resources and rewards. Uda's lavish entourage to Ishiyama Temple in this narrative is a far cry from his travels in story 2, which emphasizes loneliness and seclusion; his journeys as presented in story 172 were extravagant enough to cause economic anxieties for the governor of Ōmi. This sole instance of Uda's appearance as a prosperous imperial figure might be explained by the fact that story 172 is likely a later addition by an unknown editor (Katagiri et al., *Taketori monogatari*, 431–32); we might speculate that sometime after the completion of the core collection of stories (1 through 171), someone decided to add story 172, a narrative that depicts a much more robust vision of this retired emperor, possibly to offset the relentlessly weak portrayal of this emperor in the rest of the text. The narrative that provides the single exception to the figure of Uda, then, may actually reinforce the striking degree to which the rest of the text undermines the status and power of this imperial personage.

14. For instance, the appearance of very young emperors has led some to argue that aristocrats, not emperors, were increasingly responsible for the actual day-to-day execution of national governance, while the emperor's individual capabilities became less important. The Jōwa Incident in 842 is said to mark the beginning of relative standardization of imperial succession, which now embraced patrilineal succession (as opposed to successions that allowed for alternating fraternal lineages to take power) as the norm; in turn, this standardization allowed for some emperors to take the throne before the age of ten, setting the stage for regency, a phenomenon that continued until the end of the Heian period. The incident itself involved Emperor Junna (r. 823–33), who abdicated the throne to his nephew, Ninmyō (r. 833–50); Junna's son, Tsunesada, became the crown prince. However, secret plans implicating Prince Tsunesada in a coup surfaced, and he was removed from the line of succession. Ninmyō's son became the new crown prince, and this lineage went on to dominate imperial succession. The details of the secret plot and its circumstances—possibly a trap by those who supported Ninmyō's line—remain murky, but the incident sheds light on the complicated and unstable politics of imperial succession during this time (Kawajiri, *Heiankyō sento*, 52–54).

15. Ibid., 96–98. *Sesshō* refers to the position before the emperor comes of age, and *kanpaku* after.

However, if aristocrats as a group were gaining power vis-à-vis the emperor, the competition *among* the aristocrats remained fierce and volatile.[16] The political climate of these times was characterized by intense struggles for dominance and rapid shifts in balances of power among male elites, particularly the efforts of the Fujiwara family to acquire and monopolize authority. It is this instability that *Yamato* selectively highlights, with many examples of aristocratic men in uncertain circumstances, particularly when they are involved in movement from place to place. Women are not shown to travel to other provinces frequently, but when they do, the portrayal of their trips is various; their journeys are not always prosperous, but neither are they consistently tinged with melancholy.[17] In contrast, male figures embark on trips to other provinces much more frequently than female figures, which may not be surprising; however, the most striking aspect of *Yamato*'s male travelers is that often they fare poorly.[18] Obviously, travel was challenging in the Heian era, and it was likely not surprising to encounter difficult—often fatal—situations while on the road. However, *Yamato*'s representation of upper-class male travel is fraught with tragedy that suggests, in the context of male instability found

16. The Ōtenmon Incident (866), in which the major counselor Tomo no Yoshio was charged with the crime of arson and exiled, cleared the way for Fujiwara no Yoshifusa (804–72) to dominate court politics as the maternal grandfather of Emperor Seiwa (850–80; r. 858–76). Yoshifusa's heir, Mototsune, sought to challenge and control Uda, as stated above; however, his daughter Onshi's failure to produce a male heir to the throne delayed the institution of the *sekkan* system of rule, in which the maternal grandfather of the emperor would control national governance, until later in the tenth century, when it would finally take root. Mototsune's son, Tokihira, successfully ousted his rival, Sugawara no Michizane, in 901, but he and his direct descendants were unable to achieve full prosperity; it was rumored that this failure was the result of Michizane's vengeful spirit. It is Tokihira's brother, Tadahira (880–949), whose descendants go on to establish the so-called golden age of Fujiwara dominance in the late tenth century through *sekkan* rulership.

17. For example, an imperial princess who has been sent to Ise to serve as the *saigū* is portrayed neutrally, her move presented even as an indication of her good fortunes (story 36); the travels of the second wife from Tsukushi, detailed later in this chapter, are not unhappy for the woman herself. Less fortunate is the fate of a woman who is abducted from the capital and brought to Mutsu Province in the distant northeast (story 155); she grieves over her changed appearance—possibly due to her pregnancy, possibly due to her now-rustic condition—and kills herself.

18. The most notable cases in which men do *not* face some sort of tragedy on the road seem to be official dispatchings of provincial governors (stories 73, 75, 87, and 88).

elsewhere in the text, that here, too, male figures are specifically constructed as leading precarious, mobile lives.

For example, story 168 focuses on the figure of Yoshimine no Munesada (816–90), better known as the priest-poet Henjō, one of the *rokkasen* (Six Poetic Immortals) of the *waka* genre. The narrator states that he had been a dashing, flourishing figure at court as one of Emperor Ninmyō's favorites, but when that emperor passes away, Munesada disappears, leaving his friends, family, and others in the capital frantically searching for his whereabouts. He had, in fact, taken the tonsure and become a monk by the name of Henjō, now unrecognizably haggard and dressed only in a straw raincoat as he journeys widely as part of his ascetic practice. Since Henjō has shed the dust of this-worldly concerns, he tries to avoid contact with those he used to know, and the stories of his near and actual encounters with past relations are wrenching. For instance, at the Hasedera Temple in Yamato Province, he happens upon his wife and children, who have come to pray for a reunion with him. Henjō, though, hides himself like a good recluse monk, even though he cries tears of blood all through the night, wanting to see his family. In another passage, we hear that Henjō eventually settles at a temple called Kazan in the eastern hills of the capital. When his family finally gains word of his whereabouts, they send the eldest son to see him. The reunion, however, does not end happily: much to the son's resentment, Henjō forces him to also take the tonsure on the spot, saying, "It is best for a monk's son to also become a monk."[19]

Henjō, however, seems to have led a life significantly less desolate than the *Yamato* passage suggests. True, he took the tonsure after the death of Ninmyō, possibly due to power struggles at court, and because his father had died young, leaving him with little backing. On the other hand, he proceeded to achieve prominence within the Tendai school of Buddhism, and his seventieth birthday was grandly celebrated at the imperial palace; until his death five years later, he seems to have enjoyed much prosperity.[20] Like the case of Uda, then, *Yamato*'s version of Henjō's supposed life story is one that ignores successes of a highly influential male protagonist and instead emphasizes the unfortunate moments of his decline.

19. Imai, *Yamato monogatari hyōshaku*, 2: 320–30.
20. Abe, *Henjōshū zenshaku*, 3–27.

Another striking example is that of Ariwara no Shigeharu (dates unknown) in story 144. Born as the third son of the famous poet Ariwara no Narihira,[21] Shigeharu was a poet in his own right, with compositions that were included in *Kokin wakashū* (A collection of *waka* poetry old and modern, 905), the first imperially commissioned *waka* anthology. The *Yamato* narrative states: "Was it because the middle captain [Narihira] had traveled east? His children also journeyed to other provinces once in a while. [Shigeharu] was one with feeling, and at desolate places in other provinces that stirred his sense of *aware*, he did things like compose *waka* and write them down."[22] Shigeharu is thus shown to engage in courtly poetic exercises in his family's tradition; however, unlike his father Narihira, who returns to the capital after his travels, Shigeharu "walks and walks" through various provinces, reaching the province of Kai, where he falls critically ill. There, he is said to have composed the following poem:

karisome no yukikaiji to zo omoishi wo
ima wa kagiri no kadode narikeru

"A temporary trip to Kai," so I had thought—
but my last journey's beginning, this trip has become.

Shigeharu is thus the unhappy double of his father's figure; like Narihira, he is said to have composed moving poetry at appropriate poetic landmarks as he traveled, but unlike his father, he is here cast a permanent traveler destined to die on the road. What is more, Shigeharu's poem renders even his death a mobile act; he positions himself as being adrift in the middle of his travel, which now marks the start of his wanderings from this life to the next.

In contrast to the treacherous terrain traveled by male elites, who face abdication, the rise and fall from power, and uncertain ends, *Yamato* constructs a positionality for the woman attendant at court who is empowered precisely because of her potential to remain stationary. She

21. Despite his being the third son, Shigeharu was known as Zaiji no kimi (Second Son of the Ariwara Family) because his older brother had been adopted into the Takashina family.

22. Imai, *Yamato monogatari hyōshaku*, 2: 167.

is portrayed as having the possibility to occupy the same role for years, perhaps even decades—across multiple imperial reigns, across the fluctuations of aristocratic competitions for authority. That *Yamato* begins with this vision of the woman attendant is, I believe, crucial: it gives her a quasi-transcendent positionality that is an exclusively gendered domain. In other words, the woman attendant in this text is shown to already possess one of the things the male Fujiwaras crave the most: the possibility of a multireign presence and influence at court. The woman attendant can potentially achieve what emperors cannot: to stay at court beyond a single reign. In other words, in this particular text, the position of the woman attendant is privileged through the opening narrative that endows this position with an exceptional sense of continuity with regard to the realm of the male ruling class. The text's claims about the relationship of power between men and women are thus specific and strategic: the author(s) of *Yamato* construct(s) that positionality as something potentially stationary and therefore stable, and suffering far less from the negative aspects of mobility to which upper-class men were subjected.

Engendering Genres: Movement, Stasis, and Spatial Politics

It is, of course, not just in the opening sequence of *Yamato* that we find gendered stasis as a privileged position. Story 147 is another clear example; it is one of the longest and most elaborate stories in this collection. The narrative is rich in variety, with a cast of characters of different backgrounds centered upon a gripping story of love, tragedy, and revenge. It is also a text that is intensely concerned with two distinct modes of movement: not only do characters journey from one bounded geographic space to another, but the telling of the tale itself moves rapidly between textual spaces demarcated according to the genres of prose and poetry. Such flurries of motion, though, contrast starkly with significant moments in the story that come to a metaphorical standstill. Let us examine this text in detail, with close attention to these shifts at both the narrative and metanarrative levels. This story not only presents the figures of women at court who are empowered through their ensconcement, and male figures in motion who are closely associated with uncertainty and death; it also engenders literary genres, and even challenges conventional conceptions of territoriality.

COURTLY WOMEN, METANARRATIVE, AND POETRY

Story 147 has a striking tripartite structure. The first section introduces a love triangle between one woman and two men. One suitor hails from the woman's own province and has the surname Mubara (also read Ubara), which is a name for the southern coastal area of Settsu Province. The other man is identified as having moved to Settsu from the neighboring Izumi Province, and is aptly named after an area in the coastal part of his home province, called Chinu. The narrator relates that the woman is unable to decide between the two men, who plead their devotion to her in identical displays of earnestness—timings of visits, the giving of gifts, and so on. A contest to see which suitor can shoot down a waterfowl results in a draw; the woman, at a loss for what to do, throws herself in the Ikuta River and dies. Adding to the tragedy, the two distraught men follow her fate and drown together with her. The narrative then shifts to an interlude-like second section, to which I will turn in a moment; the third section rather suddenly returns to the tale of the two suitors, who now exist in the realm of the dead. In this last section, the spirit of one of the suitors approaches a traveler in a dream, asking for his help in defeating his bitter rival; the traveler provides the suitor with requested weaponry, permitting him to finally emerge victorious over his foe.

The world of the unfortunate maiden and her embattled suitors frames the second section of story 147, in which a cast of women at court, who have no direct connection to any of the characters featured in the love triangle, makes a sudden appearance. It turns out that the romance, an "old tale," is presented here as an explanation of a narrative painting that is being given to an empress. The audience is informed that the very occasion for telling the prose story arises from a courtly, aesthetic exercise: a certain person had given paintings depicting this tragic love triangle to Empress Onshi (as noted previously, daughter of Fujiwara no

Mototsune and consort of Emperor Uda), and those present composed *waka* about the old romance; the majority of this section consists of the ten poems composed by those who were in the empress's presence. In other words, the prose telling of the story in the first and third sections can be understood as background information for the poetic sequence, and the courtly women are shown to be examining the romantic tale from an extradiegetic space.

At first glance, story 147 appears to present a configuration of movement that reinforces the familiar gender binary of men in motion and women in static confinement. The prose sections featuring the old romance cast the two male suitors as protagonists; they are both engaged in various types of movement from place to place, ranging from the Chinu man's move from Izumi to Settsu, to the men's courtship visits to the woman's abode. In contrast, the woman remains at her home, and her suicide could be read as an ultimate display of her inability to escape—both physically and metaphorically—from the bind into which she is placed. Furthermore, the second section of the story is populated entirely by female figures in the depths of the imperial palace; these women appear to remain stationary for the duration of the textual passage as each of them takes a turn composing *waka* poetry, totaling ten poems. On the surface, then, story 147 seems to affirm what we understand to be the normative configurations of gendered movement—that is, male figures are mobile and free to pursue their various interests, whereas female figures are confined to their fates of staying put in one place.

Yet, here, too, a closer reading indicates that matters may not be as they seem. First and foremost, let us keep in mind that the female characters in the second section exist at a metanarrative level—that is, they are situated in a textual space from which they are able to examine and comment upon the story that involves the male figures in motion. It is a privileged space, since it is a one-way relationship; the Chinu man and the Mubara man are allowed to function solely within their own narrative world, whereas the women have access to two worlds—the world of the narrative being told and the courtly "reality" they occupy. The women's lack of mobility, therefore, is here less an undesirable state of confinement than a superior seat from which to view a tale and to comment upon it poetically.

In fact, we can compare the relationship between the male prose protagonists and the female poets in story 147 to the opening sequence of *Yamato* discussed at the beginning of this chapter. In story 1, the woman attendant at court is positioned as potentially more desirably stationary than an emperor, who faces abdication, departure from the palace, and ensuing uncertainty. Her position is therefore akin to that of the metanarrative commentator: she remains in one place and observes the comings and goings of emperors; the latter, on the other hand, is unable to escape the drama and transiency of imperial succession, and can never cohabit the metaphorical space of the woman attendant. In the case of story 147, the female figures at the palace—this time, a mix of both attendants and women of imperial descent who share a strategic camaraderie with their attendants vis-à-vis male figures—are similarly depicted as occupying a secure space from which to produce their own texts, whereas the men must dance to the commands of the prose plot, which has them engrossed in various types of movement under difficult—often deceased—circumstances.

What is more, this metanarrative space is one that is imagined as having a particular literary genre associated with it, in addition to attributions of gender and movement/stasis. Story 147 privileges poetry as the mode for metanarrative; furthermore, poetry is here presented as a genre that *belongs* to the courtly woman, who exhibits her powers through her stationary condition. Such an imagining stands in contrast against contemporary trends: in the span of the tenth century when *Yamato* was likely composed and subsequently edited, the realm of *waka* poetry was becoming increasingly male-dominated. *Waka* poetry, of course, was routinely composed and recited by both men and women; important poetry contests were sponsored and attended by both sexes, as were personal poetry collections. However, larger male visibility in the *waka* realm, particularly in official arenas, was becoming established as the norm: for instance, male aristocrats were being entrusted with the task of compiling imperially commissioned anthologies, and far fewer female poets are represented in such anthologies than male poets. In contrast to this tendency, what we see in story 147 is an all-female cast of *waka* poets, and it is they who are endowed with the power to compose poetry that comments upon the prose narrative that they are viewing. Indeed, it is in this context that the woman attendant and imperial princesses are represented as forming a textual alliance in this story; although the circumstances of the two positionalities differ significantly, they are here shown to exist harmoniously and motionlessly in the same space and same literary genre because of their gendered relationship to *waka* poetry.

No other story in *Yamato* has a structure that divides narrative from metanarrative so clearly. Through this contrast of registers, the second section of story 147 comes to be imbued with the power of commentary that is marked as existing at a level that is different from the comings and goings of the narrative itself; the metanarrative thus becomes a discursive space that permits various types of reflections. The details and implications of these reflections are, it turns out, ones that challenge normative practices that govern other passages in the work—that is, story 147 generates a special textual location that can distinguish itself as being above and beyond the ordinary, a special extradiegetic space that can diverge from the expected.

PLACE, TERRITORY, AND THE LOGIC OF CONQUEST

What, then, are some of these unexpected utterances? Let us first turn our attention to the prose passages of story 147—that is, the first and third sections, which present the "old romance" of the Ikuta maiden and her two suitors. The contours of the love triangle resemble a well-known story that appears in texts ranging from *Man'yōshū* (A collection for ten thousand leaves, ca. 8th century) to the medieval noh play *Motomezuka* (The sought-after burial mound, ca. 14th century), but the *Yamato* version is striking both for its degree of detail and for its explicit focus on the questions of territory.[23] I will argue that these sections of story 147 are,

23. *Man'yōshū* includes poems that feature the main cast of characters, the man from Chinu and the man from Unai (an older reading of Ubara/Mubara) who fight over a maiden. The anthology includes a *chōka* (long-format poem, also based on the five–seven syllabary) as well as two *tanka* by Takahashi no Mushimaro (vol. 9, poems 1809–11) and a *chōka* by Ōtomo no Yakamochi (vol. 19, poem 4211). The strong focus on the physicality of place that is central to *Yamato*'s narration of this tale, however, does not exist in the earlier poetic references; in Mushimaro's poem, the three principals are buried next to each other without any discussions of their places of origin, and Yakamochi's elegy

in fact, less a love story than a narrative about the politics of geography and movement between territories.

As noted above, the home provinces of all three members of the love triangle are clearly marked at the very beginning of the text: the woman is a native of Settsu Province, as is one of the suitors, the Mubara man. The other party, the Chinu man, hails from Izumi Province. The narrator then talks of the suitors' competition for the maiden's hand, and their subsequent suicide. So far, there seems to be nothing particularly unusual; the geographical identification of the characters and the courtship's unfortunate outcome are narrated in a manner common to other texts of this period. However, there is a crucial passage that distinguishes story 147 from its other tellings, and illustrates *Yamato*'s keen interest in the understanding of places and movements between: it is the scene in which the parents of the two men argue over the burial locations of their respective sons.

The narrator states as follows:

> When they were about to bury the suitors in the two grave mounds flanking the woman's, the parent of the man from Settsu Province said, "Indeed, a man from the same province [as the woman] should be buried in the same place [as the woman]; how can it be the case that a person of another province is allowed to defile [*wokasu*] the earth of this province?" and tried to interfere, so the parent[s] of the man from Izumi brought over earth from Izumi Province on a boat and brought it here [to Settsu Province], and finally buried their son. Therefore, the two men's grave mounds flank the woman's on both sides to this day.[24]

Clearly, the fact that the Chinu man had journeyed from his home province to settle in another has become an urgent issue for the parties concerned. The key verb in the passage cited above, *wokasu,* has a

---

mentions only the woman's grave, not the grave of the two men (Satake et al., *Man'yōshū,* 2: 398–401, 4: 311–13). Nor can we explain *Yamato*'s fixation on place as part of a linear temporal progression in the development of the love triangle narrative: the noh play *Motomezuka* (attributed possibly to Kan'ami [1333–84]), which is said to be based on the *Yamato* text, claims that both suitors hail from Izumi Province, and makes no mention of burial location disputes that hinge on the men's home provinces. See Koyama et al., *Yōkyokushū,* 2: 174–87.

24. Imai, *Yamato monogatari hyōshaku,* 2: 188.

number of different meanings that range from desecration, transgression, and cooptation, to admonition. In the particular phrase *tsuchi wokasu,* the word seems to indicate a literal violation of the physical integrity of the earth itself.[25] Place, therefore, is far from an abstract, imagined bounded entity upon which a community is established. Undoubtedly, it is a concrete materiality here: place is situated as a tangible substance as well as an object that is laden with territorial meaning. Burial is an apt occasion for highlighting the importance of terrain itself within this discourse of place, since a corpse comes into close contact with the soil. The understanding that renders inseparable the notion of geographical boundary with the earth contained within it brings a sense of physicality to anything that happens above this soil and within its borders, be it movement from place to place, or attempts at aesthetic, political, or military subjugation—that is, although the logic of soil is still a discourse, its tangibility pulls the politics of geography from a symbolic space to a material one.

If territory is rendered concrete in this manner, then the solution to the problem of the foreignness of the Chinu man is most intriguing: the narrator tells us that the burial dispute is resolved when his parents decide to *move* dirt from Izumi aboard a boat to Settsu in order to encase their son within his homeland's earth even as he is buried in a foreign province. The Chinu man is thus both isolated and protected from the terrain of another land by a layer of his own familiar province's soil; the "cocoon" of earth plays a dual role, as it shields him from otherness and shields the terrain from his otherness. One might even argue that the bringing of soil from one province to another represents the establishment of an unusual

25. The *Kadokawa kogo daijiten*, vol. 5 (ed. Nakamura et al.), specifically highlights the usage of the verb *wokasu* in the compound *tsuchi wokasu*, which refers to a violation of the earth deity's territorial governance in the yin-yang belief system (1059); digging into the earth for construction purposes, for instance, could commit this offense if not done properly at appropriate times. The examples given in the entry include the "Haizumi" chapter of *Tsutsumi chūnagon monogatari* (see Matsuo, *Tsutsumi chūnagon monogatari zenshaku*, 306–9) and the third chapter of *Kagerō nikki* (see Hasegawa et al., *Tosa nikki, Kagerō nikki, Murasaki Shikibu nikki, Sarashina nikki*, 198), both of which use the compound in the context of a taboo to be avoided (e.g., building a new structure would violate the earth taboo and thus commit *tsuchi wokasu*). The above passage in *Yamato*, however, stands out as an example that specifically refers to the use of this term in the context of the *burial* of those who are foreign to a particular place.

variant of extraterritoriality: it produces a miniature, metonymic Izumi Province amidst the land of Settsu.

How might we read this act in the context of provincial relations—that is, what does the transporting of soil and the creation of extraterritorial space say about the way this text situates the provinces of Settsu and Izumi with respect to each other? On the one hand, the fact that a part of Settsu (albeit small) is dug aside to make room for the foreign earth of Izumi suggests that the latter quite literally displaces the former's territory and takes over the space that used to be occupied by the earth of Settsu. It is within this newly created zone of Izumi-within-Settsu that the Chinu man is allowed to rest; he is no longer an alien in this extraterritorial space, as this invasive groundwork has allowed him to claim a niche in a province that is not his own. On the other hand, bringing one's own earth for a mini-conquest renders awry that very logic of conquest: the Chinu man makes no claim upon the territory that is not imported from his home province, and taking the soil of one's home land in order to put that soil in a foreign land makes for an equation of equilibrium that goes against the grain of the conquering logic—that is, subtracting from home to add it elsewhere does not compute to an increase in power for the phantom invader. The case of the Chinu man thus suggests that not only is materiality a key component in boundary production but also that the act of ensconcing oneself in different territory, not originally one's own, does not necessarily have to be understood straightforwardly within a dominator/dominated binary paradigm. The Chinu man's family's bringing of earth from Izumi for the purpose of their son's settlement in another location can be understood as both invasive *and* respectful of boundaries: the act blatantly exhibits the displacement of one territory by another, while at the same time, it shows deference to Settsu soil, which would have become tainted from coming into contact with a foreigner's skin.

It makes sense, of course, that the two provinces are treated in a balanced manner in this story; both Settsu and Izumi were part of the Kinai region (see map 2), which consisted of five provinces that constituted a group with special nearness to the capital—physically, politically, religiously, and economically, though Izumi was a relative latecomer to the group.[26] Both provinces were particularly important for capital dwell-

26. Izumi was added to the Kinai group of provinces in 757.

ers for their lengthy coastlines, along which transportation routes ran. Furthermore, the story's attention to provincial relations makes sense in this era, as the 900s were a time in which increased emphasis was being placed at the provincial level of territorial management, as opposed to smaller units of governance that had been more important previously.[27] However, a look at the details of the third and final section of story 147 suggests that, in fact, there may be even more to the debunking of the logic of conquest in this text than first meets the eye.

In this segment, the narrative returns to a prose rendering of the romantic tragedy, this time to outline a violent battle between the two men who are buried on either side of the woman. The section begins with the phrase "Now, as for this man." However, to which of the two men the term "this man" refers is not at all clear from the context.[28] What we learn is that one of the suitors was buried together with clothing as well as weapons, whereas the other was not, due to his parents' neglect. One day, a traveler stays at an inn near the three grave mounds, and is approached in a dream by one of the deceased men, now covered in blood. The apparition begs the traveler to lend him his sword so that he can fight with his

27. Wayne Farris, discussant comments, February 6, 2015, "Rethinking Premodern Japan: Territory, Embodiment, Exposure" workshop, Center for East Asian Studies, University of Chicago.

28. Kakimoto Tsutomu interprets "this man" as the Mubara man—that is, the one buried with proper accouterments is the Mubara man, whereas the one who lacks proper weapons for self-defense and must therefore ask the traveler for assistance is the Chinu man (*Yamato monogatari no chūshaku to kenkyū*, 389). He does not give an explanation for this reading, but it is perhaps based on previous versions of this legend such as the one in *Man'yōshū* that influenced his understanding: poem 1811 in this anthology, one by Takahashi Mushimaro, explicitly states that the maiden was most likely more taken with the Chinu suitor; thus if we believe this poem we would be more sympathetically aligned with this man rather than his rival. Kakimoto also notes that the name Chinu, which can be written with characters that mean "blood marsh" and is associated with a princely deity's washing of his wounded, bloodied hands in the ocean at that place, may have inspired this gruesome story of bloodshed through imagistic association. While these theories are plausible, the words "this man" do, I would argue, remain starkly ambiguous. The male subject of the poem that immediately precedes the opening line of the third section is simply identified as "one of the men"; thus we are unable to gain any knowledge about his identity there. One might think that perhaps the third section begins where the first section left off, and look for clues there; however, the end of the first section is equally elusive, stating only, "Therefore, the two men's grave mounds flank the woman's on both sides to this day."

hateful enemy. The traveler grants the ghostly man his wish; sounds of fighting are heard, then he is visited once more by the same apparition, who now joyfully reports that he has taken vengeance upon his rival and will now devote himself to being the traveler's protective deity. The next day, the traveler finds streaks of blood by the grave mounds as well as on his sword. The third section thus embroils the suitors in further trajectories of movement: one or the other suitors is expelled from his gravesite, and the remaining suitor now pledges to accompany the traveler as his divine protector.

The ambiguity in the identities of the victorious and the defeated in this afterlife battle continues the destabilization of discourses of conquest that punctuate the narrative up to this point: without a clear delineation of who beat whom, the significance of triumph is radically diluted. Did the Chinu man, a foreigner buried in the soil of a foreign land brought over to Settsu, defeat the man who is native to the province? If so, we could read the narrative as one of successful territorial invasion; though the burial rendered complex the paradigm of conquest, the Chinu man's victory would suggest that such nuances were ultimately overcome by sheer force. Or was it the man from Mubara who was able to slay his opponent? If that were the case, then we could read the result of the battle as a successful defense of one's land: the Mubara man drives out the offending alien presence in his province, punishing the enemy for having dared to displace native soil with earth from elsewhere. These interpretations and implications, however, are on shaky grounds if we cannot know for certain the identities of the winner or the loser of the bloody battle. The *Yamato* passage presents us with an unexpected paradox: the seemingly straightforward story of a duel turns out to undercut the very workings of a narrative of triumph and defeat, of conquest and submission.

The politics of place in story 147, therefore, is a diverse rubric: by generating a complicated vision of material territoriality and struggles for domination, it levels the playing field for proponents hailing from different locations. The ambiguity infused in the text's sense of geographical hierarchy unravels the center-periphery paradigm of power relations; by featuring two provinces in the manner that it does, the text allows for an alternative conceptualization of "belonging to a place" that is more evenly empowered, materially grounded, fluid, and transportable (in small amounts).

SUBVERTING POETIC GEOGRAPHIES

I now return to the second section of story 147 for a more thorough look at the actual poems composed by the women who populate this extradiegetic space. If the first and third prose sections of this story present its audience with a complex view of place and territory, the second section echoes this tendency. The privileged metanarrative positionality is used here to subtly comment upon a popular courtly aesthetic that is imbued with politicogeographical implications: the poetic strategy of *utamakura*, or "poem pillows," which is one of the fundamental techniques of the *waka* genre and a major element of court culture more generally. Edward Kamens, in his definitive book on *utamakura*, explains the term as "place-name(s) [and other names] frequently used in poetry to invoke specific associations and sentiments."[29] *Utamakura* takes a place-name and engages in an aesthetic exercise of tropic associations—in other words, *utamakura* renders a place into a form of wordplay that endows the name with purely phonetic value, then infuses it with symbolic value that is relevant only within elite literary groups. *Utamakura* was not just a *waka* phenomenon; among courtly circles, for example, tropic places were brought to life symbolically through the construction of gardens such as the famous one at Kawaranoin, the residence of Minister of the Left Minamoto no Tōru (822–95) and a site that hosted a number of Uda's literary gatherings, which was said to invoke the scenery at Shiogama in Mutsu Province.[30]

While *utamakura* can certainly be found in the proximity of the capital, such as the famous Ōsaka Pass, or Saga in the western part of the capital (story 8), many are located in distant provinces, a number of which were involved in territorial disputes between the central government and those native to the region. *Utamakura*, therefore, was not an innocent game of words; rather, it was part of the discourse of political and aesthetic dominance that the court was seeking to establish over these contested places, as I will discuss in greater detail in chapter 2.

29. Kamens, *Utamakura, Allusion, and Intertextuality*, 5.

30. Kawaranoin was known as a site for many of Uda's literary banquets after his abdication, and after Tōru's death the property is given to Uda by Tōru's son, Noboru. Kudō, *Heianchō*, 197–212.

For the purposes of the current discussion, what I wish to delineate is that an *utamakura* severs a place-name from its concrete materiality, resituates it in the realm of pure signifiers, and subsequently endows it with literary significance; in turn, the aestheticized place-name serves to erase the subjugation to which that place must submit by suppressing any "realities" of a place and molding its nomenclature into a linguistic exercise. And, indeed, *Yamato* does contain many such standard uses of the *utamakura* technique.[31]

The second section of story 147, however, is striking in its resistance to the discursive forces of *utamakura*, despite the fact that the tale is crucially concerned with questions of place. Out of the ten poems in the sequence by Empress Onshi's entourage, only one weaves a place-name into its imagery; what is more, that place-name is one that is notable for vagueness. Haruzumi no Amaneiko, a daughter of the scholar of Chinese learning Haruzumi no Yoshitada (797–870), is here identified as chief of the Sewing Office and noted as having composed the following:

kachimake mo	*nakute ya haten*	*kimi ni yori*
omoi kurabu no	*yama wa koyu tomo*	
Without either winning, or losing	am I fated to die?	Though, for your sake
I crossed Mt. Kurabu,	comparing my rival's thoughts to mine.[32]	

31. For example, in story 152, the narrator relates that an unnamed emperor was presented with a hawk of unrivaled quality from the hamlet of Iwate in Michinoku. He entrusted an unidentified major counselor to take care of this hawk, but the latter mistakenly lets the bird escape; the major counselor looks for the lost hawk everywhere, but to no avail. He warily reports the state of affairs to the emperor, who remains completely silent upon hearing the bad news. The major counselor nervously asks why His Majesty has not said a word, to which the emperor replies with the second line of a *waka* poem:

iwade omou zo	*iu ni masareru*
Longing without speaking/Iwate	surpasses speaking.

The emperor, through the pun on the hawk's homeland, Iwate, and the verb *iwade* (to not speak), expresses his grief over the loss of the bird; here, the northeastern place-name is subsumed into the linguistic play of the poem that chastises the major counselor's carelessness.

32. Imai, *Yamato monogatari hyōshaku*, 2: 194.

Since there is no mountain with the exact name of Kurabu, there has been much speculation over its identity: it may refer to Mt. Kurama or Mt. Kibune in the northern outskirts of the capital, but some poets have used the name as if it refers to the entire mountain range that includes both of the above mountains. Other poets have invoked the name Kurabu in a poem about a mountain not far from Sagano in the western fringes of the capital and a mountain in a completely different province.[33] Mt. Kurabu is, therefore, a slippery *utamakura*: while it enmeshes a place-name in the web of linguistic play in a manner quite similar to numerous other *waka* topoi, the murky identity of the mountain destabilizes the very logic of this play. In other words, the mountain resists aesthetic appropriation by not being a "real" topographic feature in the first place; the court's cultural reach over the terrain is unexpectedly deflected when that geography is already in the realm of discourse—an empty center of sorts, one that is difficult to pinpoint and thereby appropriate.

Another feature of the *waka* series in the second section is that none of the poems mentions the actual name of the river, Ikuta, even though many openly invoke water imagery that refers to the river in which the three drowned, and despite the fact that Ikuta appears as an *utakamura* elsewhere.[34] It is as if there is a refusal to bring a concrete, actual place-name that also functions as an *utamakura* into this courtly aesthetic exercise of *waka* poetry. In fact, the omission of Ikuta's proper name in these poems complements the appearance of Mt. Kurabu, whose challenges to the operations of geographical cooptation I have just delineated. Reading the absence of the name Ikuta in the poem series together with the instability of the mountain-as-*utamakura* as symbolized by Mt. Kurabu permits us to see a moment of textual resistance to dominant courtly poetic practices: this section of story 147 challenges the conceptualization of poetic composition as an occasion to bolster and reinforce the court's linguistic dominance and political rule over places abstracted into names-as-play.[35]

33. Kubota and Baba, *Utakotoba utamakura daijiten*, 310. For example, *Nōin utamakura* (ca. Heian period, dates unknown) lists Mt. Kurabu as an *utamakura* of Iga Province (Sasaki Nobutsuna, *Nihon kagaku taikei*, 1: 93), and *Shitagōshū*, the *shikashū* of Minamoto no Shitagō (911–83), hints that Mt. Kurabu was possibly not too far from Sagano (Wakashi kenkyūkai, *Shikashū taisei*, 1: 433–34 and 441).

34. Kubota and Baba, *Utakotoba utamakura daijiten*, 86–87.

35. In story 147, there is one occasion in which we can find an example of standard

With the degrees of nuance expressed by story 147 concerning the conceptualization of place established, let us now take a brief moment to consider how "place" is invoked in *Yamato* as a whole in comparison to the specific narrative I have been analyzing. An array of places appear in the collection, ranging from the immediate capital region and its surrounding provinces, to the far reaches of what the court considered to be "Japanese territory" at the time (the Tsukushi region in the south, and the Michinoku region in the north). *Yamato*'s structure is such that the main focus of the first 146 narratives is upon specific, named individuals at court and people associated with them, all of whom populate the capital, whereas the rest of the stories are concerned mostly with nameless individuals who reside outside of the capital, with story 147 crucially marking the divide between these two sections. The two-part structure thus clearly exhibits the text's awareness of place and its ontological significance: the stage for action is classified as belonging to two distinct spaces, the capital and not-capital. This method of dividing national space seems certainly in keeping with standard discourses of the day, such as the one represented by the *utamakura* technique discussed above.

However, once again, story 147 represents a textual moment in which such divisions are rendered less stark. Take the term used to refer to "another province" in this story, for instance. Elsewhere in *Yamato*, the most commonly used term to refer to a province that is not the capital

---

utamakura usage: in the first section, the poem that the tragic maiden composes right before she throws herself into the river focuses on a pun on the river's name, Ikuta, which literally means "living rice field"; she laments over the irony of ending her life in a river whose name contains the word "life"/[to] "live." On the one hand, we can read the presence of *utamakura* in a poem attributed to the maiden herself as proof of her figure's subjugation to courtly aesthetic standards. On the other hand, the appearance of the maiden's poem in the first section and the absence of any poems that feature Ikuta as an *utamakura*—or any other "normal" usage of *utamakura* at all—in the second section is, I believe, significant. It is this middle section that is clearly marked as a courtly space in which poems are composed as commentary to the "old tale"; the textual insistence on avoiding *utamakura* usage in this section, when read together with the contrastive presence of an *utamakura* in a poem attributed to a person native to the regions, again subverts the conventional context of *utamakura*. In other words, the Settsu maiden is allowed to compose a poem that turns her own landscape into manipulated language, whereas the women who reside at court clearly refrain from doing so. What we see is that differences in the positionality of each character affect what she produces textually, as well as the implications of those productions.

is *hito no kuni* (other people's province), a term used in other Heian texts such as *Ise monogatari.* Annotators gloss this term as follows: Imai Gen'e likens it to the modern-day term *chihō* (the "regions"), Kakimoto Tsutomu uses the same gloss and also sometimes translates it as *inaka* (countryside), and Takahashi Shōji explains that the term places the speaking subject in the position of a capital-dweller (thus the term refers to a province away from the capital).[36] In other words, the term *hito no kuni* is enunciated from the positionality of someone who lives in the capital and is looking "outward" toward the provinces. The term appears in eight stories, and in these passages, *hito no kuni* is almost always associated with the desolation that arises out of one's distance from the capital, and is situated as an undesirable destination.[37]

In contrast, what we find in story 147 is the term *kotokuni* (different province), not *hito no kuni.* I would argue that *kotokuni* here is a term that allows for a subject position that is other than that of "capital dweller"; the term does not necessarily privilege the capital as the only spatial positionality from which one can speak. It recognizes difference through the use of the word *koto*, but does not carry with it the connotation of simple binary distinctions contained within the term *hito no kuni.* My point is that here, the assertion of difference does not automatically put one half of a binary over the other in the same way that *hito no kuni*'s "othering" situates the capital-dwelling self in a normative position vis-à-vis those in "other provinces."

That story 147 is the first of the noncapital narratives in *Yamato* is, I would argue, paramount in understanding the significance of this term; the appearance of *kotokuni* in this text likely signals a shift not just in the content of the stories, but also a change in the collection's geographical attitude. In other words, up to story 147, the viewpoint of the narrator-editor is that of the capital dweller; thus all but one of the terms like *hito no kuni* appear in this section. Story 147, however, shifts the reader to another viewpoint, one that allows for geographical difference with less emphasis on hierarchy. The unusual complexities of this story—its movement between narrative registers, views on territorial conquest,

36. Imai, *Yamato monogatari hyōshaku*, 1: 36; Kakimoto, *Yamato monogatari no chūshaku to kenkyū*, 35; Katagiri et al., *Taketori monogatari*, 258.

37. Stories 6, 54, 55, 57, 73, 141, 144, and 167.

unexpectedly opaque *utamakura*, and so forth—can thus be understood as attention-grabbing signposts marking this shift, alerting the audience to the start of multivalent discourse.

In the time of *Yamato*'s likely composition and compilation, there were strong attempts at geographical consolidation and expansion. Uda's abdication of the throne signaled the rise in power of Fujiwara no Tokihira, who came to be known for his reforms of land management at the national level, such as the ground-breaking edict that attempted to regulate *shōen* holdings in 902. He was also a chief compiler of the famous *Engishiki* (Regulations and laws of the Engi era, 907–27), which delineated the rules and regulations of governance, and includes a prominent chapter on the designation of provinces and subregions within provinces. Tokihira also had a hand in editing the *Sandai jitsuroku* (True record of three reigns), which will turn out to be the last in the series of national histories that had been compiled since the eighth century.[38] In the cultural realm, Tokihira saw the commissioning of the *Kokin wakashū*, which can be understood as a move to establish a national order in the realm of *waka* and larger aesthetic norms.[39] At the same time, it was an era for notable rebellions and territorial disputes: revolts by Taira no Masakado (?–940) in the east, and Fujiwara no Sumitomo (?–941) in the west enlivened the mid-tenth century, while in the northeast, the central government struggled to subjugate local populations, as I will discuss in detail in the next chapter. Conquest and the issue of territorial boundaries, therefore, were on the forefront of the central government's concerns of the day. Against these trends, we can read story 147's nuanced stance with regard to places and the act of conquest as one that critiques the consolidationist vision of certain male elites in the first half of the tenth century.

What, then, might have made it possible for the narrative to have taken this critical stance? Here, I invoke a text from roughly the same time period as an example for comparison: the famed *Tosa nikki* (Tosa diary), authored by none other than Ki no Tsurayuki, the main compiler of the above-mentioned *Kokin wakashū*; the opening states that the "diary" is

38. Oboroya, *Fujiwarashi sennen*, 76.

39. See Okada, *Figures of Resistance*, 85–111.

being written by a female character who is traveling from Tosa Province back to the capital in 934 as part of the provincial governor's entourage. As Tomiko Yoda's pioneering analysis of this text has shown, Tsurayuki's invocation of the woman's persona should be understood as a textual strategy that attempts to privilege one poetic language form over another.[40] Here, I propose that this strategy—that of the gendered persona—also enables the text to represent *places* in the ways that it does. In terms of pronouncements about place, the overwhelming majority of *Tosa* is devoted to the privileging of the capital as the location to which everyone on the trip longs to return as soon as possible; the narrator and the others in the entourage are relentless in expressing this desire, while other provinces are depicted as being clearly inferior. The very end of *Tosa*, however, radically undercuts this discourse of the capital as a coveted land: when the travelers finally get home, they find that everything is in disarray and are deeply disappointed.[41] The final impression of the text is thus one of sudden surprise; what had seemed like a work dedicated to singing the praises of the capital and its elite culture turns out to have an abrupt ending that pulls the rug from under these praises.

Story 147, though less straightforward in its problematization of the capital as a locational object of desire, is equally subversive in the way it unravels some of the foundations upon which the project of territorial conquest is built. What is analogous about *Tosa* and this text is the strategy of the gendered metanarrative—and it is this strategy that creates a space that permits such disruptive counterdiscourses, here specifically about places and the meanings attributed to them. In other words, the construction of the gendered narratorial persona in *Tosa* is similar to the production of the metanarrative layer in story 147: certainly because they are both gendered as female, but even more vitally because the additional layer of subjectivity allows for the creation of a critical space—one that is more free to offer alternative understandings of the relationship between geography and power.

Indeed, in this light, we might even say that the persona of the female narrator was necessary for Tsurayuki, who seems to otherwise have been an active participant in capital-privileging cultural projects, to be able to

40. Yoda, *Gender and National Literature*, 81–110.
41. Hasegawa et al., *Tosa nikki*, 32–33.

render places in the ways that he does in *Tosa.* Thus in that text, the node of gendered critique is the constructed persona of a woman traveling in the service of the former governor of Tosa; in story 147 of *Yamato*, the corresponding space is a literal one: the palace room full of high-ranking women who comment upon the actions of characters in an old romance through the powers of poetry. Thus what at first glance appears to be a straightforward, almost stereotypical scene depicted in *Yamato*'s story 147—women in the depths of the palace composing poetry—turns out to be far more than what meets the eye: their stationary status is a privileged, gendered space for textual commentary, and the generic mode through which the critique is made challenges a male-centered scene of poetic authority; furthermore, the commentary itself is one that interrupts the standard operations of courtly aesthetics and geopolitics.

When Women Do Move

We have established that *Yamato* features a significant presence of narratives that construct courtly women's stationary status as a coveted and privileged position. The collection, however, is not devoid of female figures from other social classes. Although the stories about these lower-ranking women do not bring together diegetic and extradiegetic mobility in the ways examined above, I discuss them here nonetheless, because when such figures do engage in acts of movement, they often subvert the iconic image of the waiting woman and the commuting man from a different perspective. Narratives that feature women on the move therefore tend to contrast sharply with those about men; whereas the latter, as I have shown above, are frequently strongly associated with tragic ends and a sense of uncertainty, the former's female protagonists are cast in a more neutral fashion, and some even manage to improve their life conditions significantly as a result of their willingness to step out.

One such example is story 141, which relates the following: a man who called himself a middling official of Yamato Province brings a second wife to live at home together with him and his first wife; the narrator states that the two wives go on to become excellent friends.

What is interesting is that the second wife starts to see other men during the husband's lengthy absences, and she becomes the subject of rumors among neighbors. She then composes the following poem in response to such talk:

yowa ni idete	*tsuki dani mizu wa*	*au koto wo*
shirazugao nimo		*iwamashi mono wo*
Going out into the night,	if only the moon had not seen me,	about my tryst
an "I know nothing of it" face		I would be able to don.[42]

This poem clearly situates the speaker, the second wife, as the one who leaves her home "into the night" to meet her lover. Perhaps it would have been too awkward for her to receive her extramarital suitors at her husband's residence; perhaps she was exceptionally aggressive in her pursuit of multiple lovers. Whatever the reason, it is she who is cast as the subject of movement in this multiple-partner configuration.

The second wife continues to carry on with other men, while confiding to the first wife about her affairs; the first wife keeps everything secret from the husband to protect her best friend. When the husband eventually discovers the truth, it turns out that he is not terribly concerned. It takes a while for him to grow tired of the second wife, who does not stop seeing her suitors even after she knows that he is aware of the situation. She finally decides to leave, in order to return to her home province of Tsukushi to live with her family. At the end of the story, both the husband and the first wife are distraught with grief upon the second wife's departure, thinking nostalgically about their years together. The narrative ends with the scene of the three's parting, with the couple in tears watching the boat on which the second wife has boarded disappear into the offing.

The figure of the second wife is therefore far from that of a wife who patiently waits for her neglectful husband; rather, she is cast as an irreverent lover who does as she pleases, actively engaging in nocturnal journeys in pursuit of adventure. The first wife, who appears to play a more normative role of the stay-put wife in a uxorilocal marriage, is here transformed into the second wife's silent accomplice, enabling her friend

42. Imai, *Yamato monogatari hyōshaku*, 2: 146.

to venture forth on her affairs. What is more, despite her irreverence, the second wife is shown to forge strong ties not only with her friend, the first wife, but also with her husband, even when he discovers the truth of her secret trysts. In the final scene, it is the second wife who is again engaged in movement: she chooses to leave, and her departure affects the couple she leaves behind in a profoundly emotional manner. In all of these ways, story 141 subverts the normative trope of polygynous uxorilocal relations through the figure of female movement: the second wife's mobility is acknowledged and permitted, and the narrator makes it clear that she was greatly liked by those to whom the marriage bound her.

Story 148, on the other hand, fully reverses the trope of the woman who waits in one place and the man who wanders off, promising a return. A couple living in Naniwa in Settsu Province, described as being "not too lowly in status"—that is, not among the most elite, but not exactly commoners—falls upon hard times. At a loss for what to do, the man encourages the woman to go to the capital to find employment, stating that once they regain their footing they could be reunited. She thus makes her way to the capital, where she succeeds in becoming an attendant for a certain high-ranking noble. She still earnestly longs for her home province and her husband, but her courtly service improves her dress and makes her beautiful and attractive. When her employer's wife passes away, her employer decides to marry the woman from Naniwa. The union, moreover, does not appear coerced; the narrator states that she came to have loving feelings for the nobleman and became his wife (*omoitsukite tsuma ni narikeri*). Her new life seemed to be splendid and "without worry."

The woman, despite her good fortune, continues to be concerned about what has become of her former husband. She finally manages to arrange for a trip to Naniwa on her own; when she gets there, however, she finds no trace of her home, nor word about the whereabouts of her former spouse. Fate, though, would have it that she comes across a destitute reed seller—her former husband, now barely recognizable in rags. They realize each other's identity and engage in a requisite exchange of *waka*. His poem:

kimi nakute ashikarikeri to omou nimo
itodo naniwa no ura zo sumiuki

Without you I harvest reeds/times are bad— so I feel;
Naniwa Bay: how desolate it is to live here.

Her poem:

ashikaraji *tote koso hito no* *wakarekeme*
nani ka naniwa no *ura mo sumiuki*

"It wouldn't be bad"— because we thought so we parted, didn't we?
How could Naniwa Bay be a desolate place to live?[43]

Here, the man expresses grief over having been left behind by his former wife and his subsequent destitution; the woman responds with a rhetorical rebuttal, refuting his accusations over her departure to the capital, pointing out that it was an act of mutual agreement.[44] She therefore justifies her actions and deflects blame, even as she is depicted as deeply saddened by the man's poem and his current condition. In the end, she gives him her own robe and an undisclosed letter before going back to the capital.

Story 148 thus casts a man in the waiting, stationary mode in contrast to the woman who travels to the capital and attains prosperity. For the man who chooses to stay put in Naniwa, the fall from his original social position that is "not too lowly" to that of a poverty-stricken reed seller is striking; the woman's departure has brought him not only emotional grief but a substantial economic decline. On the other hand, the woman on the move gains not only physical advantages, such as improvements in clothing and general appearance, but also a livelihood that far surpasses her former lifestyle in Naniwa. It is significant that although she is clearly touched by her former husband's duress, she nevertheless returns to the capital, where a more comfortable life with her new husband awaits. The lesson seems to be, then, that when men stay still, the outcome is negative, whereas when women engage themselves in movement, many good things can happen. If we read this story in the context of other narratives in *Yamato*, then, male figures

43. Ibid., 2: 215.

44. The various versions of *Yamato* disagree over the order of these poems, and some only present one or the other of the pair (for a full discussion, see Katagiri et al., *Taketori monogatari*, 380–81, and Imai, *Yamato monogatari hyōshaku*, 2: 218–22). If the woman's poem had been presented first, it would be less of a rebuttal than in the textual example here; however, the force with which she points out that they had both agreed to her departure remains constant.

find themselves in a lose-lose situation vis-à-vis the trope of movement: when they are in motion, their life courses are uncertain and potentially quite tragic, but if they stay in one place, matters can be equally problematic.

Both story 141 and story 148 involve female protagonists who do not reside in the palace as women attendants, who were the central characters of the narratives discussed in the earlier parts of this chapter. It may be, then, that mobility is ascribed to female figures who exist outside of that special, exclusive imperial space; one might say that *Yamato* endows relatively more ordinary women who inhabit such out-of-palace, less exclusive places with the power of movement. Whereas in the privileged world of those within the palace, power is shown to be derived from their stationary status, these women who do not dwell in the palace assert themselves through successful journeyings. In other words, various female figures in *Yamato* are empowered through their associations with different manifestations of the trope of movement, depending upon their class and occupational backgrounds; some remain still at court while others embark on purposeful trips, and many attain something—ranging from a continuous presence at the palace to the ability to seek other partners—as a result of their engagement with the rubric of movement.

One final narrative needs examination before I end this chapter; it is one in which a protagonist named Yamato, a woman attendant to one of Uda's sons, Prince Atsuyoshi (887–930), engages in a willful act of motion. Story 171 states that when Fujiwara no Saneyori (900–970) was young, he courted Yamato, who was in service at the residence of the imperial prince. When Saneyori had not visited her for a while, Yamato decides to take matters into her own hands. She secretly gets into a carriage, and heads for the imperial palace, where her lover would be at work. She parks the carriage at one of the palace gates, and asks a number of people who come through to please tell Saneyori that there is someone who wishes to speak to him. People are surprised or appalled by her request; finally, she succeeds in getting someone to deliver the message to Saneyori, who is amazed and amused. He has her come into the guard station at the gate, then asks her how this has happened. She replies defiantly: "What could be the problem? I thought it was an appalling matter that . . . "; the story trails off there.[45]

The abrupt finish to the story is likely a technique called "severed format ending" (*matsubi setsudan keishiki*), in which a narrative is cut off in the middle of a sentence on purpose. The presence of this technique in a narrative can indicate that it is the last of a text as a whole, although it can finish off a chapter in a longer work.[46] As disruptive as such a sudden ending may seem to an unfamiliar audience, modern annotators point out that the audience at the time would likely have known the rest of the story, whose exact contours remain unclear to the readers of today. Poem 788 in *Gosen wakashū* (Later collection of *waka* poetry, ca. 951), the second imperially commissioned poetic anthology, provides a possible clue about how things turned out; it is said to be composed by Saneyori and sent to Yamato:

imasara ni *omoi ideji to* *shinoburu wo*
koishiki ni koso *wasure wabinure*

Now, I will no longer think about you— I thus try to contain myself, but
because I long for you, it grieves me to forget.[47]

Although it is not clear whether the poem was sent before or after Yamato's excursion, the poem suggests that he felt strongly about her, possibly even after the "unusual" event of her sudden visit at his workplace.

The identity of this defiant woman attendant, Yamato, is unknown except for her above appearance in *Gosenshū* as well as in the *Yamato* story under discussion; thus it is difficult to surmise further about the implications of this narrative based on her exact background. Much more is known about her partner, Saneyori, a prominent courtier born as the

45. Imai, *Yamato monogatari hyōshaku*, 2: 360–61.

46. The "severed format ending" was not an uncommon technique, and variations can be seen in other texts such as the slightly later *Genji monogatari*. Because *Yamato*, like many texts of this period, was composed, edited, and reedited, it is difficult to discern which story was the last of the collection at any given time. Story 169 ends in a "severed format" as well, suggesting that it may have been the last story of *Yamato* in its earliest form. See Katagiri et al., *Taketori monogatari*, 418.

47. Katagiri, *Gosen wakashū*, 230–31.

eldest son of Tadahira (880–949), who was a younger brother of the above-mentioned Tokihira, and the first of the Fujiwara to establish the *sekkan* system of rule, in which a male aristocrat would control the court as the maternal grandfather of an emperor. Saneyori rose steadily in the ranks, and eventually reached the highest position of prime minister (*daijō daijin*). Story 171, therefore, features a woman attendant in an audacious act with not any man, but one of the most powerful in that era.

Saneyori himself, however, is a complicated figure, much like Uda and other male aristocrats that populate the rest of *Yamato.* Although he achieved the pinnacle of power, he was unable to wield his influence through the *sekkan* pattern that his father had established: his daughter, a consort of Emperor Murakami, failed to produce an imperial heir, thus voiding the possibility of his influence as maternal grandfather to an emperor; compared to his younger brother Morosuke (908–60), Saneyori's lineage was much less able to secure power through this system of rule.[48] By the time of *Yamato*'s earliest compilation date of 951, there were already seeds of uncertainty about Saneyori's ability to sustain the strength of his political prowess; his figure is thus an embodiment of both the potential for power and its fragility, once acquired.[49]

Given these features concerning Saneyori's circumstances, the fact that the narrator has Yamato visiting him while he is on the job at the palace is, I would argue, an interesting and ironic statement about male and female positionalities, continuity, and movement. In story 171, it is the man who is at the palace and is being visited by a mobile woman; this configuration is a reversal of the more expected situation of a man who comes calling to the place of the woman attendant who is serving at court. Even more significant, however, are the nuances of this reversal: whereas the "stationary woman" trope has been established all along in *Yamato* as an empowering positionality, the stationary man is not necessarily so stationary. Saneyori simultaneously symbolizes male political success and the difficulty of its maintenance; his physical presence at the

48. Morosuke's descendants, such as his sons Koretada (924–72), Kaneie (929–90), and grandson Michinaga (966–1027), all famously attained their powers through the *sekkan* system.

49. For example, Morosuke's daughter, also a consort of Murakami, had produced an heir by the time of *Yamato*'s earliest date of compilation, whereas Saneyori's only daughter had already died while in service at court.

palace one day is not a guarantee that he will be able to enjoy continuity in receiving imperial favors and asserting dominance over other courtiers with whom he is in constant competition. In other words, the narrative suggests that male figures lead uncertain lives not only when they are on the move, but also when they appear to occupy the position of the one-who-waits-at-the-palace.

The woman attendant, in contrast, is here cast in what seems to be an unusually willful, mobile undertaking. Her daring physical movement across space, contrasted with the uncertainties of Saneyori's future career and familial trajectories, engenders different types of movements that either empower or destabilize. The figure of Yamato thus embodies the subversive potential of female movement: while story 1 argued that a palace woman attendant could choose to remain stationary through multiple imperial reigns, story 171 suggests that on the other hand, if a woman attendant—located elsewhere yet still within the most elite circles of society—were to decide to engage herself in specific types of movement, she could do so without necessarily facing censure. If, as proposed earlier, the "severed format ending" of this narrative implies that at least at one point, this story crowned the finishing spot of the entire collection of *Yamato*, it is the woman in motion—whose name coincides with that of the text itself—who brings gender and movement full circle. *Yamato* reads normative movement-configurations of its day—upper-class women remaining still—as an empowering paradigm; the last story shows that exceptions to this configuration can still, in the end, have a potential for empowerment. This reading is not a reidealization of movement as a symbol of "freedom for the individual"; rather, it is a strategic appropriation of mobility into a specific gendered realm as something that can be positive, *alongside* the privileged status of remaining stationary.

Indeed, let us revisit the figure of the woman attendant Ise, who began the collection with her poetic exchange with the about-to-abdicate Emperor Uda. Her life contours remain mostly unknown, and it does not seem that she actually returned to the palace after Uda's abdication, despite the possibilities raised in the opening exchange of the collection. However, after she accompanied her employer, Onshi, out of the palace, Ise proceeded to enter into a relationship with Uda's son, Prince Atsuyoshi—who, coincidentally or not, is the employer of the attendant named Yamato in story

171. Ise and Atsuyoshi have a daughter, Nakatsukasa (dates unknown), who goes on to join the ranks with her mother as one of the *sanjūrokkasen* (Thirty-six Poetic Immortals). Meanwhile, Uda appears to have continued to hold Ise in high regard as a poet, inviting her to poetry contests and maintaining friendly ties.[50] The figure of Ise—who outlived Uda and even Atsuyoshi, who was likely more than ten years her junior—thus embodies both the powers of the stationary woman (while she serves at the imperial palace) and those of the woman free to move (to and from literary circles, as well as between lovers both current and former).

Since we are concluding with a story about a woman named Yamato, let us take a final moment to speculate on the title of the text: *Yamato monogatari.* To what "Yamato" refers has been a mystery, and various possibilities come to mind. It could refer to the province of Yamato; this province had housed the imperial palace during the sixth through eighth centuries, before the capital was moved to the location of present-day Kyoto at the beginning of the Heian period in 794. Such an invocation of the "old capital" might seem to praise the continuity of the imperial institution, and thus represent a deferential acknowledgment of the longevity of the powers that be; however, as I have argued above, *Yamato* reveals that this institution is, ironically, dynamic in composition—that is, the personnel sometimes shifted rapidly, even if the system itself had managed a semblance of continuity, at least discursively, through the centuries. Or perhaps this text came to be called by its name when story 171 was the last of the collection, and people simply chose to refer to the text by the name of the unusual woman attendant. If so, the title is whimsical, yet also significant: the willful woman attendant comes to synecdochically represent the collection, which is, I have argued, itself a willful interpretation of the positionality of such women.

On the other hand, yet another possibility for the title is that the term "Yamato" also refers to the nation, as in the famous invocation of "'Japanese' poetry" (*yamato uta*) that opens the *kana* preface of the *Kokin wakashū.* Such an understanding is apt for this sizable collection of narratives that span the geography of what the courtly government deemed to

50. For details about Ise's life, see Yamashita Michiyo, *Ōchō kajin Ise.*

belong to Japan at the time; from nameless characters in the provinces to imperial and aristocratic players whose identities are clearly marked, *Yamato* narratives encompass the gamut of society during the era in which it was created, as perceived by those who occupied the court. It is, then, a vision of the nation according to the narrating persona; this vision is clearly and firmly concerned with the production of courtly culture—specifically, the genre of *waka* poetry and its associated rubrics—as a crucial medium through which social and political relations are negotiated. However, the familiarity of such court-centric productions in the eyes of the modern readers should not prevent them from seeing the different lens through which this vision of the nation in *Yamato* is filtered; this lens allows for an alternative understanding of how power, gender, and movement are related. *Yamato*'s nation of Yamato is a place where the Achilles heels of the most powerful men are starkly revealed, and the advantages of the courtly female positionality are strongly put forward.

Yamato remains a mysterious text with much about it unknown—the identity of the compiler(s), the exact circumstances of its compilation, and other basic features of the work remain in the realm of speculation. It is possible that it was authored and/or edited by one or more men, instead of by one or more women; my intent here is not to essentialize a "feminine camp" of authorship that sought to destabilize consolidationist politics or imperial authority by assigning a necessary, biological correlation between gendered occupation and political sympathy. Rather, my point is that *Yamato*'s narratorial alignment with the positionality of women at court permitted the creation of a *textual space* from which to challenge dominant discourses, whether the authorship is female or male. It is not that *Yamato* takes a blanket feminist stance against all things male; rather, it is that the text points to a strategic invocation of a potentially critical gendered subjecthood, rather than to an overdetermined gendered authorship. Through tropes of movement, *Yamato* designates this classed, gendered subject position as a place from which one can reflect upon various discourses in mid-Heian politics, cultural and otherwise.

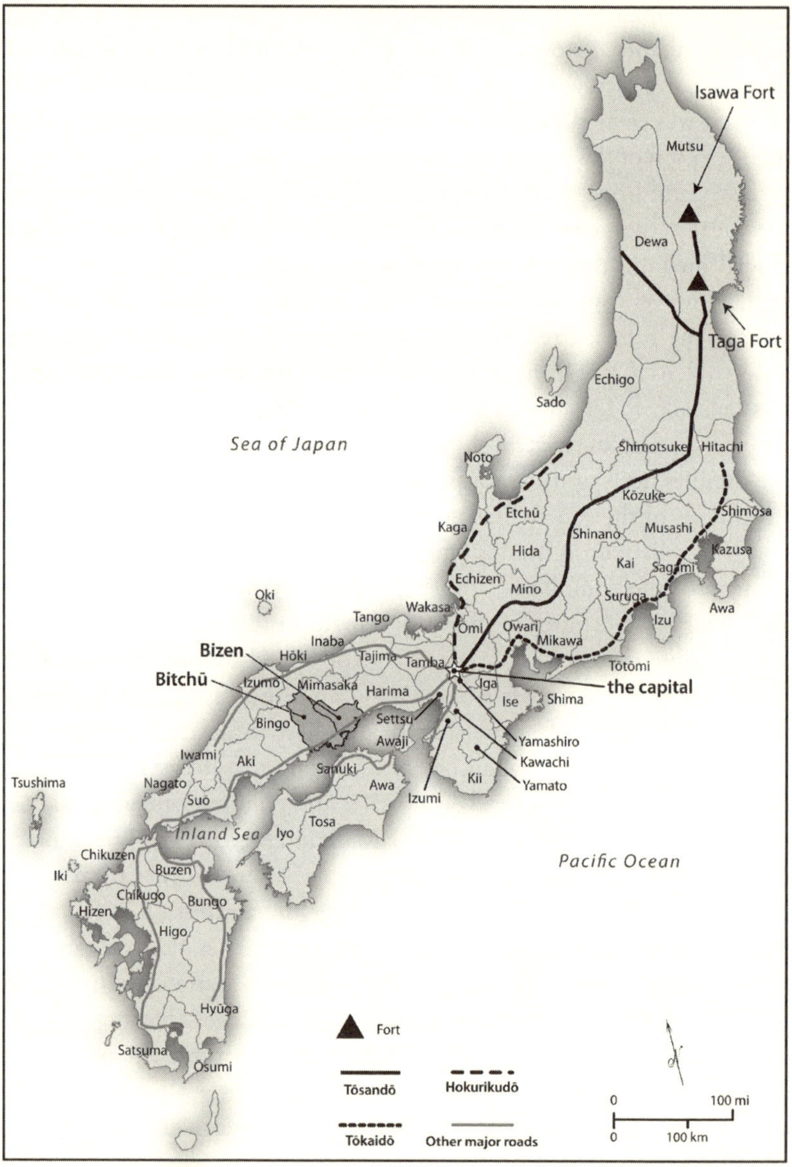

Map 3 Heian and medieval Japan: the Mutsu Province forts (Taga and Isawa) and *Genpei jōsuiki* locations (Bizen and Bitchū Provinces).

TWO

Sanekata

Poetry, Territory, and the Exilic

I have argued so far that *Yamato monogatari* illustrates the ways in which power—even at what should be the pinnacle level of emperorship—could be rendered contentious; such subversions, in the case examined in the first chapter, came from competing gendered factions among those who shared the very core space of an imagined national terrain. In this chapter, I turn to a different moment of discursive fracture, which manifests itself in texts featuring an aristocrat by the name of Fujiwara no Sanekata: this time, the setting ranges from the capital to the distant lands in the northeastern areas that were considered frontiers of Japan by those at court. At first glance, it may seem that the players and issues involved in this relationship are familiar: the center-region paradigm often tells a story of dominance and resistance, and indeed, that narrative is an important part of the configuration between the Heian capital and the provinces of Mutsu (also called Ōshū or Michinoku) and Dewa (see map 3).[1] However, when we closely investigate how such discourses of dominance are crafted, we find that such claims to power in fact point most importantly to radical fissures *among* the supposed dominators—once again, problematizing claims to the stability of authority at its very source.

In chapter 1, I explored some of the means by which poetics play a role in the defining of places; the current chapter examines the particular technique of *utamakura* more closely, specifically as a trope of movement that figuratively transports places across space to the terrain of the courtly

1. Mutsu roughly corresponds to the present-day prefectures of Aomori, Iwate, Miyagi, and Fukushima, and Dewa to Akita and Yamagata.

aesthetic. As we have already seen, this textual device is one that takes place-names from locations across Japan and forcibly brings them into the exclusive linguistic playing field of *waka* poetry, thereby rendering these geographic locations abstract and detached from materiality. Such a maneuver commands attention as a literary technique that enables imagined, tropic travels on the part of those in aristocratic circles of the capital; in the case of the protagonist we are about to investigate, these tropes and associations come to be laden with even more authority, since he is said to have been sent to distant lands for the express purpose of viewing the *utamakura* locales firsthand. The poetic invocation of place-names, then, here becomes a doubly reinforcing trope of movement: *utamakura*, inherently a technique involving movement in its symbolic deliverance of physical place into the space of abstract wordplay regulated by the rules of the ruling elite, is deployed and confirmed by a figure traveling through those very named places.

Such a strong reinforcement of the task of *utamakura* might suggest that its aims are obvious: the assertion of the supremacy of court culture, and the establishment of an infallible national geographic hierarchy. However, perhaps the *utamakura* doth protest too much; I will argue that, in fact, this insistent discourse is formulated precisely to disavow a different source of authority that was very much at play in matters northeastern in the mid-Heian period and beyond: the rising group of families among the ruling classes of the capital whose strength stemmed from their military capabilities. The Heian court relied on a system of appointed provincial governors to rule various parts of the nation, and such posts were filled by aristocrats dispatched from the capital; the protagonist of the texts that will be discussed in this chapter belongs to this cohort. Particularly in provinces that were contentious, however, a civilian outpost was not enough for governance. As we will see in more detail below, the government established separate offices for the control of the northeastern region, one civilian and one military; elites with strengths in the latter category were sent from the capital to oversee matters concerning security. Relations between these two offices were, at times, less than collegial; yet we see no hint of discord in texts that rely heavily on the aesthetics of courtly poetics. In fact, we hear nothing about military engagements in the discourse of *utamakura*; it is as if the northeastern region existed in a calm and timeless tropic terrain that is obediently governed by the power of cultural practices alone. *Utamakura*, then, here function as a trope of movement that becomes a fetish, disguising a lack of harmonious unity among those who sought power with national reach. And it is this very lack that foreshadows large-scale conflicts to come in later centuries, ones that will change the fundamental structures of power in medieval times.

Fujiwara no Sanekata was born around the year 958 into the powerful Koichijō lineage in the northern branch of the Fujiwara family, who dominated the court in the mid-Heian period. His paternal great-grandfather, the famous Tadahira, served as prime minister, and his grandfather, Morotada, ascended to the rank of minister of the left. Although his father had died before Sanekata was born, he was taken into the custody of his paternal uncle, Naritoki, and appears to have spent the childhood and youth expected of the offspring of such a lineage, progressing relatively smoothly up the ladder of ranks and promotions until his mid-twenties. Texts such as *Eiga monogatari* (A tale of flowering fortunes) attest to his amorous popularity, especially with the likes of Sei Shōnagon, the author of *Makura no sōshi* (The pillow book).[2] He was also known for his elegant sensibilities; indeed, it is no accident that Sanekata was conflated with the legendary paramour Ariwara no Narihira in a number of medieval texts.[3]

It is not entirely clear why the course of Sanekata's career began to slow down. Some scholars blame it on his ineptness at the art of writing government documents and his ignorance of government and court rituals (*kuji*).[4] Others assert that his career suffered from his status as one of the favorites of Emperor Kazan, who was deposed in 986 due in part to the political machinations of Sanekata's relatives, Fujiwara no Kaneie and his three sons, Michitaka, Michikane, and Michinaga.[5] The rise of Michinaga in particular as the dominant force in court politics may have assured that anyone still associated with an undesirable retired emperor was looked upon with disdain. In any event, texts suggest that Sanekata stopped being promoted at a rate comparable to that of his powerful great-grandfather, grandfather, or his uncle and guardian.

2. Matsumura, *Eiga monogatari zenchūshaku*, 4: 436–37.

3. For example, *Kokinshū chū* by Kitabatake Chikafusa states that it was Sanekata who had the exchange with Ono no Komachi regarding the pampas grass in her skull's eye socket; *Tsurezuregusa* lists Sanekata's name right next to Narihira's.

4. Takehana, *Sanekatashū chūshaku*, 537.

5. For a critical discussion of this view, see ibid., 541–42.

The culmination of this tendency was his appointment as the provincial governor of Mutsu, the northeasternmost territory at the time. This distant region had interested ruling elites for centuries prior to Sanekata's lifetime, and was seen as a crucial frontier, as I will outline in more detail below. It was not, however, a post that was normally desired, due to its extreme remoteness from the capital, and because it had no particular prestige. Indeed, before Sanekata's appointment, it appears that someone of his rank and family background would have been considered too elevated to be assigned such a governorship.[6] This suggests that something was likely amiss; it represented a demotion in rank and an expulsion from the capital, even if it was meant to be temporary. Of course, an unwanted mission does not automatically equate with exile, since Sanekata was given this official appointment in a manner quite different from the treatment one would receive if one were being expelled as a criminal, for instance.[7] There are, though, concrete reasons why we might consider his post a form of banishment.

We can find several earlier examples of powerful individuals who were suddenly ordered to occupy significantly inferior positions in faraway provinces; within the Heian and medieval contexts, this fate was generally understood as being a form of exile. Perhaps the most famous case is Sugawara no Michizane, the *kanshi* expert who had risen to the rank of minister of the right before being sent away to Dazaifu on the island of present-day Kyūshū as a result of a power struggle at court. He is said to have become a fierce vengeful spirit and thunder deity after his death due to his deep resentment at being banished from the capital in this manner; texts such as *Ōkagami* (The great mirror; unknown author, ca. 11th–12th century) use the term *nagasaretamō* ("exiled") in referring to Michizane's fate.[8] Another example is Minamoto no Taka'akira (914–82), who had reached the rank of minister of the left but was deposed by none other than Sanekata's grandfather, Morotada, who usurped the

6. Ibid., 553.

7. Texts such as *Gonki* (by Fujiwara no Yukinari, who comes to be featured prominently in the *Genpei jōsuiki* section below) and *Nihon kiryaku* state that he was sent off with a banquet at court, given direct words from the emperor, a salary raise, and a promotion in rank before his departure, suggesting that he was far from being an exiled criminal or a stigmatized outcast (Nio, "Sanekata no setsuwa," 131).

8. Tachibana and Katō, *Ōkagami*, 74.

post; like Michizane, Taka'akira was demoted and sent away to Dazaifu. Morotada's sudden death only seven months after he occupied his new post was rumored to have been caused by Taka'akira's vengeful spirit, who resented his exile to the distant western lands.[9]

Sanekata's mission to the northeast might thus be understood as being comparable to the cases of Michizane and Taka'akira; although he was not called an exile outright, the lackluster quality of the position, its remoteness, and the pattern of failing to be promoted smoothly in the years prior to this de facto demotion, together suggest that his positionality may have been understood as a form of exile by his peers. Indeed, perhaps even more important, later generations of writers come to embrace Sanekata's figure *as* an exile, regardless of the actual circumstances of his assuming the provincial governorship of Mutsu; medieval texts specifically cast him in this role. His time spent in the northeast adds to the tragic quality of his life story: he was assigned this position in the first month of 995, and he embarked on his trip to Mutsu in autumn of the same year, only to pass away a short while later, in 998, while still in that province; the causes of his death are not known.

Sanekata's figure can thus be situated as exilic—that is, as one who has been ascribed properties of an exile; this positionality, as we will see in this chapter, comes to play an important role in the production of discourses that situate the capital and the northeast in specific ways. *Sanekatashū* is a collection of *waka* poems mostly attributed to this courtier; it belongs to the genre of *shikashū* ("personal" poetry collection) and contains his poems as well as poetic exchanges with others in his social domain. These poems invoke a particular relationship between the capital and other provinces, which is generated through the repeated use of a narrow range of tropes. Through these poems, his figure emerges as one who affirms the supremacy of court culture through expressions of

9. This incident is known as *Anna no hen* (969). Taka'akira's daughter was married to Prince Tamehira, who was a likely candidate for becoming crown prince to succeed Emperor Reizei. However, the Fujiwara backed Prince Morihira, whose mother, Anshi, was a daughter of Fujiwara no Morosuke (908–60; brother of Morotada); they succeeded in making Morihira the crown prince in 967. There were still fears of Tamehira's influence and his powerful father-in-law; thus members of the Fujiwara family, headed by Morotada, are said to have entrapped Taka'akira by claiming that he had rebellious plans to depose Morihira in order to institute Tamehira as the crown prince. See, for example, Oboroya, *Fujiwarashi sennen*, 94–97.

a series of self-reflexive chains of unattainable desire: the exilic positions himself *as* exilic through the articulation of such cultural vocabulary, and fundamentally contributes to the production of the capital—which is here defined exclusively by its courtliness—as the most desirable place, to which one always longs to return. The unequivocal quality of this capital, however, becomes suspect when we read *Sanekatashū* against other texts of this period; what we find elsewhere, in fact, are struggles within the very structure of national governance in these so-called remote regions. The exilic's project of affirming the supremacy of court culture is thus neither leisurely nor an end in itself.

H. Richard Okada, in his analysis of *Genji monogatari*, has shown the extent to which the exilic and other tropes of displacement come to be fundamental to courtly literature of the mid-Heian period, and the ways in which such tropes expose and critique the radical violence of court politics.[10] More recently, Jonathan Stockdale has put forward a nuanced understanding of Heian-era exile as a multivalent node of meaning, one that could be asserted or appropriated by different segments of society for different reasons.[11] In keeping with these scholars' assertions, I suggest that the exilic is not a category with a preexisting set of consistent attributes, but rather a strategic and variable positionality that here, in the form of Sanekata, works to bolster the court's territorial reach. Furthermore, that bolstering is a complicated project: we must, at the same time, pay attention to how Sanekata's figure trumpets the efficacy of cultural projects as a means to pacify and rule over a territory precisely to deny other means of conquest. The battle, therefore, is one that exists among the subjugators of Mutsu and Dewa; this exilic figure indicates that the fraught arena is not one that merely involves the center-region dichotomy but one in which the "center" itself implodes. I will then end the chapter by turning to two more moments of complexity: a prose narrative that was produced in the medieval period, many years after Sanekata's death, which introduces new features to the legendary figure of Sanekata and points to further possibilities for the exilic figure in the northeast, and slippages in the deployment of *utamakura* itself.

10. Richard H. Okada, "Displacements of Conquest," 63–79.
11. Stockdale, *Imagining Exile in Heian Japan.*

I Long for What I Am: Place, Power, and the Exilic

Sanekatashū was compiled in stages by various individuals between a few years before Sanekata's death and the late Heian period. Although a number of versions exist, at least parts of the collection are thought to have been edited by Sanekata himself, and contain poems that appear to have been composed before he embarked on his mission to Mutsu; later, expanded versions that were likely compiled soon after his death augment the collection with poems about his time in Mutsu.[12] This *shikashū* is rich with references to places, which is not surprising for a poetry collection of and about someone who was rendered exilic and sent from one place to another; the specific manners in which places are invoked, however, are what interest us here, since they illustrate the ways in which the exilic positionality is constructed.

The following is a linked-verse exchange between Sanekata and an attendant of a retired empress:

142 [He] was to travel to [Mutsu] Province, thus he went to pay his respects to Retired Empress Senshi[13] [at Higashi-sanjō-in]; at that time, the assistant handmaid[14] Jijū, while granting him a gift of parting, [composed]:

michinoku ni	*koromo no seki wa*	*tachinuredo*
In Michinoku	the Koromo "robe" barrier	for which you depart/ which I have sewn/ severs us/stands clear;

Before she even had a chance to finish [Sanekata composed]:

mata ōsaka wa	*tanomoshiki kana*
that we will meet again at the Ōsaka Barrier	I feel confident.[15]

12. My analysis below is based on Takehana Isao's annotated edition of *Sanekatashū*, which presents an expanded version, the *Kunaichō shoryōbon*. For a detailed discussion of the various versions, see 495–509 of this work.

13. Fujiwara no Senshi (962–1001), daughter of Fujiwara no Kaneie, consort of Emperor En'yū, mother of Emperor Ichijō.

14. *Naishi no suke*; also assistant palace attendant.

15. Takehana, *Sanekatashū chūshaku*, 283–85. The slashes that appear here and in subsequent translations indicate multiple possible meanings for a single original line.

In this sequence, the attendant Jijū first raises the place-name, Koromo Barrier, located near the famed city of Hiraizumi in Mutsu Province; she spins a quadruple pun, weaving together Sanekata's imminent departure, the sewing of the robe which is the retired empress's parting gift to Sanekata, and the barrier as that which severs the world and stands clearly between the capital and Mutsu (even though many miles and provinces lie between the two locations). Sanekata, however, responds "before she even had a chance to finish," by presenting another barrier much closer to the capital (Ōsaka) and hinting at his eventual return to the capital region. Here we can detect a double-layered attempt at appropriating the trope of Koromo Barrier, and by extension, the northeastern region: first, by pitting a more "central" barrier against it, Koromo is situated as a distant and less desirable location from which one tries to flee, and second, by making Koromo into a pun with "robe," the location is rendered into one that exists mainly in the realm of courtly poetics: just as the nearby Ōsaka Barrier functions frequently as an *utamakura* rather than a "real" place in the imagination of Heian aristocrats, Koromo is similarly coopted into the same rubric, obeying the commands of the *waka* aesthetics and wordplay. In fact, the Koromo Barrier became well known as an *utamakura* only after Sanekata's time; the invocation of this trope in poems pertaining to or attributed to him no doubt contributed to its canonization.[16]

Another poem featuring Koromo reinforces this point:

273 *wakaru tomo* *koromo no seki no* *nakari seba*
sode nuremashi ya *miyako nagara mo*

16. Ibid., 464. Takehana states that the first appearance of the trope "Koromo Barrier" seems to be in *Gosen wakashū* poem 1160 (unidentified poet, nontopic poem):

tadaji tomo *tanomazaranan* *mi ni chikaki*
koromo no seki mo *ari to iunari*

Though it is a straight road do not count on me; near my person
there is even the Koromo Barrier, they say.

The poet, perhaps humorously, states that he or she cannot be relied upon to visit regularly, since she or he is in a faraway place near the Koromo Barrier; the pun on "robe" suggests that the poet is referring to chances of intimate encounters being hindered by public decorum (i.e., the donning of clothes). Katagiri, *Gosen wakashū*, 348. Already in this instance, Koromo is positioned as a distant locale, though the sense of radical divide prominent in *Sanekatashū* is not as strong here.

Even if we were to part, if the Koromo Barrier did not exist,
would one's sleeve be drenched, though one remains in the capital?[17]

The authorship of this poem is not entirely clear; it may be by Sanekata or it may be a poem sent to Sanekata, speculating on whether or not people would shed tears of longing for him if the Koromo Barrier did not sever the two realms so decidedly. There is a pun on *seki* ("barrier" and "dam"); it regulates traffic, but also blocks the flow of tears. Koromo here serves an interesting double, contradictory function: its fundamental existence causes people to cry since it divides the northeast region from the capital and makes Sanekata's presence distant, but its existence also obstructs the stream of tears shed because of this very divide. This doubleness is somewhat analogous to the two subject positions Sanekata occupies while in the northeast, which I will theorize in detail below; here I note that again, Koromo's association with the heavily symbolic icon of the robe in *waka* aesthetics helps to transform its signifying capacity from that of an opaque proper name into that of a constituent element of the realm of culture recognized by courtly poetics.

This sort of appropriation of place-names occurs with particular frequency in poems concerning Sanekata's departure for Mutsu. We see that Koromo is invoked elsewhere in *Sanekatashū* as a marker of the boundary between "here" and "there" (poem 147). Other Mutsu locales are invoked as well: for example, poem 164 concerns a similar incident regarding a robe given as a parting gift by his cousin, Emperor Sanjō's consort Seishi (972–1025), which puns on the Hakogata shore with the *hakogata* pattern found on fabric, and the Habakari Barrier makes an appearance in poem 167 as wordplay on "hesitation."[18] The practice of coopting place-names into the realm of the aesthetic is, of course, not at all unique to *Sanekatashū*; as I noted in chapter 1, *utamakura* as a category is devoted to this act, and it was apparently fashionable for courtiers to incorporate scenery known almost exclusively as poetic tropes into their garden landscapes. What makes Sanekata's case intriguing, however, is the combination of aestheticization and the exilic; poems pertaining to his figure help us envision places not as static, timeless entities, but

17. Takehana, *Sanekatashū chūshaku*, 463–64.

18. Poem 164: ibid., 317–18; poem 167: ibid., 322–23.

as something derived from relations between one imagined space and another. The exilic functions as a mobile agent who renders this point evident.

If places in the northeast are named in poems that emphasize their distance from the capital, in contrast, the capital itself is presented as something for which one constantly longs when one is away:

162 As he was about to depart for Michinoku, Fujiwara no Kintō gave him an under-saddle:

azumaji no *ko no shita kuraku* *nari yukaba*
miyako no tsuki wo *koizarame yawa*

On the road east as the shadow of trees/ the under-saddle becomes dark,
the moon over the capital— won't you miss it?

His reply:

kotozuten *miyako no kata e* *yuku hito ni*
ko no shitakura ni *ito tomadou to*

Please carry a message, traveler to the capital:
that the dark shadow of the trees/ the under-saddle puts my mind in disarray.[19]

Here, the one who will remain in the capital, Kintō, asks an almost rhetorical question: won't Sanekata miss the moon over the capital? Sanekata responds by affirming the paradigm of desire established by the gift giver, whose gift is meant to remind Sanekata of that to which he no longer has direct access, thereby propagating yet another cycle of desiring and not attaining. A similar example is the exchange between Fujiwara no Takaie (979–1044) and Sanekata before the latter's departure: Takaie (who, ironically, will spend a great deal of his time away from the capital later in life) states that this autumn is particularly sad because of his friend's departure, and Sanekata responds that his thoughts are in disarray because he must leave for the distant lands even though he has regrets (*kuyuredomo*).[20]

19. Ibid., 313–15.
20. Ibid., 315–17, poem 163.

Sanekata further reinforces the trope of the capital as an object of desire:

280 In Michinoku, since [he] could not hear the *hototogisu* [cuckoo], around the fifth month he sent to a person:

miyako ni wa *kiki furinuran* *hototogisu*
seki no konata no *mi koso tsurakere*

In the capital it is so commonplace to hear the cuckoo;
on this side of the barrier, this body—indeed it is in pain.

In reply:

hototogisu *nakoso no seki no* *nakari seba*
kimi ga nezame ni *mazu zo kikamashi*

The cuckoo— if the Nakoso "don't come" Barrier did not exist,
you, as you lie awake would be the first to hear it.[21]

The first poem by Sanekata links the familiar image of the *hototogisu* with the capital; the speaker is clearly positioning himself as one who misses the capital and its culturally constructed seasonal rhythms. The person who sends the reply reinforces the distance and the divide between the exile and the capital: by invoking a place-name, the Nakoso Barrier, which lies between Mutsu and Hitachi Provinces, the poet firmly establishes the boundaries of the "civilized" world from which Sanekata is excluded. It is no accident that barrier names are invoked frequently in poetry about the exilic: they serve to create the cultural and geographical chasm between the faraway and the "cultured." At the same time, the poem incorporates the place-name "Nakoso" into the realm of linguistic play appreciated by those who are aware of the courtly cultural codes. Here, Sanekata suffers twice: first, in composing his own poem, he laments that he can no longer hear the familiar sounds of the place where he desires to be again, and second, in receiving the reply poem, even as his correspondent tries to console Sanekata, he or she reminds him of the existence of the barrier, physically (i.e., its very existence) and poetically (through the pun "don't come"), which prohibits Sanekata's access to the object for which he longs (or the object's access to Sanekata).

21. Ibid., 474–76.

In another example, the figure of the *hototogisu* appears again:

> 278 From the province, around the fifth month, [he] sent the following to the crown prince:[22]
>
> *haruka naru miyama gakure no hototogisu*
> *kiku hito nashi ni ne wo ya nakuran*
>
> Far away, in the deep mountains, hides the cuckoo;
> although no one is there to listen it sings its song, I think.[23]

This poem has been interpreted as Sanekata making an analogy between the *hototogisu* and his own condition: deep in the distant provinces, there is no one around him to appreciate him and his sense of courtly elegance.[24] If this were the case, the speaker establishes those surrounding him as ignorant, and in the same stroke elevates those in the elite circles of the capital for being able to properly appreciate the bird's song. The ornithological trope is also a well-known symbol for longing; Sanekata-as-*hototogisu* would then be expressing his longing for something he misses: the crown prince, and probably court culture as a whole. Tokumitsu Sumio notes that during Sanekata's time, it was the fashion among aristocrats in the capital to compete against one another to see who could hear the sound of the *hototogisu*'s song first in a given spring.[25] Within this context, the poem truly becomes one about a lack: the absence of such games, and the overall aesthetic matrix that gave meaning to such activities. Furthermore, the *hototogisu* was also understood to serve as a messenger between this world and the netherworld. It is almost as if the bird's surroundings, deep in the mountains, are cast as "another world," in which the rules are different (no one appreciates its song). At the same

22. Prince Okisada, later emperor Sanjō (976–1017).

23. A similar poem attributed to Sanekata also exists in *Shūishū,* poem 1073:

> *toshi wo ete miyamagakure no hototogisu*
> *kiku hito mo naki ne wo nomi zo naku*
>
> The years have passed in the deep mountains; there hides the cuckoo.
> There is no one there to listen, it alone sings its song.

Koyamachi, *Shūi wakashū*, 307.

24. Takehana, *Sanekatashū chūshaku*, 471–72.

25. Tokumitsu, "Fujiwara Sanekata kashū no kenkyū," 48–49.

time, Sanekata-as-*hototogisu* is also the messenger that connects the capital to the northeast, bringing news to the crown prince that the lands far afield are missing the cultural grounds upon which privileged aesthetic codes can flourish. One might even stretch this argument so far as to claim that the poem can be read as an invitation for the forces of the crown prince to "un-countrify" and "civilize" the "deep mountains" of Mutsu. The poem hints that it is a waste for the *hototogisu* to continue singing when its audience, the "locals," cannot understand the web of meaning associated with the bird; perhaps someone should teach these people how to properly understand the song of the *hototogisu*, long a major poetic trope in the courtly literary tradition.[26]

In such ways, the trope of the exilic in *Sanekatashū* produces a double construction: it generates *both* the desiring subject *and* the subject of desire and consolidates them into a single figure. In other words, through his exilic movement, Sanekata comes to represent the desired (culture and aesthetics of the ruling class) as a personification of courtly practices in a setting away from the capital, and *at the same time,* he is made to desire that which he represents—that courtly culture to which he no longer has direct and immediate access. Just as he is both the only correct appreciator of the *hototogisu* as well as the *hototogisu* itself, he performs the roles of the courtly nobleman *and* the exiled without access to the culture to which he belongs in these poems. Homi Bhabha's discussion of mimicry is useful here; he states: "Mimicry represents an ironic compromise. . . . [T]he colonial mimicry is the desire for a reformed, recognizable Other, *as a subject of a difference that is almost the same, but not quite*. . . . [I]n order to be effective, mimicry must continually produce its slippage, its excess, its difference."[27] Bhabha is, of course, talking about the colonial context, in which colonists, on the one hand, want to see the colonized subjects "reformed" according to the guidelines of the colonizing society (such as through the imitation of "civilized" dress, behavior, etc.) but, on the other hand, reject the possibility of a "perfect" mimicry since it would erase the fundamental distinction between colonizer and colonized. It is for this reason that mimicry insists on a difference—the

26. For example, the majority of summer poems in the *Kokinshū* contain the *hototogisu* imagery; this and other symbolic significances of the *hototogisu* cited here are listed in Kubota and Baba, *Utakotoba utamakura daijiten*, 790–91.

27. Bhabha, *The Location of Culture*, 86.

colonized should mimic, but mimicry must never be confused with the "real." Analogously, we might think of Sanekata's figure as performing a type of mimicry as well. As an exilic, he still represents the courtly—yet "he is almost the same, but not quite" compared to his counterparts back home. His poems continually produce that difference—the "not quite": the *hototogisu* are not appreciated properly, or he feels pain on hearing them sing because he is not in the proper location (i.e., where his cohorts reside and work in the capital). Simultaneously, however, he is also in the role of the colonizer, as the official provincial governor dispatched from the capital. He is therefore analogous to *both* the colonist and the mimicking colonized; he is at once the courtly *and* its "not quite" double. And it is the *waka* in his *shikashū* that effect this curious identity.

Furthermore, the very medium through which Sanekata's figure is constructed, *waka* poetry, ensures that the rhetoric of desire for the courtly be expressed in a format regulated by that realm's aesthetic discourses. Here lies the paradox of the exilic: the figure is trapped in a cycle of self-reflexive unattainability that ultimately locates the exiled within the paradigm that privileges court culture as its very reinforcer and propagator. To put it another way, because the exilic is fundamentally cast, in Sanekata's case, as performing both the "colonized" and "colonist" roles, this positionality guarantees that attempts at the fundamental subversion of this paradigm cannot succeed: the "colonized" is unable to rebel against the "colonizers" precisely because both are embodied in a single figure, and because both positions are manufactured according to the aesthetics of the court, which is cast as the monolithically desirable. Even those unruly exiles who return to the capital's elite circles to wreak havoc, such as Sugawara no Michizane, support the discourse of the court as a coveted entity worthy of attempts at usurpation.

The figure of Sanekata-as-exilic continued to have currency for many years after the completion of *Sanekatashū*.[28] One such example can be

28. The establishment of Sanekata's exilic figuration is complemented by an increasing tendency to portray his journey northeast as a de facto form of exile. One such example can be found in chap. 24 story 37 of *Konjaku monogatari* (ca. mid-12th century), "On the courtier Fujiwara no Sanekata's composing *waka* poetry in Mutsu Province." The narrator provides his brief biography; quite notably, the text states that he "became the governor of Mutsu unexpectedly" (*omoi kakezu mutsunokami ni narite*). The surprise expressed at Sanekata's appointment shows that already in the late Heian period, at least

found in the text *Imakagami* (The mirror of the present, ca. 1170), a "historical" *monogatari* attributed to Fujiwara no Tametsune (1113–?), a courtier known for his *waka* poetry and his friendship with the famous poet Saigyō (1118–90).[29] This passage is particularly striking for its discussion of a custom in Michinoku that Sanekata had supposedly imported from the capital: when Tachibana no Tamenaka (d. 1085) was appointed governor of Mutsu and assumed his duties, he noticed that on festival day on the fourth day of the fifth month (*tango no sekku*), the locals were displaying from their eaves some grasses that were not irises, the traditional plant for the day's decoration. When he asked those around him why this was the case, the explanation he was given is as follows:

> When the middle captain [Sanekata] was governor, he asked, "Irises are supposed to be hung from eaves today—why is this not being done?" [Someone] answered, "There is no such custom here," to which [Sanekata] replied: "Around the time of the spring rains in the fifth month, the droplets achieve their serene beauty in both sight and sound *when they fall from the irises*. Quickly display them." [Someone] said, "[Irises] do not grow in this province," and [Sanekata] ordered, "But how can we not engage in this practice? At Asaka Marsh, there is something called the *hanagatsumi*. Display those."[30]

Here, we see the full force of this exilic individual as the enforcer of courtly sensibilities: Sanekata insists that irises be displayed not only because it is the custom of the capital, but since it is vital to his correct,

---

some regarded this transfer as an unusual decision on the part of those in power, if not something of a stark demotion. Indeed, the narrative proceeds to list other "unexpected" events in Sanekata's life: the untimely death of his friend, the passing away of his infant son, and his own departure from this world only three years after arriving in Mutsu. The fact that this courtier's becoming the governor of a distant northeastern province is linked together with these other sudden and devastating events suggests that his being asked to embark on his post was regarded with deep sympathy akin to that expressed on the occasion of someone's death. Sanekata's governorship thus comes to be understood as a form of banishment from this world into a different realm. Komine, *Konjaku monogatarishū*, 4: 455.

29. He is also known as the former husband of Fujiwara no Teika's mother; she married Fujiwara no Shunzei after Tametsune took the tonsure.

30. Unno, *Imakagami zenshaku*, 2: 474–75.

elite aesthetic appreciation of spring rain. When he discovers that actual irises are unavailable, he emphatically orders that the practice be carried out with a substitute plant. These are the signs of his exilic condition: the simultaneous embodiment of power (as a firm authority figure who makes certain that the customs of the capital are carried out) and lack of it (although he wants irises, he must make do without the "real thing" since he is away from the capital—again, a form of mimicry, the almost-the-same-but-not-quite).[31] Sanekata understands and desires courtly culture, but the "authentic" is beyond his reach; the proof of his culturedness is his awareness of this lack. Whereas the natives of the northeast do not realize that there is a lack in the first place because of their ignorance of this court practice, Sanekata exemplifies the proper "aesthetic person" through his performance of one-who-lacks. As an exilic, he is destined to be confined to this role; he can never be fully whole (i.e., at one once again with court culture), and he must forever orchestrate the awareness of his incompleteness in order to maintain his stature as a privileged person from the capital. The passage thus exemplifies the two traits that I have identified in Sanekata's figure as an exilic: double positionality and the cycle of desire and unattainability.

A postscript to Sanekata's trope of the exilic is the group of narratives that claim that his ghostly spirit made a return to the capital, even though he had expired while on duty in Mutsu. Tale collections such as *Kojidan* (A discussion of past matters, 1212–15), *Jikkinshō* (Ten lessons explained, ca. 1252), as well as the above-mentioned *Imakagami* contain stories about how Sanekata, resentful that he had failed to reach the rank of head chamberlain in his lifetime, became a sparrow after his death and flew into the imperial palace in order to peck at some food on a footed tray.[32] Sanekata's figure is thus transformed into a nonhuman entity who possesses human grievances; as a sparrow, he can only express himself by consuming scraps of food as an uninvited guest at the place that used to be quite familiar to him. It is notable that the bird into which he transforms is specifically identified as a sparrow; it is far from being a species that is loaded with poetic significance like the

31. Interestingly, the narrative cites a *waka* poem that claims that irises *do* grow in Asaka Marsh, and wonders about the truth of the poem (ibid., 2: 475).

32. Kobayashi Yasuharu, *Kojidan*, 1: 182–83; Asami, *Jikkinshō*, 355; and Unno, *Imakagami zenshaku*, 2: 474–79.

hototogisu, or a more menacing variety. Sanekata is thus like an emasculated version of Sugawara no Michizane: he becomes not an angry thunder god who instills great fear in those who caused his suffering, but a small creature with little power beyond the ability to steal a taste of imperial cuisine. Indeed, *Imakagami*'s reference to this story explicitly states that "later generations would consider his behavior as a sparrow embarrassing and pitiful."[33] These narratives thus amplify the dilemma of the exilic's lack: Sanekata's desire for an official post he can never attain is expressed through a virtual parody of his frustrations, in which his revenge is rendered trite. In this way, his figure not only affirms the importance of the capital and its courtly ruling structure by returning to it even after his death, but also performs his own powerlessness as an exilic. Another example can be found in *Tsurezuregusa* (Essays in idleness, ca. early to mid-1300s), which cuts a less pathetic figure for Sanekata by noting his spirit's enshrinement at Kamo Shrine in the capital; according to the narrator, people saw his ghost reflected in the water of the hand-washing basin at the shrine, thus he came to be worshiped there as one of the deities.[34] Even this instance of homecoming, though, represents the domestication of the exilic: he shows attachment to the capital even after his death, as a nonviolent reflection; he is then given a divine function and ensconced (and thus contained) at a place of worship.

Culture Rules: The Exilic and the Military

So far, I have outlined specific ways in which *Sanekatashū* and its literary legacy crafted the subject position of this exilic: we see his figure acting as the government's colonizing agent while being tormented by the elusiveness of his home terrain and its elite culture. What is virtually absent from these texts, however, are concrete references to the materiality of Mutsu and Dewa Provinces; the northeast is mentioned only metaphorically, as a place that enables the exilic expressions of a nobleman. We will now look elsewhere in order to consider other textual representations of

33. Unno, *Imakagami zenshaku*, 2: 475.
34. Kidō, *Tsurezuregusa*, 87.

Sanekata and his destination so that we may situate the implications of his figure in a broader fashion.

We can begin with an example from the story collection *Konjaku monogatari* (Tales of times now past; unknown compiler, ca. mid-12th century): chapter 25, story 5. If our impression of Sanekata so far is typified by an elegant, poetically performed sorrow, this narrative gives us a different vision of his time as the governor of Mutsu. In one of the lengthier tales of the collection, Sanekata's name appears at the very beginning of a drama involving an intense military conflict between two individuals, Taira no Koremochi and Fujiwara no Morotō (both dates unknown).[35] The text states:

> In the past, a person called Middle Captain Sanekata became the governor of Michinoku, and traveled to that province; this person was a high-ranking aristocrat, so the key warriors of the province treated him in a special manner distinct from the treatment of previous governors, and ceaselessly served him day and night.[36]

Sanekata is thus enthusiastically welcomed, but it appears that his effectiveness as governor was far from optimal. Koremochi and Morotō had a skirmish over territorial matters and filed their grievances with Sanekata, but since both parties had legitimate arguments, and since they both wielded strong influence over local matters, Sanekata hesitated in making any decisions about their grievances and died after only three years at his post without making further progress. As a result, relations between the two warriors deteriorated even further, until outright war broke out. Here, Sanekata is clearly not a sympathetic exilic figure who continuously reinforces *waka* regimes while attempting to shape the cultural practices of those in Mutsu. Instead, he appears in the role of a pampered aristocrat who proves incapable of properly handling crucial political matters at his assigned province. The narrative thus gives us a chance to break

35. Known as Yogo, Koremochi later goes on to become the *chinjufu shōgun*, described below. Both Koremochi and Morotō were descendants of warriors who defeated Taira no Masakado; thus they were hybrid in their ties to the region and allegiances to the capital. Seki, *Tōhoku no sōran to Ōshū kassen*, 25–28, and Seki, *Setsuwa no kataru Nihon no chūsei*, 198–215.

36. Komine, *Konjaku monogatarishū*, 4: 503–12.

away from the northeast of courtly poetics; the terrain in Mutsu is here tumultuous, and the text shows that the central government struggled to maintain a semblance of control in this area, often unsuccessfully.

Such revelations of conflict are, in fact, not surprising. The northeast has drawn considerable scholarly attention in the modern era. It was romanticized in the early part of the twentieth century as a place that harbored the timeless and unchanging "essence" of Japan by the likes of Yanagita Kunio (1875–1962).[37] However, recent scholars have focused on less idealized, more complexly fraught concerns: for example, Bruce Batten's innovative monograph investigates the multiple processes through which the northeast was "pacified" by imperial forces, while Mimi Yiengpruksawan's pioneering art historical study of Hiraizumi brought to light the interplay between northeastern and courtly cultural milieus.[38] Japanese-language scholarship that narrates the history of the Heian period in broad terms now routinely discusses conflicts between the court's forces and the native peoples of this region, called Emishi by the court, in terms of projects of conquest and attempts at resistance.[39] Such scholarship has effectively highlighted the problems in trying to cast the multivalent premodern landscape ("Japan") as either a bounded or uniform entity.

Indeed, archaeological evidence suggests that interactions between more southerly peoples and northerners were quite frequent even in the centuries before the strengthening of court-centered governance that took place from the mid-seventh century into the early eighth century.[40] These efforts, including the establishment of the *ritsuryō* legal codes, represented attempts to consolidate power in the hands of the court government; one of the techniques for centralization involved the consolidation and organization of territorial governance. Policies toward the northeast were

37. See, for example, Yanagita's classic work *Tōno monogatari*.

38. Batten, *To the Ends of Japan*, and Yiengpruksawan, *Hiraizumi*.

39. For instance, Kawajiri, *Heiankyō sento*, 164–70; Sakaue Yasutoshi situates the court's dealings with the Emishi as part of international relations in *Ritsuryō kokka no tenkan to "Nihon"* (chap. 3, particularly 108–10). A notable work that explores the significance of the northeast as a discourse in early modern and modern Japan is Kawanishi Hidemichi's work *Tōhoku: Tsukurareta ikyō*.

40. The objects unearthed from this region point to an impressive network of trade with both the southern, court-ruled areas and present-day Hokkaido. Hosoi et al., *Iwateken no rekishi*, 52–53.

newly shaped as a part of this plan: in the years following the reform, fences were built in these regions, thus physically and publicly demarcating what the court considered to be its territory from the lands which the Emishi inhabited. Throughout the eighth century, these fence borders were pushed further northward through strategies such as *sei'i*, or "barbarian-conquering" expeditions, which were both provoked and unprovoked ventures.[41] Among the numerous wars between the court government and the Emishi, undoubtedly the most famous is the revolt lead by Aterui (?–802) and More (?–802), who fought the imperial forces and emerged victorious in the battle at Isawa in 789. The government in the capital, shocked by the defeat of its forces, sent second and third waves of assistance, and finally succeeded in forcing the surrender of the Emishi forces in 802, bringing the two leaders of the revolt to the capital for execution.[42] Less major uprisings and "pacifications" continued to plague the region in the ensuing decades; the tenth century represented a brief period of comparative calm (at least in terms of documented battles), with Sanekata arriving as the governor of Mutsu after skirmishes that took place in the first few decades were quelled, and a few years before the start of significant conflict in the eleventh century.

Open confrontations, therefore, are highly conspicuous aspects of the relationship between the northeast and the court government; however, as I have shown above, *Sanekatashū*'s poetry effectively masks warfare and territorial gains through the use of force by ignoring such strategies altogether and focusing exclusively on cultural domination. On the one hand, this may sound like a familiar situation in the history of imperialism: the denial of violence by suppressing its mention, and the justification of colonialism through assertions of cultural superiority by those in power. On the other hand, however, focusing our attention solely upon the conflicts between the Emishi and the court government would cause us to miss a vital chance to examine a different, equally important strug-

41. Suzuki, *Emishi to tōhoku sensō*, 12–18. The imperial court's territorial expansion included the relocation of population as well: Emishi who surrendered to the court's forces were called *fushū*, and were forced to live in designated provinces far away from home, while residents of regions controlled by the court government were brought to inhabit newly conquered Emishi lands (ibid., 22–33; see also Shimomukai, *Bushi no seichō to insei*, 26–43).

42. For an in-depth discussion, see Ni'ino, *Tamuramaro to Aterui*.

gle that is emerging during the mid-Heian period. I would argue that the most important aspect of Sanekata's figure is, in fact, not directly related to the struggle between the court and the Emishi, although this conflict plays a significant role as a backdrop. That is, the crucial battle fought through his figure is not a center-region clash, but rather, one that takes place within the central government itself. In other words, if battles between the invading forces of the court and the locals had tapered off at least to some extent in the late tenth century, ironically, it was competition *among* the agents from the capital that increasingly became more prominent.

It was in the eighth century that the central government first devised a two-pronged approach in administering rule over the northeast: the civilian and the military. The *kokufu* (office of the provincial governor) had been in place for many years already. It was this office that oversaw civilian administrative matters, and Sanekata, as governor, would have been dispatched to head the *kokufu* of Mutsu Province. In 724, after a significant uprising by the Emishi, a separate government office called the *chinjufu* (office of pacification) was created as a permanent military presence charged with maintaining order in the region, and housed the *chinjufu shōgun*, the general appointed to lead the operations.[43] At first, these two offices were closely intertwined: the *chinjufu* was located alongside the *kokufu* at Taga Fort in Mutsu Province, and one individual could be expected to serve as both the governor and the *shōgun*.

Matters changed, however, in the ninth century: after Atcrui and More's defeat in 802, a new fort was established at Isawa, which lay almost one hundred kilometers to the north of Taga, and in 808, the *chinjufu* moved out of Taga into the new Isawa Fort (see map 3). The immediate reason for this move may have been due to the increased administrative duties associated with territorial expansion; the roles of governor and the *chinjufu shōgun* could no longer be effectively played by one person alone, and instances of separate appointments increased. What is most

43. After the first major Emishi revolt in 720, the court government developed a strategy that included tax reform, expanded regional conscription, and the creation of an office for overseeing this expanded army: the *chinjufu*. There were other military positions, such as the *sei'i shōgun* who could be dispatched on specific missions, but the *chinjufu shōgun* was considered to be the standing officer permanently stationed in the region. Suzuki, *Emishi to tōhoku sensō*, 44–60.

significant, however, is that the clear division of the two offices signaled the start of increased independence of the military governing arm from the civilian one, as the former gained control over the surrounding areas of its new domain.[44]

The roots of *bushi*, or warriors, have been a topic of great concern and much debate among scholars for many decades, since this category of people comes to effectively rule Japan in the centuries after Sanekata's lifetime. Whereas older theories tended to locate the beginnings of *bushi* among local military-minded groups in the provinces, whose activities became more visible as security conditions deteriorated in these areas after the mid-Heian period, newer hypotheses assert that *bushi* were born out of conditions in the mid- to late tenth century as military duties became hereditary occupations within the central government's structure of authority.[45] Originally, military pursuits held far less prestige than civilian paths to power, but the tenth century was a time of transition.[46] By this time, there had developed a complex, symbiotic relationship among the most powerful, elite aristocrats, the warrior families in the capital who served those elites and were rewarded with mid-level aristocratic

44. Ibid., 212–13 and 224–25. The roles of governor and *chinjufu shōgun* come to be played by one individual once again in the mid-eleventh century; Minamoto no Yoriyoshi (988–1075) occupies both posts in 1053, and successfully quells the Abe clan's uprisings during the Zenkunen disturbance, discussed later in this chapter. In this new context, the combining of the offices symbolized a tipping of power toward the military-minded; the *chinjufu shōgun* became a coveted prestige position for warriors, and a tool for the Minamoto to forge their eventual domination (Seki, *Tōhoku no sōran*, 50–52).

45. Kawajiri, *Taira no Masakado no ran*, 188–205. Kawajiri argues that to be precise, it was the descendants of those who quelled Taira no Masakado's major-scale rebellion (931–40) who became the first *bushi* family lineages. Shimomukai Tatsuhiko agrees with Kawajiri's thesis, and adds that by the middle of the eleventh century, *bushi* had a clear self-identity, asserting that the *professions* of letters and martial arts were the dual pillars that support the nation (Shimomukai, *Bushi no seichō to insei*, 99–105). For a concise summary of the "*bushi* origins" debate, see Seki, *Tōhoku no sōran*, 17–30.

46. See Kawajiri, *Taira no Masakado no ran*; Shimomukai, *Bushi no seichō to insei*; Seki, *Tōhoku no sōran*; also, in a well-known passage in *Kagerō nikki*, a mid- to late tenth-century text by the Mother of Michitsuna, the author narrates the appointment of her husband, Fujiwara no Kaneie, to the War Ministry as follows: "He was given a position he did not particularly like as assistant to some stuffy sort of ministry." Sonja Arntzen notes that "the low esteem in which this ministry was held in the Heian period can be seen in the author's dismissive tone here and by Kaneie's own lack of interest in his post" (Arntzen, *The Kagero Diary*, 100–101).

ranks, and powerful military families based in the provinces; interactions among these groups were mediated through court interests in the arenas of peacekeeping and tax collecting.[47] Indeed, after two major rebellions were successfully quelled in 941, a few of the most notable warriors were promoted to become provincial governors themselves.[48]

The northeast, with its physical bifurcation of power between the two forts, is a particularly interesting case that magnifies the delicate balances of power between those with and without military prowess: the warrior families depended on the patronage of the highest-ranking courtiers for political support and financial favors, but these elites necessarily relied on the martial capacities of the warriors for the protection of both personal and national security. One concrete example that hints at the rise in power of the military office is that by the early tenth century, the *chinjufu shōgun* came to be routinely granted the same send-off rituals in the capital that were the privilege of provincial governors dispatched to their assigned provinces.[49] The court's generous treatment of those who were named *shōgun* illustrates the extent to which military power was being recognized by this time as a crucial method for controlling the northeast, on a par with and competing with civilian efforts. By 1018, we even see open warfare between the provincial governor of Mutsu, Fujiwara no Sadanaka, and the *chinjufu shōgun*, Taira no Koreyoshi.[50]

How might we, then, position the figure of Sanekata that is specifically generated through *Sanekatashū* and its legacy within the complex configurations of power in the northeast in his lifetime and the immediate years that followed? I propose that we read this exilic figure as serving a function that is symbolically analogous to the provincial governor's office in the late tenth century, in opposition to the *chinjufu*. As we have seen above, the strategy through which Sanekata subjugates the northeast is solely textual and nonmilitary; it is a "soft" conquest, whose logic

47. See Friday, *Samurai, Warfare and the State in Medieval Japan*.

48. In the 930s, two major rebellions occurred, as mentioned in chapter 1: Taira no Masakado rose up in arms in eastern provinces, and Fujiwara no Sumitomo rebelled in western provinces. Both were quelled by government forces, and the most prominent warriors on the winning side received significant promotions, such as Fujiwara no Hidesato (also known as Tawara Tōda; dates unknown), who was appointed governor of Shimotsuke and Musashi Provinces (Shimomukai, *Bushi no seichō to insei*, 100).

49. Hosoi et al., *Iwateken no rekishi*, 82.

50. Ibid., 84.

involves the inculcation of the notion that the courtly culture of the capital is to be privileged above all else. In other words, instead of engaging in violent battles to "protect" or expand territories, the exilic affects the imaginary through the simultaneous incorporation and othering of places through the aesthetic invocation of their names, and the situating of the capital's elite culture as the pinnacle of desirability. Sanekata performs the exilic's double-pronged subjectivity, and administers "correct" customs in the faraway lands even as he laments his exclusion from the location of cultural authority.

We can return to the place-name Koromo to get a good sense of how civilian and military approaches to geographic significance might differ. Whereas in *Sanekatashū*, as I noted above, Koromo existed solely as an *utamakura*, *Mutsu waki* (Account of the Mutsu rebellion), a late Heian *gunki* (military chronicle) narrative by an unknown author, envisions the place as a crucial factor that instigated the mid-eleventh-century Zenkunen disturbance.[51] *Mutsu waki* claims that the local strongmen, the Abe, had engaged in inappropriate behaviors, one of them being the expansion of their influence southward beyond the Koromo River.[52] We see that from the point of view of military and political discourse, Koromo marked not a conceptual barrier that marked off "this world" of the civilized and "that world" of the hinterlands and made possible stylized expressions of longing, but a contested barrier that barely contained untamed forces that were not happily ruled by the structure envisioned by those further southwest.

The cultural side of conquest, as typified by the figure of Sanekata-as-exilic, may thus have served as one-half of the imperial strategy in the northeast, and was supposed to work together with the other half, the military venture, to maximize the appearance of control over the region. However, the complete absence of references to the violent histories of Mutsu and Dewa or of any military engagements in the exilic trope is striking; it is as though no force is or has been necessary to quell the population, nor have there been conflicts among the officials sent from the capital to govern the area. To be sure, one can interpret this lack as the aversion of the eyes from a messy and bloody aspect of colonization

51. See note 65.
52. Yanase et al., *Shōmonki, Mutsu waki, Hogen monogatari, Heiji monogatari*, 135.

that could be sanitized by its denial. I believe, though, that there is more here: the trope's radical erasure of the northeast's fraught military history can be understood in light of the tensions between the civilian and military structures of governance at a time when the latter was poised to rise in power. One could go so far as to suggest that the figure of the exilic denies the need for military pacification, or military professionals; cultural ventures, such as the intoning of *utamakura* and the hanging of iris replacements, are enough to render an area controlled.

Of course, suggesting that a wholesale, clean division of power existed between the civilian and the military offices in the mid-Heian period would be inaccurate: most provincial governors hailed from the middle ranks of the aristocracy, to which the militarily capable also belonged; as noted above, some provincial governors were none other than the so-called military aristocrats themselves.[53] However, Sanekata's case is somewhat unique: he is not a member of the middle-ranking aristocracy, but a demoted member of the most elite. As a provincial governor, then, his exilic figure represents the worldview of the upper echelons of the civilian court; unlike more typical provincial governors who rubbed elbows with warriors, or were themselves militarily able, Sanekata's specific positionality enabled his figure to be detached from martial matters and thus to deny, with relative ease, their contributions to the conquest and management of frontier territories.

Indeed, we must remember that those who were most deeply affected by the contours of the exilic trope were those who belonged to or were familiar with the courtly cultural sphere; it is not clear from textual evidence to what extent such tropes had an effect upon those who lived in the northeast, outside the elite circles of dispatched officials from the court. The exilic thus points inward: its role is to reassure those in ruling circles of the superiority and efficacy of the court-based standard of aesthetics by suppressing references to other modes of exercising authority that could disrupt this paradigm, including the use of force to physically control the regions in question. Sanekata thus becomes a symbol of the triumph of court culture not only over those in the northeast, but more important, over the rising powers of militarily skilled competitors who worked for the very same court; his figure argues for

53. See Friday, *Samurai, Warfare and the State*; also, Farris, *Heavenly Warriors*.

a literary utopia in which the invocation of aesthetics alone can effectively maintain order. It may have constituted a form of disavowal, as events in the ensuing centuries show; however, the lasting impact of the discourse that privileges court culture, to which the exilic trope contributed significantly, is undeniable. Throughout the medieval period and even beyond, courtly aesthetics maintained its place, albeit in complex, shifting, and refracted ways, as a standard honored by the ruling classes, both civilian and military.

Land as Theater: Exilic Battles in the Northeast

After the Heian period, Sanekata's figure continues to appear in various guises in the medieval period; I now turn to a specific textual moment that focuses on conflict between those who strive for power *within* the rubric of courtly governance, even though at first glance, the problems may appear to be center-region issues. *Genpei jōsuiki* (Chronicle of the prosperity and decline of the Minamoto and Taira clans; also called *Genpei seisuiki*), which is considered by some to be a variant text of the better-known *Heike monogatari*, tells of the sweeping civil wars of the late twelfth century.[54] As I will explore in more detail in the third chapter of this book, this text's dates and authorship are widely debated; it is likely to have been completed sometime between the late thirteenth and early fourteenth centuries, nearly three hundred years after Sanekata's death. Sanekata appears prominently in chapter 7, whose focus is the fallout of the Shishigatani conspiracy, a failed plot by the retired emperor Goshirakawa (1127–92) and his circle to overthrow the ruling Taira family in 1177. The overarching theme of the chapter is exile: the narrator begins with the story of Fujiwara no Narichika (1138–77), who had risen among the ranks to a powerful position at court, but was exiled to Bizen Province, and eventually killed there, for his involvement in the plot. Soon after the

54. Sanekata is also mentioned in more standard versions of *Heike* as well; see, for example, Tomikura, *Heike monogatari zenchūshaku*, 1: 329–32. Like *Jōsuiki*, *Heike* explicitly calls him an "exile," but the story about Sanekata's confrontation with the *dōsojin* deity appears exclusively in *Genpei jōsuiki*.

devastated Narichika arrives at his destination of banishment, the text abruptly shifts to the story of Sanekata, here explicitly called an exile.[55]

The narrator provides the following explanation of the reasons for Sanekata's exile: one day, when he was in court service, Sanekata suddenly took his *shaku* (a piece of wood that courtiers held in their hands) and without a word, struck the hat worn by Fujiwara no Yukinari (972–1027), sending it flying and landing in the courtyard. This act left Yukinari's topknot exposed, considered a highly embarrassing state of disheveledness. All around the two were stunned, but Yukinari quietly had his hat retrieved, straightened his hair, put on his hat, and asked why Sanekata had done such a thing. No explanation is given.[56] Sanekata's "impulsive" rudeness is contrasted with Yukinari's model behavior; the latter's mature handling of the situation is praised by Emperor Ichijō (r. 986–1011) with the words "Yukinari is a marvelous, calm person," and he was given an immediate promotion to head chamberlain (*kurōdo no tō*)—the position for which Sanekata had been next in line, and would never attain in his lifetime. At the same time, the emperor is said to have "summoned Sanekata, and commanding him to go record and expound upon[57] *utamakura*, he exiled him to the depths of the east."[58]

55. *Genpei jōsuiki* uses the word "exiled," or "*nagasare keru.*"

56. Scholars have speculated on the reasons for this rather sudden, strange incident; for example, Nio Masanobu theorizes that Yukinari had been angry at Sanekata because he believed that the latter had plagiarized a poem that the former's father had once composed, and also because Yukinari, Sanekata, and Sei Shōnagon were involved in a love triangle. Nio speculates that these resentments caused Yukinari to call Sanekata a "fool," according to a passage in *Senjūshō*; after this insult, Sanekata thought ill of Yukinari, and the animosity culminated in the incident involving Yukinari's hat (Nio, "Sanekata no setsuwa"). Alternatively, there may have been family competition; the younger Yukinari belonged to a much more prosperous lineage of the Fujiwara family: his great-grandfather was Fujiwara no Morosuke, grandfather to the powerful Michinaga. Yukinari himself eventually rose to the rank of *gon dainagon* (additional major counselor) and served Emperor Ichijō closely. Sanekata, in contrast, descended from Morosuke's less fortunate younger brother Morotada, whose claim to power was brief.

57. The verb here is *chūsuru*; as it can mean both "to note" and "to annotate and interpret," I included both senses in the translation.

58. Matsuo Ashie, *Genpei seisuiki*, 2: 21–22. The fist mention of the quarrel incident between Sanekata and Yukinari is thought to be *Kojidan*. The *Kojidan* version states that "[the emperor] appointed Sanekata as the governor of Michinoku, saying, 'Go have a look at the *utamakura* there" (Kobayashi Yasuharu, *Kojidan*, 1: 144); the word "exiled" is not yet used.

Readers might be baffled by this striking moment of literary movement: why is there a sudden narrative shift in which a story about a tenth-century figure like Sanekata abruptly materializes in the midst of a thirteenth- or fourteenth-century text about a civil war that occurred in the twelfth century? One possible answer may be that his figure, who seems to have acted rashly in public at court, is pegged as an analogy for Narichika, who was also known for his arrogant behavior; in each case, the exile of a courtier is shown to be justified and deserving. I would argue, however, that the unexpected insertion of the story of Sanekata in *Jōsuiki* warrants closer examination; this text presents a complex narrative flow leading up to the introduction of his figure, and it is one that is crucially concerned with paradigms of place, its political administration, and fraught relations among those in power.

Let us examine the narrative surrounding Sanekata's appearance more closely. The exiled Narichika had been settled into his rustic residence in Bizen Province, when his son, Naritsune, is also sentenced to exile, this time to the neighboring Bitchū Province (see map 3). Naritsune, wishing to see Narichika, wonders how far his place of banishment is from his father's; he knows that Bizen and Bitchū used to be part of a single province centuries ago, and hopes that perhaps they are close by.[59] In fact, it so happens that the huts of the father and son are only about four kilometers apart, despite being in separate provinces; however, the warrior in charge of keeping watch on Naritsune lies and tells him that they are many days' journey away from each other, so that the family would not attempt to reunite. Naritsune suspects misinformation, yet the fact that he and his father are exiled to separate provinces makes the false claim of distance plausible; his struggle with the believability of the lie leads him to ponder about the very structure of geographical division that marks off Japan into myriad provinces.

Naritsune notes that in ancient times, there existed a number of large provinces, but in subsequent centuries they were subdivided; he names numerous examples, including the provinces to which he and his father are now confined. He then turns his attention to the northeast: long before, Mutsu had been one large province, but in 708, the area was

59. The original province was Kibi, which was divided into Bizen, Bitchū, and Bingo Provinces in the early 700s.

redistricted and a new province, Dewa, split off from Mutsu. It is this division that brings Sanekata into the picture: the narrator, after explaining how Sanekata came to be exiled to the northeast by the emperor as outlined above, focuses on the courtier's search for an *utamakura* called *akoya no matsu*, or the Pine of Akoya. Sanekata had been looking for this place high and low in Mutsu, since it is a well-known *utamakura* said to belong to that province, but had failed to locate it; the incarnation of the deity at Shiogama Shrine in Rikuzen Province comes to his rescue, and informs him that the famous pine is, in fact, now located in Dewa Province. The pine tree had become a famous *utamakura* of Mutsu before the provincial division occurred, thus it was not renamed as an *utamakura* of Dewa even though it now technically belonged to that province. Naritsune, after pondering these issues, gives up asking about his father's whereabouts.[60]

Thus what at first may appear to be an unexpected, rather random insertion of a tangential-at-best anecdote in the middle of an otherwise linear narrative turns out to represent a significant moment of textual motion. When we read Naritsune's thoughts about the division of one province into Bizen and Bitchū, together with the story of Sanekata's frustrating quest for an *utamakura* in the wrong province, a picture begins to emerge: first, it involves changes in territorial administration, and the ways in which such changes affect those who function within the rubric of centralized governance; and second, it highlights the disjunction between artificial boundaries and the materiality of the landscape itself. The audience is shown how large provinces of the long-ago past have been split into smaller units, causing trouble for the tenth-century figure of Sanekata and the twelfth-century figure of Naritsune. In the case of the former, the mismatch between the *utamakura*'s supposed and actual addresses lays bare the gaps between the physical terrain, the organizing principles of its governance, and cultural imagination. Sanekata's quest

60. Matsuo Ashie, *Genpei seisuki*, 2: 19–22. There is a noh play entitled *Akoya no matsu* (attributed to Zeami, 1363–1443?) that focuses on this exchange between Sanekata and the Shiogama deity. In the play, Sanekata is a rather haughty character who at first looks down upon an old villager, who turns out to be the deity in disguise; he doubts the explanation that the famous pine is now in Dewa. The deity then reveals his true self and dances in celebration of various august pine trees across Japan. See Yokomichi and Omote, *Yōkyokushū*, 1: 138–46.

for the Pine of Akoya is thwarted *not* because the actual tree had been transplanted from its former location to a different place, but because new boundaries were created on the national administrative map. It is therefore the changes that occurred within the central governing institution that stood in the way of Sanekata's mission, not the concrete materiality of the regions themselves. His quest to visually confirm *utamakura*, the artifacts of privileged courtly aesthetics, enhances the very importance of those aesthetics; yet, the quest is disrupted by changes that were established by the very members of that same court. The pine tree and the earth from which it grows are the backdrops against which conflicts among the ruling members of society play out.

Similarly, in the case of Naritsune, dividing lines are shown to be subject to manipulation by interested parties: he is kept apart from his father by a deliberate misuse of provincial borders to create a falsely augmented distance between geographic points that are actually quite close together. Thus the fragmentation of territory is here shown to produce a purely conceptual, though significant, barrier; this barrier, in turn, is utilized for political purposes by those in power in order to keep the defeated in line. Both Sanekata and Narichika therefore suffer in their exilic states due to borders that are drawn and redrawn by the central government—which is, ironically, a political entity to which each of them belonged at a highly influential level just a short while before.[61]

There is a second vital aspect to the tale of Sanekata in *Jōsuiki* that complicates matters further; it is a story about relations among those in the northeastern lands that surfaces in the last half of his story in this text. The narrator, after providing the above explanation for his exile, states that Sanekata faithfully followed the emperor's command and for three years, adhered to his mission to look for *utamakura*, until one day he happened to encounter a local deity in a place called Kasashima in Mutsu Province. The event is related as follows:

> In the end, [Sanekata] was kicked to death by a *dōsojin* at Kasashima in the district of Natori in Mutsu Province. When Sanekata was about to pass

61. This striking representation of volatility in one's status is, of course, an important concern of *Heike* narratives more generally, in which families rise to and fall from power very quickly, and open competition for power is the norm.

> in front of this *dōsojin* while still on horseback, someone chastised him saying, "This deity is one who is unparalleled in its power, and her rewards and punishments are clearly designated. Dismount from your horse, pay respects to her, then proceed." Sanekata asked, "What sort of deity is this?" The answer: "This is a daughter of the *dōsojin* of Izumo Avenue at the northern part of Ichijō, west of the Kamo River in the capital. She was raised with great respect and care, with the intent that she would be matched with a good husband, but she married a merchant and was disowned by her parents and chased down to this province. The people here regarded her with awe and worshiped her. If anyone, high or low, male or female, has a wish, that person should craft a phallus and put it in front of the deity as an offering and pray; there has never been a time when a worshiper was not granted his or her wish. You are a person of the capital, too; surely you must really want to return there. Why don't you pay your respects to the deity and worship her, and go back to your home town?" Sanekata, saying, "Then this is a lowly female deity; there is no need for me to dismount from my horse," whipped his horse onward and proceeded forth. The deity became angry, and punished both the horse and its rider by killing them. [Sanekata's] grave is said to exist near this deity's shrine today.[62]

Sanekata's life thus comes to a rapid end; his death certainly foreshadows Narichika's eventual fate, and we could draw a parallel between the causes of both exiles' fatal downfalls, which are linked to their conflicts with religious authorities.[63] But again, we can read more into the narrative of Sanekata's demise in *Jōsuiki*; the contestation for power in this passage involves figures with complex positionalities.

At first, it may be tempting to understand the passage as an example in which two poles in a dichotomy intersect in a straightforward manner: the regional divine female triumphs over the arrogant male dispatched from the center, and Sanekata's death represents a subversive textual moment in terms of both gender and geography. However, let us recall that the narrator states that the *dōsojin* deity herself, like her aristocratic foe, is an exile from the capital. It would seem that a *dōsojin*, deity of specific crossroads and spatial borders as well as of sexual union, would be

62. Matsuo Ashie, *Genpei seisuiki*, 2: 22–23.

63. Narichika's exile is said to have been a possible consequence of his conflict with Hieizan monks; see ibid., 2: 15–16.

intimately and fundamentally tied to the concrete location it is supposed to protect. Contrary to this expectation, what we see here is an example of a diasporic *dōsojin* who loses her status in her homeland, the capital, but regains it quite impressively in Mutsu; she is not a native deity of the regions. This divinity might thus be better understood as a figure who functioned within the capital's cultural matrix, who then migrates to the northeast and establishes herself as a powerful presence among the local populace; her identity as a *dōsojin* ties her powers specifically to control over crucial aspects of the landscape, such as roads and borders. The deity's triumph over Sanekata in Mutsu, therefore, represents not a perseverance of the regions over forces from the center, but rather, a display of dominance by a religious figure from the capital who has infiltrated the northeast. In other words, what we have here is not so much a "capital versus regional" battle as an "exile versus exile" showdown.

Second, we might note that the competing figures are represented as having power derived from completely different sources; this becomes the main point of contention. The *dōsojin* is described as an efficacious deity, able to bring immediate material gratification to her worshipers, for which she has gained much local devotion; she is said to be capable of granting the courtier's return to the capital if he so wished. The newer arrival Sanekata, on the other hand, has no religious capacities but possesses all of the class-based clout the *dōsojin* lacks. Whereas the female deity is said to have married a merchant and was therefore banished from the capital, Sanekata still functions within the capital's courtly cultural matrix, remaining in contact with those of his rank while diligently following imperial orders to investigate *utamakura*, a key component in the particular poetics privileged by the ruling class. The deity's punishment of Sanekata, therefore, can be understood as a challenge to class-based distinctions that are generated by those in the capital; his derision toward a "lowly" deity is met with swift and fatal retribution. In other words, the paradigm being subverted in this narrative, again, is not "center-region," but that of "elite–not so elite" within the capital's social framework. Indeed, a brief comparison with another Heian-era aristocrat's figure presents an interesting contrast: Ki no Tsurayuki, mentioned in chapter 1 as the author of *Tosa nikki* and one of the main compilers of the *Kokinshū,* is featured in texts from various eras as having encountered a similar situation in which his horse suddenly refuses to move as he passes near a shrine dedicated to the Aridōshi deity in Izumi Province. Whereas Sanekata, in a province much more distant from the capital, treats an exilic female deity with class- and gender-based contempt, Tsurayuki respectfully composes a *waka* poem dedicated to the Aridōshi deity, who is often portrayed in texts as an old man, and successfully revives his horse, leaving the shrine with the deity's blessings.[64] The sharp contrast between Sanekata's audacity and fate and Tsurayuki's deferential poetic offering and resulting goodwill highlight the complex violence featured in *Jōsuiki* as a pointed and purposeful portrayal.

The last half of *Jōsuiki*'s narrative about Sanekata, therefore, is very much about the conflict of power within the political, social, and cultural spaces that make up the capital. Rather than being a tale about the center's domination and the region's subjugation and/or resistance to it, this story of the two exiles is about the struggle for legitimacy within the framework of power structures at the political center; the exchanges between Sanekata and the *dōsojin* remain focused on concerns that carry over from their former lives in the capital. Add this to the first half of the narrative, in which the figures of Sanekata and Naritsune both suffered from intragovernmental conflict ranging from the comparatively benign-seeming act of redrawing borders on the national map to battles at the innermost circles of rulership, and we can see that the figure of Sanekata in the

64. The story of Tsurayuki's encounter with the Aridōshi deity can be found in a number of different sources. *Tsurayukishū*, a collection of poetry by Tsurayuki compiled during and after his lifetime (ca. 10th century), prefaces a poem with a story in which Tsurayuki's horse suddenly dies on the road. People nearby inform him that this occurred because he had crossed the territory of the Aridōshi deity, and that he should dedicate a prayer to the divinity. Tsurayuki purifies himself and composes a *waka* poem, stating that his disrespect was inadvertent and due to bad weather. Thereupon, his horse suddenly revives (Tanaka, Hirasawa, and Kikuchi, *Tsurayukishū*, 156). *Toshiyori zuinō* (ca. 1111–14), a *waka* handbook by Minamoto no Toshiyori (1055–1129), includes a similar tale as well, but significantly augments the narrative by emphasizing that Tsurayuki was on horseback when trespassing (Hashimoto et al., *Karonshū*, 73–75). By the medieval period, Tsurayuki's horse no longer needed to die first before being saved: the noh play *Aridōshi* (by Zeami, ca. late 14th–early 15th century) closely follows the turn of events described above, but the horse merely stops moving in front of the shrine and is allowed to proceed again after the poetry dedication (Yokomichi and Omote, *Yōkyokushū*, 1: 318–23). Similarly, the medieval tale collection *Shintōshū*, which locates the Aridōshi deity in Tanabe in Ki'i Province, tells a similar tale of the horse's recuperation from paralysis (this narrative provides a slightly different poem from the other texts above; Okami and Takahashi, *Shintōshū*, 193–94).

context of *Jōsuiki* highlights the fraught and fragmented qualities of what may appear to be an intact institution for national governance.

What, then, is the role of the northeast in this narrative? On the one hand, *Jōsuiki* states that Sanekata came to be buried in Kasashima, right next to the *dōsojin*'s shrine. The deity thus causes the courtier to be physically rooted in the region, forever removing him from his former base in the capital. The exiled *dōsojin*, therefore, forcibly takes the newly exiled arrival and converts him into a permanent presence in her environs; the courtier is now literally surrounded by and absorbed into the soil of Mutsu Province. In this way, she wrestles Sanekata into a positionality more similar to her own: bound to the terrain of the northeast, she as a deity of geographic junctures and he as a corpse, the exiles are inescapably severed from the capital and enmeshed into the materiality of Mutsu Province. At one level, then, the "regional" could be said to have conquered one exile with the help of another; identities and allegiances in the northeast were complex and hybrid, and it is no surprise to find an expression of its complexity and hybridity here.[65]

65. Already in the mid-Heian era, cases of aristocrats who are dispatched from the capital as governors or his aides, enter into relationships with women in those areas, and produce descendants who reside in the northeast were not uncommon; sometimes the officials themselves chose to remain after their terms had expired (Kawajiri, *Taira no Masakado no ran*, 26–29). Examples of intermarriage and hybrid identities are abundant in the years soon after Sanekata's lifetime: two eleventh-century rebellions that occurred in the area, the Zenkunen and Gosannen disturbances (1051–62 and 1083–87, respectively), illustrate this point. In the Zenkunen case, the Abe clan, whose native power base was in Mutsu, came into conflict with both the provincial governor and the *chinjufu shōgun*, and matters escalated into major warfare that dragged on for twelve years. The end result was victory on the side of the central government, but the ramifications were far from the simple center-beats-region scenario suggested at first glance. It was the Kiyohara family, a *fushū* (Emishi who had surrendered their authority to the court's forces) leader who hailed from Dewa Province, who came to the aid of the *shōgun*'s forces in the crucial battles against their regional comrades, the Abe. When the latter was defeated, the Kiyohara took control over the former territories of the Abe, and the head of the family, Kiyohara no Takenori, became the first northeasterner to be granted the title of *chinjufu shōgun*. The Gosannen disturbance adds further nuances to the configuration of power in this geographical area: mostly an intrafamilial strife among the Kiyohara that escalated into a significant disturbance, it was the provincial governor of Mutsu, Minamoto no Yoshi'ie, who interfered and consequently destroyed most of the Kiyohara. This turn of events may sound like a case in which the center's agent takes advantage of regional strife to eliminate the influence of local strongmen; however, matters are again more complex than they

On the other hand, however, Kasashima itself becomes a new *utamakura* to be visited by poets in centuries to come; thus although Sanekata's courtly project was cut short by the *dōsojin*, he is himself transformed into an *utamakura*, thus contributing to the continuation of the aesthetic legacy. For example, take poem 872 of *Sankashū* (A collection from a mountain home, ca. 1178), the poetry collection of Saigyō, who was famous as a traveler. The preface to the poem states that when Saigyō reached Mutsu Province, he found an uncommon grave among the pampas grass, and asked the locals about its identity; a person said that it was a middle captain's grave, and when prodded for more specificity, the person answered that it was Sanekata's. In sadness, Saigyō composed:

kuchi mo senu　　sono na bakari wo　　todome okite
*　　kareno no susuki　　katami nizo miru*

His undecayable　　name is the only thing　　that remains;
　　pampas grass in the desolate field　　I view as a memento.[66]

---

seem. First, the court treated Yoshi'ie with a certain degree of wariness, as they viewed the disturbance as a possibly unnecessary, personal interference into local matters on Yoshi'ie's part; second, the positionality of the sole main Kiyohara survivor, Kiyohira (1056–1128), provides an apt opportunity to rethink geographical dichotomies. Kiyohira was a son of Fujiwara no Tsunekiyo, who had come from the capital to Mutsu as an official who was part of the provincial governor's entourage. Tsunekiyo settled into the area by marrying the daughter of Abe no Yoritoki (also known as Yoriyoshi), the leader of the Abe family; she gave birth to a son (Kiyohira) soon afterward. Tsunekiyo was then executed for having sided with the defeated Abe in the Zenkunen disturbance, and his widow was forced to marry Kiyohara no Takesada on the winning side. The young Kiyohira accompanied his mother and was adopted into the Kiyohara family; he later sided with his half-brother in a conflict with Takesada's heir, then fought against that half-brother to become the sole remaining member of the Abe or Kiyohara families at the end of the Gosannen disturbance. He reclaimed his father's surname and called himself Fujiwara no Kiyohira, and went on to establish a powerful dynasty, known as the Ōshū Fujiwara, whose command over the northeast lasted for a century until it was eradicated in 1189 at the end of the Genpei wars. The figure of Kiyohira is thus a striking example: he is half from-the-capital (his father), half local in the form of the Abe family (his mother), was raised in another local family (Kiyohara), but in the end reclaims the surname closely associated with elite power (Fujiwara). The hybridity of his lineage and the constantly shifting nature of his allegiances illustrate that a "northeastern identity" can be far from being monolithic or stable. For details about and recent scholarship on the Zenkunen and Gosannen wars, see Seki, *Tōhoku no sōran*, particularly 34–155.

66. Watanabe Tamotsu, *Saigyō Sankashū zenchūkai*, 463–64.

The first line of the poem denies the existence of any material evidence of Sanekata's legacy at his gravesite: the middle captain is rendered solely abstract as a name—that is, his nomenclature, and his reputation as a poet and courtier within the social circle of the ruling class. Sanekata thus lives on in a realm that is completely noncorporeal, according to the first line of the poem; as a name, he is liberated from the physicality of being dead and trapped underground in Mutsu, and is instead allowed to prosper in abstract posterity. In this way, the exilic comes to be disassociated from the specific terrain in which he met his end; this severance can be interpreted as an insistence upon the privileging of Sanekata's figure as a famed poet (which makes sense from the point of view of Saigyō, a fellow poet), and as someone who really *belongs* in the cultural arena of the court, not that of the "hinterlands." Interestingly, the second line of the poem then undercuts the resistance to materiality so firmly established moments before; the memory of Sanekata comes to be literally grafted onto the view of the field that stretches out in front of Saigyō's eyes. This affirmation of the landscape adds nuance to the abstractness privileged in the first part, even though the barren scenery that Saigyō claims he sees before him gains significance only as a visual souvenir due to its association with Sanekata, who is said to be buried there.[67] As an *utamakura,* then, Sanekata's grave comes to attract generations of literary pilgrimages, including the likes of Matsuo Bashō (1644–94) and beyond, ensuring that although his figure is made one with the landscape, the ways in which Sanekata-as-place is appreciated and propagated continue to be enmeshed, at one level or another, in the traditions of court culture.

In the *Jōsuiki* narrative, there is little agency in the northeast for those who are not from the capital. The terrain does, however, become a theater for the enactment of open conflict: no longer pacified by the awesome cultural prowess of the civilian, exilic governor, the realm has now become a place in which struggles among the colonists take center stage. Indeed, it is not a surprise that the northeast as a literary

67. Similarly, the noh play *Sanekata* (dates and author unknown; performance records exist from the mid-15th century) features a dialogue between the ghost of Sanekata and Saigyō when the latter is on a journey through Mutsu Province. After the intoning of the above *Sankashū* poem at the gravesite, the play proceeds to focus exclusively on court culture, such as poetry collections and Sanekata's participation in court ceremonies (Haga and Sasaki, *Kōchū yōkyoku sōsho*, 2: 70–74).

figure comes to signify such a landscape: *Jōsuiki* as a whole, of course, is all about the twelfth-century battles between powerful families and individuals that seek to usurp power at the national level. Moreover, the circumstances leading up to and during the late thirteenth to early fourteenth centuries, the era in which this text was likely produced, are distinctly different from those of the mid- to late Heian era in which the civilian government's dream of dominance through aesthetics was interrupted only intermittently. I will explore these differences in greater detail in chapters 3 and 4; here, I will maintain my focus on dynamics specific to the northeastern region. After the Genpei wars (1180–85) and the ensuing fallout at the end of the twelfth century, the winning side established a new *bakufu*, or military government, alongside the existing civilian government (much like the situation in the Heian-era northeast). The *bakufu* sought to keep a tighter watch over the provinces of Mutsu, Dewa, and even beyond through national networks of authority, with limited success.[68] By the first part of the fourteenth century, however, the *bakufu* itself had become highly unstable, culminating in its overthrow via imperial command in 1333.

In that year, the winning emperor, Godaigo (1288–1339), names Ashikaga Takauji (1305–58), the warrior leader who was instrumental in the *bakufu*'s demise, as the new *chinjufu shōgun*. Godaigo also sends the courtiers Kitabatake Aki'ie (1318–38) and his father Chikafusa (1293–1354) to Mutsu, naming the former officially as provincial governor; Prince Noriyoshi, the future emperor Gomurakami (1328–68), accompanies the Kitabatakes northward. Various theories exist concerning this dual appointment; scholars assert that Godaigo may have foreseen the potential danger associated with Takauji's rise to power, and placed the Kitabatakes and Prince Noriyoshi in the northeast to counterbalance Takauji's influence. Indeed, the latter's power increases rapidly in the following year,

68. After the Genpei wars, the Kamakura *bakufu* added offices for ruling the northeast, such as the *ōshū sōbugyō*, the headquarters for regional governance, and the *ezo kanrei*, which was established as part of the *sōbugyō* for the management of the Tsugaru region in the northernmost areas of Mutsu and Dewa and for handling relations with the Emishi in modern-day Hokkaido. However, the area saw Emishi uprisings in 1268, and in the early 1300s, intrafamily warfare among the Andō, local strongmen of the Tsugaru region in northern Mutsu Province who had been entrusted with the task of keeping an eye on the Emishi, fueled further confusion. See Okada Sei'ichi, *Kamakura bakufu to tōgoku*, 375–405.

and Godaigo feels his rulership threatened; open confrontation erupts between Godaigo and Takauji, signaling the start of a second series of battles.[69] Ironically, therefore, the configuration of conflict we saw earlier in the tenth century involving the civilian and military offices in Mutsu Province comes to be repeated analogously four centuries later. In Sanekata's lifetime, the competitors were both aristocrats, some militarily capable and some not, jockeying for power but working ostensibly to further the same aims of national governance under one emperor; in the fourteenth-century scenario, however, even though the civilian-military dichotomy remains, understandings of the role of the emperor and unity of the realm differ significantly. What emerges from the latter war is an imperial house divided into the Southern (1336–1392) and Northern Courts; Godaigo, after being chased out of the capital, heads the former in Yoshino in Yamato Province, while the latter remains housed in the palace in the capital, backed by the new Ashikaga shogunate.

It is in this shifting climate of rapid changes and intense power struggles—one in which national structures of authority are overthrown and the imperial institution itself undergoes fragmentation—that the northeast emerges as an imagined space that permits such fissures to appear. The region becomes a vital symbolic theater for battles among those competing for power farther southwest, much like the ways in which Sanekata and the *dōsojin* clash in Kasashima. Such battles were, I would argue, not primarily direct attempts at subversion of a region-center dichotomy; what is significant is that the northeastern terrain is envisioned as a privileged space in which conflict can find open expression. In other words, the northeast may not have been allowed to simply "be" itself in texts such as the *Jōsuiki,* but the area achieves prominence as a landscape in which struggles for power become highlighted. Consequently, textual representations of the region contribute to the fundamental destabilization of power as that which is solid, monolithic, or long-lived. The figure of Sanekata here continues to privilege courtly culture at one level, but also significantly subverts such a discourse through visions of struggle and change that are now thoroughly interwoven into the figure of this exilic.

69. See Sakurai, *Nanbokuchō nairan to tōgoku*; also, Okano, *Kitabatake Chikafusa,* 53–94.

Utamakura Revisited

We might now reconsider the very project of *utamakura* searching in which Sanekata is said to be faithfully engaged in *Jōsuiki*. At first glance, the undertaking seems to conform to the expectations for a government agent, whose task here is to physically and geographically reaffirm the imagined poetic location tropes of the elite ruling class. However, even as Sanekata searches for *utamakura*, it is the *utamakura* themselves that are literally *and* figuratively keeping Sanekata from returning home. The very numerousness of *utamakura*, first of all, ensures that his mission is perpetually yet-to-be-completed; their endlessness prevents him from returning to the capital triumphant, with his task successfully accomplished. Even more important is the linguistic value of the *utamakura* themselves: the poetic meanings of some *utamakura* serve as ironic commentaries upon Sanekata's doomed project. For example, the *utamakura* Nakoso Barrier literally means "do not come/approach"; its meaning thus contains connotations of fundamental unreachability. Sanekata might look for the Nakoso Barrier, but it speaks to him: "Do not come." This barrier thus evades visitation by the courtly surveyor, and defers the completion of his duties and return to the location that had ordered his dispatch.

Another *utamakura* invoked in *Jōsuiki* warrants further examination, the Pine of Akoya. We are told that this poetic trope remains elusive to Sanekata for reasons outlined in the narrative section analyzed in detail above. In addition to the difficulties stemming from changes in territorial division, though, it turns out that this *utamakura* itself poses a more literary challenge. The poem cited in the *Jōsuiki* passage as the one that made this tree famous reads as follows:

michinoku no akoya no matsu no kodakaki ni
izubeki tsuki no ide yaranu kana

In Michinoku above the Pine of Akoya's treetop,
the moon that should be rising does not rise, indeed![70]

The poem presents us with an interesting paradox: the moon, which should rise on a daily basis, does not rise from the treetops of the Pine at

70. Matsuo Ashie, *Genpei seisuiki*, 2: 22.

Akoya. Perhaps this is an elegant joke about the height and scale of the tree; we can understand this poem to be a tongue-in-cheek comment about the large pine tree that appears to be obstructing a celestial object from pursuing its usual course across the sky. At the same time, the poem's emphasis on the location of this pine tree—Michinoku—suggests that in this distant land, something that one would routinely expect to happen, such as a moonrise, is prevented from happening by a force of nature. The moon is one of the most standard *waka* images, and the prevention of its appearance due to an object literally rooted in the northeast is, I believe, significant; as an *utamakura,* the Pine of Akoya resists the smooth operation of courtly poetics.

Let us now return to *Sanekatashū* once again to come full circle in our exploration of Sanekata's narrative and his *utamakura* project. Even in this text, which is the first to position Sanekata as an exilic figure and which elsewhere privileges courtly aesthetics with great force, we see that such affirmations are not seamless; there are slippages in this discourse from its earliest moments. For example, the work contains the following exchange between Ōe no Masahira (952–1012) and Sanekata:

168 Senior Assistant Minister of Ceremonies Masahira sent over to Michinoku:

miyako ni wa *tare wo ka kimi wa* *omouran*
miyako ni wa mina *kimi wo koumeri*

Among those in the capital who is it that you are thinking of?
In the capital, everyone longs for you, it seems.

In reply:

wasurarenu *hito no uchi ni wa* *wasurenu wo*
kouran hito no *uchi ni matsu ya wa*

Among those who cannot be forgotten I cannot forget [about you], but
among those who long for me are you one of those waiting?[71]

71. Takehana, *Sanekatashū chūshaku*, 323–24. This incident is mentioned in a narrative about Masahira that is contained in *Konjaku monogatari*, chap. 24, story 52, although Sanekata's reply is not quoted—it is said that there was a reply but it has not been passed down (Komine, *Konjaku monogatarishū*, 4: 475). The full exchange is featured in *Goshūishū* (ca. 1087), poem 1138, which lists these poems in variant form (Kubota and Hirata, *Goshūi wakashū*, 368–69).

In this playful exchange, the first poem states that all in the capital, including the poet, miss Sanekata's presence; in reply, the provincial governor of Mutsu chides the capital dweller by doubting his sincerity. This poetic dialogue demands our attention for two reasons within the context of Sanekata's exilic figure. First, Masahira's poem intones the word "capital" (*miyako*) not just once but twice.[72] The resulting effect is an explicit harping on the capital as a literary object (the sound of the word, the way the word looks on paper); the seat of power is invoked for its linguistic value, much like the way *utamakura* are poetically intoned. The rendering of the capital as a quasi-*utamakura* in this poem raises an interesting question about whether or not in the realm of *waka* poetics, the capital as a place was ever conceived of as a space that could be experienced with immediacy without any intervening textual mediation, in contrast to place-names in the northeast that are subsumed under the rubric of *waka* aesthetics. In fact, *miyako* is no less a tropic construction than, for instance, the Koromo Barrier or the Pine of Akoya; certain associated words and images form a web of accepted aesthetic boundaries that are far from random. However, *miyako* as a topic (*dai*) of *waka* composition is rare in the Heian and medieval periods, possibly because it was imagined as the privileged space that generates those very poetics.[73] Masahira's poem plays with such expected conventions and exposes the tropic potential of the capital by pointing to its value within the realm of language rather than its presumed ontological function as ultimate ground of the linguistic system.

Second, the poetic exchange goes one step further in subverting the significance of the capital in the realm of courtly aesthetics. Here, the capital is *defined* by its residents' abstract interactions with Sanekata: they miss Sanekata, and he misses them as well—we could even say that the raison d'être of the capital is to function as a dwelling space for those who miss Sanekata. Masahira's poem turns the trope of the exilic upon its own head: the exilic Sanekata, who represents the self-reflexive chain of unattainability, is here cast in the role of the recipient of desirous longing by the capital—the very capital for which he is elsewhere depicted as pining

72. Takehana, *Sanekatashū chūshaku*, 325. Takehana attributes this technique to Masahira's thorough and occupational familiarity with Chinese poetry.

73. Kubota and Baba, *Utakotoba utamakura daijiten*, 853.

urgently. In fact, the positionality of those "left behind" in the capital is an important loophole in the discourse of this exilic: if Sanekata's exilic figure forges the boundaries between "here" and "there," and delineates the distinctions between the capital and not-capital, then this exilic also throws into motion the chains of desire and longing for him—those who remain stationary in the capital suffer from the exilic's absence. The expressions of this longing, of course, remain within the boundaries of the courtly cultural rubric; nevertheless, the above exchange reminds us that the trope of the exilic constructs not only the exilic figure himself but other positionalities as well, including that of "capital dweller." In these ways, the poetic exchange between Masahira and Sanekata not only artfully disrupts the conventions of *utamakura*, but also suggests the extent to which all positionalities, including that of the exilic and the capital dweller, are discursive constructions that are generated through cumulative textual invocations of associated tropes.

In this chapter, I have attempted to consider Sanekata from a standpoint that neither romanticizes the figure as a tragic embodiment of courtly aesthetics, nor idealizes him as an inherently subversive hero who successfully dismantles existing regimes of power. The exilic figure is not only complicit with, but is in fact a vital part of the centuries of canon-building activities that privilege "court culture" as the most refined aesthetic standard toward which the ruling classes strove throughout a large part of Japanese history. At the same time, however, a close examination of the exilic figure suggests the extent to which he undermines his own tropic claims; he challenges the very source of power that binds him by referring to conflict, competition, and change.

THREE

Shigehira

Genres and Politics in *Heike monogatari*

The famous Genpei wars began in 1180 and lasted for over five years; in this civil war, the Minamoto (or Genji) fought not only the Taira (or Heike), a clan that had skyrocketed to the top ranks of government, but also among themselves, and finally emerged with a new governing configuration by the early 1190s. In the many years since, these wars have been narrated, performed, and theorized as a watershed moment in Japanese history, in which a clear division of power was established between the court and its civil officials, which continued its existence in the capital, and the *bakufu*, or military government, which was located over five hundred kilometers away in Kamakura and was technically in charge of managing warriors in the eastern provinces, but eventually came to exert its influence at the national level.[1]

This chapter will focus on the ways in which a particular figure is made to navigate through various states of motion in the years in which rule by these two governing bodies took shape. The story is one that is far from leisurely: the protagonist is a prisoner of war who is forced to travel from the capital eastward in order to be viewed and questioned by the shogun-to-be in Kamakura. What is striking about this constrained act of motion is that it is narrated in two distinct genres of courtly writing, where one genre abruptly follows another. The first of these two genres is one we have already encountered multiple times in this book: the world of *waka* poetry and poetics, this time a subgenre that specifically pertains

1. For a summary of past scholarly debates concerning the relationship between the Kamakura *bakufu* and the court, see, for example, Kawai, *Genpei no nairan to kōbu seiken*.

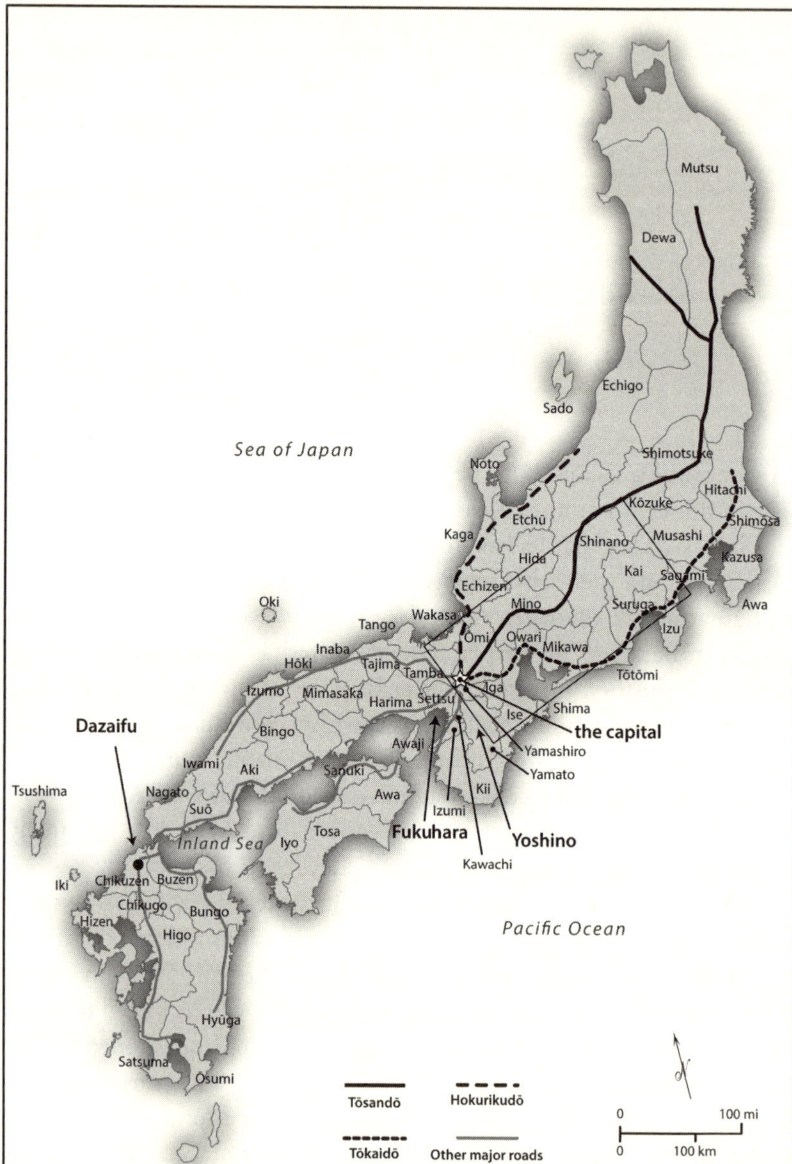

Map 4 Heian and medieval Japan: Dazaifu, Fukuhara, and Yoshino; the area enclosed by the rectangle is shown in detail in map 5.

to tropes of travel. The second genre I will address is *kanshibun*, or poetry and prose in Chinese, which was as important in the milieu of courtly literature as *waka* poetry. Through a sudden and rapid shift between these two literary genres, the text weaves a tale of radical demise for the prisoner-in-motion; I will argue that this disempowerment carries a number of crucial implications for the status of courtiers, warriors, and the double structure of power that had arisen in the early medieval landscape that is the setting for the story, as well as for the late medieval setting in which the actual text was produced.

The captive's excursion from the capital to Kamakura is narrated in what is perhaps the best-known work in the *gunki* genre: *Heike monogatari*, a lengthy epic that tells of the rise and fall of the Taira clan. The work is difficult to attribute, since it is known for its vast number of different versions that were compiled by various individuals, many of whom remain unidentified, over the course of more than a hundred years between the mid-thirteenth century and the late fourteenth. The text typically covers the span of about sixty years in the twelfth century, during which the Taira rose to prominence and fell from power; although some versions appear to have been written for the purpose of reading, the most famous variants are ones that were performed orally by a group of professional blind musicians called the *biwa hōshi*, who recited the story musically to the accompaniment of a *biwa* lute. This chapter focuses on the Kakuichibon version, which became the standard for *Heike* recitation in the middle of the fourteenth century. Its creator, Kakuichi (d. 1371), was a powerful *heikyoku* (*Heike* recitation) performer who is credited for establishing the supremacy of his school, the Ichikata, in the *tōdōza* (organization of *biwa hōshi*). The Kakuichibon is important not only for achieving the status of the standard for *heikyoku*, and for its popularity in the generations that followed its emergence, but also for its unique attention to the particular figure who is central to this chapter's analysis.

The scholarship on *Heike* is abundant, but it is notable that in recent years, this text has been the focus of a number of path-breaking English-language studies that make new efforts to situate its myriad incarnations in their political, religious, social, and literary contexts. Elizabeth Oyler skillfully traces the intricate role of *Heike* in legitimizing Yoritomo, the first Minamoto shogun, as the rightful leader of his clan and its legacy that is the Kamakura *bakufu*; David Bialock convincingly argues for the importance of paying attention to the work's multivocality, particularly in the text's portrayal of Taira no Kiyomori, usually understood as a nefarious tyrant responsible for the ultimate demise of his clan, and for the significance of China's role as both an imaginary phantasm and a place with which to engage in diplomatic and economic exchange; and Vyjayanthi Selinger pays careful attention to the ways in which ritual and material actions legitimize a particular vision of warrior rule in *Heike*, most notably in the version known as *Genpei jōsuiki*.[2] All of these studies have shown the degree to which *Heike*'s complexity radically resists readings based on straightforward, binary understandings of good and evil, victor and defeated, and those with or without power. This chapter contributes further to this reevaluation by focusing on the relationships between tropes of movement, literary genres, and elite identities: I will suggest that the fourteenth-century *Heike* tells the story of a captive's forced march in a specific, strategic manner that challenges the foundations of the authority that was thought to belong to the courtier-warrior of the late twelfth century.

My focus will be upon the figure of the aristocrat Taira no Shigehira, the fourth son of the above-mentioned infamous clan leader, Kiyomori. Texts from the medieval period suggest that before his capture, this middle captain had a reputation for being a strong and effective leader, and was instrumental in a number of victorious moments for the Taira in the Genpei wars, particularly in the burning of the Nara temples Tōdaiji and Kōfukuji in 1180.[3] Indeed, although Shigehira's figure has

2. Oyler, *Swords, Oaths, and Prophetic Visions*; Bialock, *Eccentric Space, Hidden Histories*; Selinger, *Authorizing the Shogunate.*

3. For example, *Azuma kagami* (author unknown, probably completed ca. early 14th century) depicts him as a brave warrior; in fact, this passage closely resembles the one seen in *Heike* and *Genpei jōsuiki*, to be discussed later in this chapter (Hotta, *Yakubun Azuma kagami hyōchū*, 1: 182–83). *Gyokuyō* by Kujō Kanezane (1149–1207) portrays Shigehira as a highly capable yet very sinful warrior who committed the gravest crime of burning august temples; see Takahashi Sadaichi, *Kundoku Gyokuyō*, 4: 347–48, and 5: 38 and 46. Kanezane's younger brother, the Tendai abbot Jien (1155–1225), also states in his work *Gukanshō* that Shigehira was the commanding officer in the Nara attack, and that he was consequently executed, his head suffering a humiliating public exhibit. The text includes a sympathetic portrayal of Shigehira's visit to his wife days before his execution. See Nakajima, *Gukanshō zenchūkai*, 426–30, 456–58, and 464–67. For an example of a noh

received significantly less attention in modern scholarship compared to his father or his older brothers such as Shigemori or Tomomori, when he is discussed, the focus tends to be upon his burning of these temples and his consequent role in later narratives as an enemy of Buddhism.[4] It is not, though, just the military arts in which Shigehira is said to have excelled; he is also depicted as a person of courtly refinement in *Heike* and elsewhere. For example, *Heike kindachi zōshi* (Tales of Heike aristocrats), an *emaki* (picture scroll) by an unidentified author that was probably produced in the mid-Kamakura period, focuses on his lighthearted, mischievous side as well as his good looks,[5] and *Kenrei mon'in ukyō no daibu shū* (Poetic memoirs of Lady Daibu), a *waka* collection with prose narrative (ca. 1232) by a woman who served the imperial consort Taira no Tokushi (Kenrei mon'in, 1155–1213), similarly paints his figure as a lively character who is full of interesting stories to tell, and expresses great grief when his fortunes take a turn for the worse.[6]

---

play that features Shigehira as a foe of Buddhism whose presence at a temple obstructs the forging of a bell, see *Tatara Shigehira* (dates and author unknown) in Tanaka Makoto, *Mikan yōkyokushū*, 6: 50–54.

4. For instance, Kusaka Tsutomu focuses on Shigehira as a martyr-like figure who was executed for all of the wrongs the Taira had committed (Kusaka, *Heike monogatari no tanjō*, 330–34), while Saeki Shin'ichi asserts that his figure found in *Heike* is a lesson in salvation: whereas other texts limit their views of Shigehira either to that of an enemy of Buddhism or a cultured aristocrat, *Heike* combines both types of portrayals to concoct a sympathetic figure who has engaged in evil activities but can nevertheless be saved in the generous paradigm of Buddhism (Saeki, *Heike monogatari sogen*, 329–46). Interestingly, a number of narratives claim that attempts at constructing various Buddhist metallic objects (such as a temple bell [see the previous note, note 3, for an example from a noh play], or a mirror, etc.) failed because part of the molten metal contained items pertaining to Shigehira. Other scholars make assertions similar to those made by *Heike* about the relationship between Shigehira's portrayal and Pure Land discourses that seek to save "even the most evil" (Hyōdō, *Heike monogatari: "katari" no tekusuto*, 190–93; see also Kobayashi Yoshikazu, *Heike monogatari no seiritsu*, 168–84). Yamashita Hiroaki argues that the crux of Shigehira's story in *Heike* is his moment of confession to the priest Hōnen (*Katari to shite no Heike monogatari*, 113–29).

5. Shigehira is said to have been the chief instigator of a joke in which he and his friends pretended to be thieves and raided the quarters of the waiting women of the imperial consort; he is also described as having had multiple admirers among the women at court. See the *Heike kindachi zōshi* appendix in Hisamatsu and Kubota, *Kenreimon'in ukyō no daibu shū*, 169–72 and 177–79.

6. Itoga, *Kenrei mon'in ukyō no daibu shū*, 91–92 and 103–4. *Azuma kagami* also notes that Shigehira's use of language and his skills in the performing arts were superior; see Hotta, *Yakubun Azuma kagami*, 189–91.

Shigehira thus comes across as a quintessential courtier-warrior of the late Heian period: dashing, cultured, and capable as a military leader, his figure embodies the ideals of a nobleman in times of unrest. In *Heike*, he takes center stage after he becomes a prisoner of war. When Shigehira's troops are destroyed by the cunning strategies of the famous warrior Minamoto no Yoshitsune (1159–89) at the battle of Ichinotani in 1184, he tries to make an escape but is captured by his opponents just as he gives up and is preparing to commit suicide; he is taken to the capital where his opponents deliberate his fate. At this point, the story of his life becomes the focus of the text: large parts of chapter 10 and a section in chapter 11 are dedicated to his forced travel from the capital to Kamakura at the command of the victors, his time spent in the east awaiting the final decision about his punishment, and his return trip at the end of which he is summarily executed. When we look closely at the details of how Shigehira's figure is constructed, and the implications of that construction, we will be able to trace how the narrative systematically dismantles the figure of the courtier-warrior through the use of literary genres that belonged to his class.

An Unheimlich Journey East: *Waka* Poetry and the Loss of Home

As a captive, Shigehira in *Heike* is immediately forced into a series of movements that do not stem from his own volition: the former high-ranking aristocrat is first publicly paraded across the streets of the capital as a criminal for all to see, then is summoned hundreds of kilometers away by the Minamoto leader, Yoritomo. Thus Shigehira's figure is made to embark on a long journey along the Tōkaidō (Tōkai Road), the main thoroughfare between the capital and places east (see map 4; for a detailed map of Shigehira's trip, see map 5). The literary technique through which his travel is told is commonly classified as a *michiyuki*, which might be defined as a poetic narration of a journey that is governed by established textual tropes. A *michiyuki* creates the sense of travel through the listing of well-known *utamakura*, or place-names with poetic significance, along a route, as well as "old legends" associated with those places.

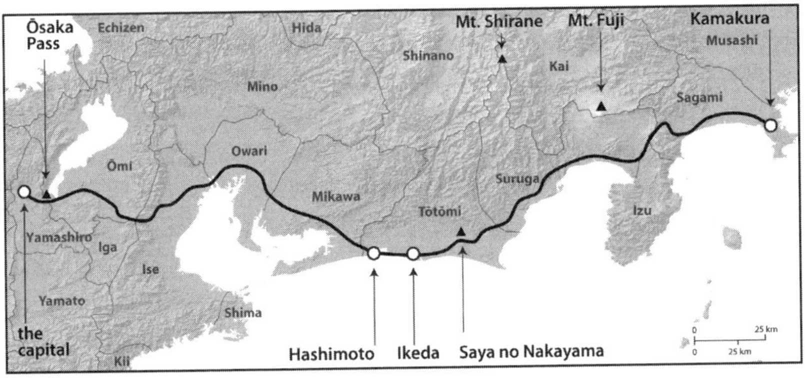

Map 5 Taira no Shigehira's eastward journey from the capital to Kamakura. Based on the map in Nagasaki et al., *Chūsei nikki kikōshū*, 13.

The *michiyuki* passage between the capital and points east along the Tōkaidō, however, is not just any *michiyuki*. This particular path is supremely famous, and is laden with multiple layers of intertextual allusions along the way. The locus classicus of *azuma kudari*, or the *michiyuki* eastward from the capital, is found in *Ise monogatari*, which is thought to tell the tale of another middle captain centuries before Shigehira, Ariwara no Narihira. In this text, the hero, thinking that he is "useless" in the capital, departs eastward with only a few companions. Narihira's journey is marked by the composition of *waka* poetry at specific places along the Tōkaidō; although the *azuma kudari* chapters in *Ise* are short and few in number, the practice of the production of poetry and the attributes ascribed to the places Narihira visits become standard courtly cultural tropes to which textual representations of the majority of trips east along this route refer for centuries afterward.[7] *Azuma kudari* thus represents an accumulation of discursively generated "realities" in which one sees what one is supposed to see and produces texts one is expected to produce at any given famous place. Locales that one notes or visits on this trip east thus tend to be quite fixed, and the narratives concerning those places equally familiar. Moreover, one of the key distinguishing features of *azuma kudari* is its viewpoint; the eastward journey in *Ise* is narrated from the point

7. The *Ise* chapters that pertain to *azuma kudari* are chaps. 7 through 13, then onto the northeast in 14, 15, and in later chapters (115, 116).

of view of an elite individual who ordinarily resides in the capital, and considers the regions—that is, the places along the Tōkaidō and points further east—as intriguing but culturally lacking.[8]

Texts from the medieval period continued to follow and augment, to varying degrees, the template of *azuma kudari*, and the numerous travelogues about one's trip from the capital to Kamakura that date from the thirteenth century are no exceptions. *Kaidōki* (An account of the Tōkaidō; unknown author, ca. 1223), the nun Abutsu's *Izayoi nikki* (The diary of the sixteenth night, ca. 1279–82), the poetry collection *Shinshō hōshi shū* (Poetry collection of the monk Shinshō, or Shioya no Tomonari, d. 1248; compiler unknown, ca. possibly a few years before or after Shinshō's death), and *Tōkan kikō* (Travels east of the pass; author unknown, ca. mid-13th century), all belong to this category. Shigehira's journey-in-captivity as found in *Heike* can be situated amid these travelogues, as the list of places mentioned in his itinerary closely resembles those found in a number of these texts mentioned above; in fact, there are exact matches in both itinerary and wording among *Heike*, *Kaidōki*, and *Tōkan kikō*.[9]

Like its predecessors, then, *Heike*'s journey east—here called *kaidō* (short for Tōkaidō) *kudari*, as it is in other medieval texts such as *Kaidōki* cited above—focuses exclusively on the familiar geotropic intonation of *waka* poetry. What sets the telling of Shigehira's eastward trip apart from those found in other texts, however, is this: although the contours of *azuma kudari* are replicated in Shigehira's travels from the capital eastward, his story, in fact, represents a quasi-parodic version of this trope. Here, it is the medium of courtly poetics that is made to perform its own difference—that is, *waka* poetry is shown to problematize its own tradition in the uncertain, shifting terrain of the new, medieval trip down the Tōkaidō.

There are a number of other distant travels depicted throughout the Kakuichibon *Heike*; however, from exiles to and from remote places,[10] a

8. See, for example, Hasegawa Masaharu's chapter on *azuma kudari* in his book *Kyōkai kara no hassō*, 29–46.

9. Sasaki Kōichi, "'Kaidō kudari' no michiyukibun," 581–84; specific comparisons will follow later in this chapter. *Nōin utamakura* (ca. mid-Heian period) also features exact matches with the *Heike* itinerary: this text, attributed to the monk-poet Nōin (988–?), consists not of prose narratives but of lists of *utamakura*, arranged according to provinces. For Tōkaidō provinces, see Sasaki Nobutsuna, *Nihon kagaku taikei*, 1: 93–94.

10. For example: the Tendai abbot of Mt. Hiei, Meiun, is exiled to Izu (chap. 2), and the monk Shunkan, Taira no Yasuyori, and Fujiwara no Naritsune are exiled to Kikai ga

retired emperor's visit to a shrine hundreds of kilometers west of the capital,[11] to troop movements on both sides across vast parts of the country,[12] we find very little in the way of references to places along the way, or of poetic tributes to famous locations. This is the case for both aristocrats and lower-ranking warrior types alike; the sole exception might be the case of Taira no Munemori (1147–85), Shigehira's older half-brother, who also travels east as a captive, yet Munemori composes but a single *waka* poem, and is caricatured as a coward who spends the journey thinking not of past literary allusions, but only about whether or not his life will be spared by Yoritomo.[13] Shigehira's *azuma kudari* therefore stands out among the entire lengthy text of this *Heike* version as the sole poetic, intertextual journey of its kind.

The first location that the *Heike* narrator notes after Shigehira leaves the bounds of the capital is Mt. Ōsaka, a short distance away at the border of Yamashiro and Ōmi Provinces through which all travelers east had to cross. This location houses what is arguably the best-known checkpoint in the realm of *waka* poetics; established as a pass in the Nara period before the capital was moved to its Heian-era location, Ōsaka was famous as a gateway to and from points east. The pass's name had been used for its meaning, "meeting hill," in countless poems from the *Man'yōshū* onward, and is routinely invoked in travelogues of the Tōkaidō, the *Heike* passage being no exception. What is interesting, though, is the exact imagistic allusions that this text generates at this geographic juncture: in *Heike*, Ōsaka calls to the narrator's mind the figure of the quasi-legendary poet/blind performer Semimaru

shima (all but Shunkan eventually return to the capital; chaps. 2 and 3). Also, when the Taira clan flees the capital (*miyako ochi*), there is much attention devoted to their sadness at leaving the capital, but no description of their trip westward is provided.

11. The retired emperor Takakura travels to the Itsukushima shrine in Aki Province, chap. 4; he repeats this trip in later chapters as well.

12. There are many such troop movements throughout the text. Notably distant ones include the first major Taira forces traveling east to counter Yoritomo's army (chap. 5) or up the Hokurikudō [Hokuriku Road] to battle Kiso no Yoshinaka (chap. 7), and Minamoto no Yoshitsune taking his forces west to battle the Taira in chaps. 9 and 11.

13. Kajihara and Yamashita, *Heike monogatari*, 2: 321–22 and 327–30. Munemori does compose one poem at the very beginning of his journey east, at the famous Ōsaka Pass, which is actually a variant of a poem elsewhere attributed to Fujiwara no Senshi (962–1001, consort of Emperor En'yū).

(dates unknown; possibly active in the mid-Heian period), who is said to have lived here in a modest hut.[14] The summoning of the specter of Semimaru, I would argue, is neither coincidental nor merely generically conventional; his presence was not mandatory within the discourse of *azuma kudari*, nor were tropic associations with his figure consistent.[15] We must examine the figure of Semimaru, then, as a purposeful presence in the particular journey eastward of the captive Shigehira as narrated in *Heike*.

The appearance of Semimaru in the *Heike* passage is, in a way, not surprising, since he was known not only for his role as the patron deity of Ōsaka Pass, but also as the originary figure of the blind performing

14. Narratives concerning Semimaru's identity are numerous and vague; *Tōkan kikō* and *Heike* passages actually call the Ōsaka Pass area Shinomiya-gawara ("fourth prince riverbed"), stating that Semimaru, who had lived in the area, was a son of Emperor Daigo (885–930), whereas *Konjaku monogatari*, chap. 24, story 23, claims that he was an attendant of Prince Atsumi (893–967), the eighth prince of Emperor Uda (Komine, *Konjaku monogatarishū*, 4: 427–30). The *Heike* passage, except for its insistence that Semimaru was of imperial origin, summarizes the *Konjaku* narrative in which Minamoto no Hiromasa (918–80), an aristocrat famous for his musical talents, commuted to Semimaru's humble abode at Ōsaka pass for three years in order to secretly hear him play two extraordinary *biwa* pieces (*Heike* puts the number at three pieces). Hiromasa remains unsuccessful until the fifteenth day of the eighth month in the third year, a night conducive to moon viewing, when he presents himself to Semimaru and finally receives Semimaru's teachings. For an extended discussion of other aspects of the Semimaru legend, particularly its reincarnations in the noh theater and in the performing arts of the Edo period, see Matisoff, *The Legend of Semimaru.*

15. For example, the *Kaidōki* narrator moves quickly past the area, with no reference to Semimaru or his poems; other versions of the *Heike* also exhibit this trait, such as the Shibu kassenjōbon, and the Nagatobon even fails to mention the area altogether. Other examples include a diary-style text by a courtier named Asukai Masa'ari, *Haru no miyamaji* (ca. 1281), which includes a travelogue section from the capital to Kamakura, and the narrator takes note of this area at the outset of his trip. However, Masa'ari makes no invocation of Semimaru; instead, he focuses on a surprise meeting with a close friend who had come to wish him a good journey. Stating with delight that indeed, the name Ōsaka ("meeting slope") is appropriate for this location, he delves into a discussion of a passage in *Nihon shoki* that explains the origins of the place name (Nagasaki et al., *Chūsei nikki kikōshū*, 369). Similarly, *Izayoi nikki*'s protagonist travels through the pass without any mention of the blind performer or his poems (Yanase and Takei, *Izayoi nikki, Yoru no tsuru chūshaku*, 65–78). Furthermore, later-era travelogues such as *Nagusamigusa* by the famed poet Shōtetsu (1381–1459) indicate that allusions to Semimaru continued to be optional (if still popular). See Nagasaki, *Chūsei nikki kikōshū*, 430–31.

artist—a category to which *Heike* reciters belonged;[16] indeed, the passage expounds upon his expertise in the *biwa* lute, the central instrument in *heikyoku* performance. My argument, however, is that his being invoked in the midst of Shigehira's story is not solely due to the performer's connection to the *biwa hōshi*. Rather, the introduction of Semimaru's figure at the outset of the captive's journey east occurs in order to allude to the following poem by the blind performer:

yo no naka wa *to temo kaku temo* *sugoshiten*
miya mo waraya mo *hateshinakereba*

This world can be lived this way or that, I suppose—
since the palace or a straw hut, one cannot live there forever.[17]

The *Heike* passage states, "In olden days, [his] bed in the straw hut—one is made to think about these things; how sad,"[18] clearly referring to the above poem. Thus Shigehira's version of *azuma kudari* begins with the problematization of spaces—here, places of residence—as having any possibility of permanency. Let us examine the poem alluded to more closely: we can understand Shigehira's stark fate as a once-prospering aristocrat who has fallen to the status of a war prisoner as analogous to the comparison between the palace and the straw hut. The appearance of a narrative of rise and fall here makes sense, since the theme of inevitable decline among those who were once powerful is a strong and recurring

16. *Konjaku monogatari*, chap. 24, story 23, credits Semimaru as being the first of the blind lute reciters (*meshi'i no biwa*). Sasaki Kōichi also emphasizes this connection; see Sasaki Kōichi, "'Kaidō kudari,'" 578–81.

17. This poem appears in *Konjaku monogatari*, chap. 24, story 23; another version, included in *Shin kokin wakashū* as poem 1851, replaces *sugoshiten* (can possibly be lived) with *onajikoto* (is the same thing), resulting in the first line "The world is the same, any which way." Annotators agree on the interpretation of *hateshinakereba*; see, for example, Tanaka and Akase, *Shin kokin wakashū*, 539, and Minemura, *Shin kokin wakashū*, 535. Minamoto no Toshiyori's *waka* commentary *Toshiyori zuinō* quotes the same poem along with an anecdote stating that Semimaru composed this poem in response to belittling comments about his hut by passersby; this version replaces *sugoshiten* with *arinubeshi*, which also translates as "can be lived, I suppose." See Hashimoto et al., *Karonshū*, 79–80.

18. Kajihara and Yamashita, *Heike monogatari*, 2: 216.

trope in *Heike* as a whole.[19] But an even more important feature of the allusion is that Semimaru's poem collapses the difference between the imperial and the humble by stating that *any* abode, whether it belongs to the most powerful or the more modest, is merely temporary—that is, not only can one fall from high to low, but even the low is an ephemeral place, because all places are transient. In this paradigm, everywhere is fluid, and nowhere is permanent; one has no resting place, no home, no place to which one might return.

Shigehira continues down the Tōkaidō, with the narrator mentioning the requisite places of the *azuma kudari* itinerary in quick succession, just as one might note passing scenery. The first pause in narrative occurs in the environs of Hashimoto in Tōtoumi Province; the audience is presented with a description of Shigehira's overnight stay on his journey for the first time. By the time of *Heike*'s composition, this region had come to be associated with a specific trope: professional female entertainers called *asobi*, and the humble residences in which they lived. For example, in *Tōkan kikō*, the narrator discusses the famous *utamakura* Hamana Bridge, which was anchored at its western end in Hashimoto, then proceeds to a discussion of his overnight stay with a few *asobi* women in a thatched roof inn that is worse for wear. He states that in the middle of the night when the rays of the moon came filtering through the cracks and crevices in the inn's architecture, one of the *asobi* women softly recited part of a *kanshi* (poem in Chinese) by Miyoshi no Yoshimune (dates unknown):

> Almost dawn, by the blinds white dew has appeared
> All night long, in bed the dark blue sky could be seen
>
> 向暁簾頭生白露
> 終宵床底見青天
>
> *akatsuki ni nannan to shite sudare no hotori ni hakuro wo shōzu*
> *yomosugara yuka no moto ni seiten wo miru*[20]

19. For example, the famous opening line of *Heike* that begins "The sound of the bells at Gion *shōja*/resounds with impermanence" proceeds to state that all who prosper must decline.

20. Sugano, *Wakan rōeishū*, 283–84.

The *asobi* intones the second line of this poem, and the narrator applauds this gesture as elegant (*kokoro nikushi*).[21] The poem is categorized under the heading "former palace/deserted residence" in *Wakan rōeishū* (Japanese and Chinese poems to sing, ca. 1012–18; edited by Fujiwara no Kintō), a section that features poetry that despondently longs for the glory of days gone by while gazing at barren ruins of buildings. In *Rōeishū*, the poem is thus placed among other verses that aestheticize desolation and reflect wistfully upon symbols of former prosperity; *Tōkan kikō* augments this nostalgia by emphasizing the aesthetic rusticity of the inn's disrepair and commenting upon the refinement of the *asobi*'s sensibilities.[22]

Heike presents a similar scenario: at a place called Ikeda, mentioned immediately after the Hamana Bridge, Shigehira also stays at a simple inn and interacts with an *asobi*. The female entertainer named Jijū ponders the tragic unexpectedness of a visit to the modest lodging by a person of such high rank, and composes the following poem—which, notably, is a *waka* instead of a *kanshi*:

tabi no sora *haniu no koya no* *ibusesa ni*
furusato ikani *koishikaruran*

The skies on the road— since the red-earthed hut is so shabby,
your hometown—how you must miss it so.

The reference to the skies and the hut in this poem renders it similar to the one recited by the *asobi* in *Tōkan kikō*; Jijū expresses her sympathy for the captive by denigrating her own residence. The assumption here is that surely Shigehira misses his home; the narrator sounds apologetic that her humble hut, by comparison, must be forcing the captive to long for the much more glorious place from which he has come.

21. *Kokoro nikushi* can have other less positive meanings; annotators, however, are in agreement on the "elegant" definition (see Takeda, *Kaidōki zenshaku*, 121–22).

22. The trope of the humble inn near the Hamana Bridge can be seen elsewhere; for example, *Kaidōki* talks about the inn's narrow grass mat upon which the narrator spends the night; see ibid., 183–90. The appearance of the *asobi* in this area was also an established event—*Shinshō hōshi shū* lists two poems, one at Hashimoto and the other at nearby Ikeda, that were sent to *asobi* at respective inns with whom the narrator was familiar from previous trips. See Imazeki, *Shinshō hōshi shū shin yakuchū*, 10–12.

In reply to Jijū's poem, however, Shigehira produces the following:

furusato mo koishiku mo nashi tabi no sora
miyako mo tsui no sumika naraneba

My hometown— I don't miss it, under skies on the road;
since the capital, too, is not one's final resting place.[23]

This verse echoes and amplifies the way in which Semimaru's poem about the transiency of dwellings had been alluded to earlier in the captive's journey eastward. In responding to his host, Shigehira is shown to very strikingly and directly negate not only his feelings for his hometown, the capital, but also the very idea of the capital as a permanent place of residence—for anyone, as the subject of the poem is left ambiguous. There is no "home" according to this poem; origin is illusory, and everything is ephemeral. One is, at a metaphorical level, always in motion, since no place in this world permits one to remain there for good—we all must ultimately take leave at the time of death; this notion of impermanence is certainly one that lies at the core of Buddhist teachings, and we can read this poem as an expression of enlightened indifference. In Shigehira's case, though, the emphasis on fluidity is not only religious, but geographically critical: through the figure of the captive, the text denies assumptions about the capital's permanency by dismantling the very logic of hierarchically arranged spatial desirability.

Shigehira's poetic answer to Jijū in this passage is, in fact, strikingly different from a poem he is said to have composed earlier in his life, before he became a prisoner of war. Previous to chapter 10, Shigehira appears only sparsely in the Kakuichibon *Heike*, with the exception of chapter 8, which tells of events a few months before Shigehira's capture. The narrator tells us that it has been a month since the Taira clan had been chased out of the capital, and they are on the run westward. They arrive in Dazaifu in the province of Chikuzen (see map 4); the future looks unpromising for them, as requests for help dispatched to area strongmen draw only lukewarm responses and their own retainers begin to dwindle in number. It is at this point some Taira visit Anrakuji, the temple that houses the gravesite of the exiled poet-scholar Sugawara no Michizane,

23. Kajihara and Yamashita, *Heike monogatari*, 2: 216.

to compose some linked verses as offerings to the now-deified exile in an attempt to garner his divine assistance in their return to the capital and to power. On that occasion, Shigehira is said to have composed the following *waka* poem:

suminareshi *furuki miyako no* *koishisa wa*
kami mo mukashi ni *omoi shiruran*

The familiar old capital in which one has lived long: the longing for it—
the deity, too, in the past must have known this feeling.[24]

The narrator states that all present shed tears upon hearing this composition. This passage plays two important foreshadowing roles: first, the invocation of the figure of Michizane here will become crucial in a scene involving a different female entertainer later on in the text, as I will discuss below. Second, this poem's open pining for the capital, a place in which he has spent most of his life and with which he has become very familiar, contrasts sharply with the sentiment he delivers in his exchange with Jijū, analyzed above, that comes two chapters later. In light of the chapter 8 poem, Shigehira's seemingly nonchalant reply to the female entertainer's sympathetic poem in chapter 10 could be read, perhaps, as a contrived façade of resignation and enlightenment donned to mask his fears about impending doom. Let us, however, remember that whereas the earlier poem is composed while he is still on the run together with his own clan, the poem in chapter 10 is composed on his journey eastward as a lone captive being transported to be viewed by the victors of war. Thus while Shigehira is at large, he is able to imagine the capital as a place of origin with which he still has hopes to recover contact, and exhibits no hesitation in painting an unconflicted vision of that space. However, as composed by a prisoner of war who is forcibly summoned on a journey, Shigehira's poem presents a different perspective. The text situates his status as a captive beckoned east, in fact, as the very proof of the breakdown of the geography of power in which authority is housed in the capital, the place he used to call his home. This dissolution thus imbues his poetry with an awareness of radical loss: he is now unable to believe that power can be stably contained in any place.

24. Ibid, 73.

Returning to the exchange between Jijū and Shigehira, we find that after composing the reply, he praises her elegant poetic skills; it is then revealed that his older brother, Munemori, had bestowed favors on her when he was the provincial governor of Tōtoumi in his youth. As if to foreshadow the destabilization of aristocratic command and the desirability of the capital as a place to reside, as already suggested by Shigehira's poem above, the narrator proceeds to recall that Jijū had been summoned to the capital by Munemori and had enjoyed his patronage, but had asked for permission to return to Ikeda after a while since she had left her aging mother at home. Munemori was reluctant to let her depart, at which point she composed, in the third month:

ika ni sen *miyako no haru mo* *woshikeredo*
nareshi azuma no *hana ya chiruran*

What shall I do? Spring in the capital, indeed, is a shame to miss,
but it is in my old home, Azuma, where the flowers fall.[25]

Jijū is quite obviously referring to her worries over her mother's life; this poem and its surrounding story come to be made famous through the noh play *Yuya*, featuring an *asobi* in the title role.[26] What is significant in the context of our current discussion is that like the preceding poem by Shigehira, in which the hometown-ness of the capital is rejected, this poem, too, challenges the capital's status as a preferred place to live by inserting a more-prioritized flower elsewhere into the scenery of spring. The word *azuma* refers to a wide region in the east, and its boundaries varied with time; in all cases, it denoted an eastern area that began a few provinces away from the capital, and Kamakura was part of the *azuma* designation. Given Shigehira's destination on this trip, it does not seem merely coincidental that a poem that includes this term is provided at this textual moment. The narration of Jijū's story and the full quotation of her poem here, then, suggest that the text is enacting and commenting

25. Ibid., 217.

26. There seems to have been confusion about the identities of Yuya and Jijū: the Kakuichibon states that Jijū is the daughter of Yuya, who is a *chōja* (leader of a group of *asobi*) at an inn in Ikeda. In the Hyakunijukkubon and Yashirobon versions, Jijū appears under the name Yuya.

on the points of departure and arrival of Shigehira's trip, as well as on the status of elite power: Munemori, the aristocrat living in the capital, had summoned a woman from the east, but she successfully breaks free of her duties and returns to her home in *azuma*; the capital's desirability is thus questioned through the presence of priorities elsewhere, be it public or private. And it is Jijū, a female entertainer, who is presented as leaving the capital of her own free will in favor of her home back east, in contrast to Shigehira, a fallen aristocrat, who is a captive forced out of the capital to march *azuma*-ward. Through the invocation of Jijū's *waka* poem, then, we find the courtly literary tradition dismantling its own keepers: the capital becomes an uncertain, unreliable host for those supposedly in power, and places east materialize as those that house strong beckoners, ones that undermine the authority of elites who want to call the capital their home.

After the encounter with Jijū, the narration continues with Shigehira's journey eastward. There is only one more scene in which the captive is allowed to pause long enough at a location to compose poetry. The passage reads as follows:

> There was a mountain laden with white snow in the distance to the north. When inquired, it is answered that [the mountain] is called Shirane, in Kai Province. At this time, the middle captain of third rank held back the falling tears, and kept thinking thus:
>
> *woshikaranu*   *inochi naredomo*   *kyō made zo*
>   *tsurenaki kai no*   *shirane wo mo mitsu*
>
> Though my life is not precious,   it is indeed due to the fact that until today
>   I have been without incident: thus I am able to see Mt. Shirane.[27]

Let us analyze the poem in detail, as it has a highly complex structure that can be read in a number of different ways. First, commentators routinely interpret the phrase *kyō made zo* (indeed, until today) in the first line of the poem as one whose grammatical structure continues into the next line, yielding the meaning "it is indeed due to the fact that until today,

27. Kajihara and Yamashita, *Heike monogatari*, 2: 217–18.

I have been without incident."[28] The translation above is based on this interpretation. However, an alternative reading would pause after "*kyō made zo*" and read the first line as a discrete unit: "Though my life is not precious, it is only *until today*"—that is, my life is not something valuable, and it will end today.[29] The two interpretive possibilities, one practically the opposite of the other, immediately produce an unsteady reading ground. Furthermore, the possible homophonic resonance between the words for "today" and "the capital" (both pronounced "*kyō*," though written differently) adds a further dimension to the poem: one could then imagine the poem meaning "though my life is not precious, only the capital"—that is, Shigehira's life has relevance solely in the context of the capital; anywhere else, it may as well have ended.

Second, another fluidity in meaning revolves around the phrase *tsurenaki kai*, the first phrase in the second line. The word *tsurenaki* has two possible meanings: (1) to be without incident and therefore be in a routine state of peace, and (2) to be heartless and unfeeling. *Kai* stands for both "due to" and the name of the province in which Mt. Shirane is located. The second line of the poem in its entirety, *tsurenaki kai no shirane wo mo mitsu*, could therefore read either as "It is due to the fact that [I] have been without incident that I am able to see Mt. Shirane," or "I see the heartless Mt. Shirane of Kai Province." This line thus paints the figure of a viewer grateful for being alive at that moment, yet simultaneously undercuts that picture of contentment with a personified mountain who cares not for the fate of the doomed viewer.

Third, we can read the term *tsurenaki* as playing a role in yet another textual instability: in the Takanobon edition of the Kakuichibon, the scribe writes this word as *tsunenaki* (impermanent, mutable), not *tsurenaki*.[30] If we insert this other term into the second line, the resulting trans-

28. For example, Ichiko, *Heike monogatari*, 2: 286; also, Tomikura, *Heike monogatari zenchūshaku*: 272–74. Kajihara and Yamashita interpret the "without incident" as an ironic commentary, meaning "I have been shamelessly living on without incident, despite the demise of my clan" (*Heike monogatari*, 2: 218).

29. Reading the first line as a complete sentence makes sense, since the particle *zo* usually initiates a *kakarimusubi* grammatical pattern in which the main verb should end in a *rentaikei* conjugation. Here, however, the verb and suffix combination *mitsu*—"to see," *miru*, conjugated and followed by the past/continuation suffix *tsu*, which is found in the last phrase of the poem, ends not in *rentaikei* but in *shūshikei* form.

30. The manuscript says *tsunenaki* with a note next to the *ne* that suggests a replace-

lations might read both "It is due to the ways of the impermanent world that I see Mt. Shirane," which highlights the rise and fall of Shigehira's fortunes that brought him to this mountain in the first place, and "I see the impermanent Mt. Shirane of Kai Province," which comments ironically on a seemingly immobile, permanent figure of a mountain's actual emphemerality.

Interestingly, the surrounding prose passage about Mt. Shirane is a very close rendition—with exact phrasing matches—of the passage in *Kaidōki* that addresses the same mountain range; Shigehira's poem is also virtually identical to the one featured in that travelogue. The *Kaidōki* poem, however, varies in crucial ways from the one Shigehira is said to have composed in *Heike*. The earlier travelogue's poem reads as follows:

woshikaranu *inochi naredomo* *kyō areba*
ikitaru kai no *shirane wo mo mitsu*

Though my life is not precious, because I am here today,
I am still alive, I am able to see Mt. Shirane in Kai Province.[31]

The terms in this poem, compared to those in Shigehira's poem, are significantly more straightforward: *kyō areba* ("because I am here today") and *ikitaru kai* ("due to the fact of being alive" and a pun on Kai Province) are words that have fewer layers of meaning than those employed in the *Heike* passage.[32] It seems, then, possible to deduce that

ment with *re*; annotators have chosen the *re* option in their interpretations. See Kajihara and Yamashita, *Heike monogatari*, 2: 218, and Ichiko, *Heike monogatari*, 2: 286.

31. Takeda, *Kaidōki zenshaku*, 253. The *Kaidōki* passage leading up to the poem reads: "*There was a mountain laden with white snow in the distance to the north. When inquired, it is answered that [the mountain] is called Shirane, in Kai Province.* I have heard about it through the years, and I am able to see it because I am still alive. Generally, during these past few days, I have been able to cultivate strength, as if my life has extended for a hundred years. Perhaps the famous longevity medicine of the deities is of no use to those who live in this world." The exact wording matches between the *Heike* passage and this passage in *Kaidōki* are italicized; we can see that *Heike* omits all of the optimistic parts of the latter, in addition to changing the wording of the *waka* poem.

32. Considering the possible circumstances of *Kaidōki*'s writing, it makes sense that the featured poem is more stable than the one Shigehira is said to have composed. Although the identity of *Kaidōki*'s author remains mysterious, and its overall arc is one

the *Heike* authors copied the *Kaidōki* prose on Mt. Shirane, but altered the poem to add nuanced interpretive possibilities; the *Heike* poem radically resists being pinned down to a consistent or single meaning, textually performing volatility and mutability through its contradictory complexity. Shigehira's poem challenges the foundations of stability at two different textual levels: a seemingly immovable, permanently anchored material object—the mountain—is rendered changeable, while the very possibility of signification, of a clear and unified interpretation, unproblematic in the earlier text, is here firmly denied.

There is one last layer to Shigehira's poem about Mt. Shirane. Shortly before the above scene, the protagonist passes over a mountain by the name of Saya no Nakayama in Tōtoumi Province. There, the narrator makes an allusion to a poem by the priest-poet Saigyō, featured in *Shin kokinshū* (A new collection of *waka* poetry old and modern, ca. 1205) as poem 987, which reads:

When [he] was traveling eastward, [he] composed:

toshi takete *mata koyubeshi to* *omoiki ya*
inochi narikeri *saya no nakayama*

In old age, to pass over it again— this is unexpected!
Ah, to be alive— Saya no Nakayama.[33]

The joyful tone of this poem would resound nicely with a positive reading of Shigehira's poem about Mt. Shirane: just as the priest-poet relates his pleasure at being able to cross over Saya no Nakayama, so Shigehira is glad to be able to see Mt. Shirane. However, the way in which the narrator alludes to Saigyō's poem is as follows: "As [he] came across Saya no Nakayama, the thought that it was unlikely that he would be able to pass over it again made everything even more heartrending, and he drenched his sleeves with his tears."[34] The contrast between the

that is tinged with a sense of impermanence and sadness, there are strong expressions of hope in formally entering the Buddhist path; unlike Shigehira's entrapped positionality as a captive, the *Kaidōki* narrator is freer to imagine religious salvation as an antidote to the inevitable ways of the world.

33. Tanaka and Akase, *Shin kokin wakashū*, 295–96.

34. Kajihara and Yamashita, *Heike monogatari*, 2: 217.

more leisurely traveler Saigyō and the captive Shigehira heightens the misfortune of the latter; unlike the former who celebrates his happiness in being able to go back and forth over Saya no Nakayama, Shigehira's chances of being able to climb over this mountain again, much less his chances of living until old age, are slim at best. The tragic character of the prisoner's crossing over one mountain (Saya no Nakayama) produces additional implications for the poem that follows concerning the next mountain (Mt. Shirane): although in the latter, Shigehira, in one possible reading, appears to be rejoicing over his survival so far and his being able to view Mt. Shirane, the allusionistic comparison between his situation and Saigyō's in an immediately preceding scene contributes a distinct sobering tone. The intricacies of Shigehira's Mt. Shirane poem already undercut a hopeful reading; the presence of the contrastive reference to Saigyō's case makes such a reading even less straightforward. This allusion reminds the audience that the prisoner of war's return trip to the capital after his *azuma kudari* is far from guaranteed, since his safety in Kamakura rests upon the whims of the victors; in fact, there is no promise that his life would not end suddenly on his way eastward.

Indeed, nothing is certain for this captive: his survival, his return home, even the very idea of home; this uncertainty is generated primarily through *waka* poetry recited or alluded to in his travels. If the tropic figure of a more conventional *azuma kudari* could be defined as an homage to a courtly vision of the capital through the medium of *waka* poetry, then the telling of Shigehira's journey is one that makes faithful reference to—but constantly and thoroughly unravels—this trope. After he ponders the view of Mt. Shirane, the passage continues with the party setting off again, and the mentions of famous places become more abbreviated as the entourage arrives in Kamakura in short order in an atmosphere of radical fluidity.

In Kamakura: Building the Prison House of *Kanshibun*

If the ways in which Shigehira's trip down Tōkaidō are represented stand for a complex unraveling of a tropic *waka* journey, matters change abruptly when the text shifts its attention to his arrival in Kamakura. Nowhere in the narration of his time spent in the eastern lands do we find a single recitation of or reference to *waka* poetry; the genre of the narrative enters completely into the *kanshibun* sphere. Courtiers had been, of course, writing in Chinese for centuries before Shigehira's time, both officially and privately, and Chinese classics were standard curriculum for the ruling class; it is this second genre of aristocratic literature that *Heike* chooses to define and construct Shigehira's narrative experience in Kamakura.

If Shigehira's figure represented an ideal of the courtier-warrior of the late twelfth century, his *azuma kudari* addresses only his courtier side, as the standard vocabulary of *waka* permits few references, if any, to the outright violence of war. The world of *kanshibun*, on the other hand, allows for an exploration of his role as warrior, as this genre contains a broader range of modes of writing, such as Chinese histories about reigns and battles of conquest. Like *waka*, *kanshibun* is obviously full of its own tropes and standard texts; what we find in Shigehira's case is not only an invocation of such references, but also depictions of radical and consistent misreading of the original *kanshibun* passages. The quasi-parodic mode of citing or alluding to past texts only to diverge from the implications of the originals parallels the fracturing of the classic *azuma kudari* that we saw in the previous section of the *Heike* passage analyzed above. This time, what we find is a series of relentless miscitings of *kanshibun*: Shigehira's figure is shown to invoke and misinterpret all *kanshibun* as proofs of what he believes is his tragic destiny: the text portrays him as insisting on understanding his positionality as one from which he cannot escape.

Let us return to where we left off in *Heike*: Shigehira's arrival in Kamakura. The section in chapter 10 titled "Senju no mae" begins with a scene in which the narrator relates how Shigehira proudly and bravely received an audience from Yoritomo. The captive argues that since the Taira had fought on behalf of the emperor numerous times in the past, it does not seem just for his family to suffer such a complete fall. He, however, acknowledges that he and his kin have now found themselves in a dire situation, and it is at this moment that he says:

> I deeply regret that it is all due to previous karmic deeds that it has come to this. However, there is the ancient text that says, "King Tang of Yin was captured and sent to prison at Xiatai; King Wen of Zhou was confined at Youli." Even in the very old days it was like this. How much the more so, then, in these latter days? Since [I] am one who takes up arms, to lose my life in the hands of my enemy may seem embarrassing but is actually not shameful at all. So be generous and make haste with cutting off my head.[35]

In this passage, Shigehira refers to two well-known Chinese kings of times past; these kings appear in a number of texts, ranging from the *Shiji* (Records of the grand historian), the first official history of China, edited by Sima Qian around the turn of the first century BCE, to subsequent writings in both China and Japan. Concerning the current analysis, it is the exact manner in which these kings' figures are invoked that is vital: it entrenches a pattern of textual interpretation that will surface repeatedly in the passages to follow—that is, a pattern in which the possibility of escape is denied despite intertextual evidence to the contrary. In the passage quoted, the captive raises examples of these past kings in order to resign himself to the fate of being executed; he states that Chinese monarchs of the past have been captured, just like himself, and he uses these characters in order to justify himself in the face of his impending end. What is interesting about the two figures that appear in his declaration is this: according to the *Shiji*, both kings eventually manage to break free of their captivity and lead powerful, productive lives. The first figure to be named, the virtuous King Tang (17th century BCE), was imprisoned by King Jie of Xia, who was reputed to be a tyrant. Jie, however, subsequently released his prisoner; later, when Tang defeated Jie, the latter is said to have regretted not having done away with the former at Xiatai. The second figure, King Wen (11th century BCE) of the state of Zhou, began his career as one of three ministers to Emperor Zhou of Yin, another famous tyrant. Emperor Zhou executed two of the ministers and turned

35. Ibid., 219–20.

their flesh into cuisine after they admonished him for killing a consort who was a daughter of one minister. After hearing of this incident, the future King Wen expressed grief over these matters, which led Emperor Zhou to imprison him. Due to the efforts of his retainers, however, Wen won freedom and returned to his home state of Zhou, where he took the throne and ruled wisely. Ultimately, the Yin ended when King Wen's son, King Wu, defeated Emperor Zhou in battle.[36]

That Shigehira is depicted as naming these kings is intriguing enough as a display of his resistance against Yoritomo, since both stories involve good kings who are imprisoned by evil rulers, and subsequently instrumental in the founding of new dynasties; the references can thus be read as his critique of the situation into which he is placed through the use of analogy. What is most striking, though, is that the text portrays him as being willful about his myopic reading—even misreading—of the kings' biographies that in fact go on to tell of the eventual escape and ultimate prosperity of the wrongfully imprisoned monarchs; Shigehira chooses instead to focus solely on their confinement without a trace of mention of their release. In this way, the *Heike* passage begins to carve out a second mode of downfall for this captive figure: he is represented as firmly entrapping himself into that positionality through misleading textual misreadings of *kanshibun*, and by expressing his acceptance of "fate" that, he asserts, comes as part and parcel with his occupation as a commanding military officer.

After this meeting, the narrator proceeds to explain that Shigehira is detained at the residence of one Kano no suke Munemochi in nearby Izu, who treats him with respect as a guest. There, the traveler from the capital is bathed and cleaned by a "serving woman about the age of twenty, very pale and pure, truly elegant and beautiful"; she is identified as a daughter of a leader of female entertainers at Tegoshi, and it is revealed that her name is Senju no mae.[37] Thus begins the romance between the tragic

36. From the "Xia *benji* [basic annals]" section in Sima Qian, *Shiji*, 88–89; and from "Zhou *benji*," in Sima Qian, *Shiji*, 116–26. Later texts also refer to both King Tang and King Wen as powerful, virtuous kings: *Yiwen leiju* (ed. Ouyang Xun [557–641]), vol. 12 includes biographies of both kings (Ouyang Xun, *Yiwen leiju*); *Hōbutsushū* and *Jikkinshō* refer to King Wen's accomplishments (Koizumi et al., *Hōbutsushū, Kankyo no tomo, Hirasan kojin reitaku*, 32, 105, and 260–61; and Asami, *Jikkinshō*, 212).

37. Kajihara and Yamashita, *Heike monogatari*, 2: 220–21.

captive and the female performer; it continues to be retold in later centuries in texts such as the noh play *Senju* (attributed to either Zeami [1363?–1443?] or Konparu Zenchiku [1405–70?]). Through scenes of Shigehira's exchanges with Senju, *Heike* delves further into depictions of the captive as one who falls deeper into textual entrapment; this time, the poetic medium is exclusively *kanshi*, or poetry in Chinese, which was known to have been set to music and sung by professional female entertainers.[38]

The narrator relates that later that evening, Senju materializes at Munemochi's house, equipped with a *biwa* lute and harp, in order to entertain the host and Shigehira, who are having drinks. She begins by singing the opening lines of a *kanshi* poem:

> The gossamer and brocade robes are heavy;
> They resent the heartlessness of the weaving maidens.
>
> 羅綺之為重衣
> 妬無情於機婦
>
> *raki no chōi taru*
> *nasake naki koto wo kifu ni netamu*[39]

38. As Wakita Haruko points out, female entertainers are shown to be musically performing *kanshi* in examples across a variety of premodern textual genres (*Josei geinō no genryū*, 147–48). Such cases include *Heike* itself, which features *asobi* singing a song about the *asobi*: chap. 12 of the non-*tōdō* line Nagatobon version features the following poem composed by Minamoto no Shitagō (911–83), included in *Wakan rōeishū* within the section entitled "Yūjo":

> [She] plays the Japanese harp languidly, looking down upon the reflected moon;
> Pushing high the Chinese oar [she] enters into the mist above the waters.
>
> 倭琴緩調臨潭月
> 唐艣高推入水煙
>
> *wagon yuruku shirabete tangetsu ni nozomu*
> *kararo takaku oshite suien ni iru*

(Kurokawa et al., *Heike monogatari*, 415); the *Tōkan kikō* example cited above in which an *asobi* at a rundown inn quotes a passage from a *kanshi* featured in *Wakan rōeishū*; and the noh plays *Dōjōji*—in which the protagonist, a *shirabyōshi* dancer, alludes to Tang poetry (Yokomichi and Omote, *Yōkyokushū*, 2: 137)—and *Giō*, about three famous *shirabyōshi* who are characters featured in *Heike*, sing the same "The gossamer and brocade robes" poem by Sugawara no Michizane that is featured in the *Heike* passage concerning Shigehira (Sanari, *Yōkyoku taikan*, 2: 867).

39. Kajihara and Yamashita, *Heike monogatari*, 2: 222.

The passage states that it was customary for another person to sing the next lines of the poem as a form of duet (*join*), which Shigehira should have done but does not do here. The lines left unrecited are:

> The string and wind ensemble's piece is long:
> They begrudge the musicians for not coming to an end.
> 管弦之在長曲
> 怒不関於伶人
> *kangen no chōkyoku ni aru*
> *woezaru koto wo reijin ni ikaru*[40]

The subject of this poem is the Gosechi dancing maidens, who were young upper-class women selected to dance at annual court rituals. The poem's author is the well-known exile and *kanshibun* expert Sugawara no Michizane, mentioned earlier, who was also revered as the deity at Kitano Shrine (Kitano *tenjin*). One might be struck by the notion that

40. The poem, included in *Wakan rōeishū* and popularly sung, is actually an extraction of four lines from a much longer prose preface for another poem found in *Kanke bunsō* (ca. 900, by Sugawara no Michizane) as well as in *Honchō monzui* (ca. mid-Heian, compiled by Fujiwara no Akihira [989–1066]). Entitled "At a *naien* banquet in early spring at Jijyūden, a *fu* poem on the frailty of beautiful maidens," the preface begins with an assertion that the history of *naien* is unique to Japan; Michizane asserts that the *naien*, a banquet for composing and reciting *kanshi*, is said to have originated in the era of Emperor Saga (r. 809–23), and to have become an official banquet held on the twenty-first day of the first month by Emperor Montoku's time (r. 850–58). The *fu* features an omniscient narrator who gazes at the heavenly delicate dancing maidens in their gossamer robes and tells us these dancers' thoughts; it follows the prose section. See Kawaguchi, *Kanke bunsō, Kanke goshū*, 221–22 and 676–77. Michizane's poem remained popular in the centuries to follow, and is quoted directly in *Imakagami*, in a passage describing the wondrous nature of Tokudaiji Kin'yoshi (a son of Tokudaiji Saneyoshi, 1096–1157; became minister of the right). It states that at a *kanshi* forum dedicated to Michizane held at Kitano shrine, Kin'yoshi stood out amid all the various scholars and courtiers by splendidly singing the poem "The gossamer and brocade robes," thus solidifying the status of this poem as one of Michizane's most representative compositions (Unno, *Imakagami zenshaku*, 2: 126–30). The trope of Gosechi dancing maidens and the heaviness of their seemingly gossamer robes was apparently popular elsewhere as well. For example, a poem by Fujiwara no Tadamichi (1097–1164) on the topic of Gosechi dancers includes the phrase 綺羅衣重舞腰低 (*raki no i omoku shite maitaru koshi hikushi*, "The gossamer and brocade robes are heavy, they dance with their hips low"; Honma, *Honchō mudaishi zenchūshaku*, 1: 190).

the poem's protagonists are burdened with both the literal weight of the robes in which they must perform as well as the necessity of performance; furthermore, the dancers direct their resentment *not* toward those responsible for organizing and managing the dance performance, but toward another category of professional women, weaving maidens, for creating a robe that is beautiful yet cumbersome. By singing this poem, therefore, we could surmise that Senju no mae is drawing a multilevel analogy between the dancers and Shigehira. First, she invokes the figures of maidens who are physically restricted to a place—the performance stage—and whose movements are constrained by their garments, much like Shigehira's captive status and current confinement at Munemochi's residence. Second, the poem suggests that the difficult situation in which Shigehira finds himself is due to his occupation, as courtier-warrior; this is similar to that of the dancers in the poem, whose role forces them into a situation in which they did not choose to be placed. While during the time that the narrative takes place—that is, the late twelfth century—the status of warrior had not solidified into an exclusive category as it did in the centuries that followed the Genpei wars, Shigehira is very clear about having followed the demands placed on an important political figure with military responsibilities.[41] A third analogy, however, represents a subtle criticism of precisely these discourses of ensnarement: the *kanshi* suggests that Shigehira, instead of directing his attention and anger at Yoritomo and the Minamoto forces for having placed him in the position of prisoner of war, is refocusing his blame on what he presumes to be past bad karmic deeds—as he had stated in his defiant speech to Yoritomo—in a way that resembles the dancers' shifting their attention to the supposedly heartless weaving maidens. In other words, Senju no mae's song points out the way in which the captive shifts the cause of his prisoner status from political and military events in his current life to predetermined karma; this shift permits him to accept the status of captive with a sigh of resignation.

41. For example, in a speech immediately before his execution, he declares: "That I, Shigehira, have committed a *gyakuzai* [a severe crime in which the lower goes against the higher in status], is not at all due to my own wishes; it is only that I had chosen the logic of following the ways of the world. What living being would make light of an imperial command? What person born into this world would disobey his father? In both cases, one cannot go against their wishes" (Kajihara and Yamashita, *Heike monogatari*, 2: 337).

Shigehira appears quite oblivious to these implications and particularly the possibility for critique; he waxes melancholy instead: "It is said that the deity at Kitano has pledged to protect those who perform this poem by making a round of the heavens three times in one day. But Shigehira has been cast aside in this life. What good would it do for me to perform the next lines of the poem? If my sins were to be alleviated, I would join in a duet."[42] The passage presents a stubborn and resentful figure of Shigehira, who refuses to perform the second line of Michizane's poem, since the Kitano *tenjin*, Michizane's divine transformation, has not delivered on his promise to the soon-to-be-executed Shigehira. We might remember that in chapter 8, he had composed a *waka* poem dedicated to Michizane at Anrakuji in Dazaifu about missing the capital, as I mentioned earlier in this chapter; here, he feels betrayed by the deity since his offering had not made a difference for himself or the rest of his clan. A *waka* tribute, therefore, completely fails to be efficacious, leaving Shigehira prisoner; instead, we are presented with a contrasting description of Michizane, the *kanshibun* master, and his stunningly agile movements across the heavens—but in a textual section laden with *kanshibun* references that together produce a discourse of inevitability for the prisoner, Shigehira.

Senju no mae, perhaps forgiving him out of professional courtesy or thinking it too harsh to blame him for being obsessed with his imminent bad end, quickly adjusts her repertoire to her customer's needs. She recites instead a Buddhist *kanshi* and an *imayō* song that focus on the rapidity and all-encompassing nature of the Amida (Amitābha) Buddha's compassion, perhaps a more soothing choice for a person facing potential execution.[43] What happens next, however, is the culminating scene

42. Ibid., 2: 222.

43. The *kanshi*, also featured in *Wakan rōeishū*, is as follows:

> Even having accomplished the Ten Evil Deeds, the Amida Buddha will guide one
> Faster than a burst of wind dispersing the mist and clouds,
> Even to one chanting of the *nenbutsu*, the Amida Buddha responds,
> Like the vast ocean embracing a tiny drop of water.
>
> 雖十悪兮猶引摂
> 甚於疾風被雲霧
> 雖一念兮感応
> 喩之巨海納涓露
>
> *jūaku to iedomo nao injō su*
> *shippū no unbu wo hiraku yori mo hanahadashi*

in which the figure of Shigehira is seen to perform a textual self-entrapment through *kanshibun* misreadings. The banquet participants return to *kanshi* singing a little later in the same scene, after Senju no mae performs another Buddhist *shirabyōshi* song suggesting that she and Shigehira had former karmic ties.[44] In return, he offers the first line of a *kanshi* featured in *Wakan rōeishū*, this time by Kisshōkō (Tachibana no Hiromi, 837–90):[45]

> The lamplight dark, in several streaks fall the consort Yu's tears;
> The night grows late, from all four sides the sound of Chu songs.

> *ichinen to iedomo kanarazu kan'ō su*
> *kore wo kyokai no kenro wo iruru ni tatou*
> —Prince Tomohira (964–1009)

The *imayō* song is as follows:

> *gokuraku negawan hito wa mina*
> *mida no myōgō tonaubeshi*
>
> All who hope to achieve rebirth in the Pure Land
> should chant the name of the Amida Buddha.

Ibid.

44. The song is as follows:

> *ichiju no kage ni yadoriai*
> *onaji nagare wo musubu mo*
> *mina kore zenze no chigiri*
>
> To stay together in the shadows of one tree,
> and to draw from the waters of the same stream—
> these are all due to ties from our former lives.

This is an unidentified *shirabyōshi* song, not found in other texts; interestingly, the same song is invoked in the "Giō" section of chapter 1 of *Heike*, when the *shirabyōshi* Giō is chased out of Kiyomori's residence due to the appearance of a new *shirabyōshi*, Hotoke gozen. Giō thinks that even chance travelers who share water and lodging for a night create ties that are difficult to break; how much the more so in her case, since she had been in Kiyomori's favor for three years (ibid., 1: 20).

45. It is interesting that the author of this poem, Tachibana no Hiromi, also suffered from unfavorable shifts in the political climate. Embroiled in the Akō Incident of 887 mentioned in chapter 1, in which a document he had drafted on behalf of Emperor Uda for the appointment of Fujiwara no Mototsune to the position of regent came under criticism for its wording, Hiromi failed to prosper after the dispute and was only posthumously awarded the title of *chūnagon* (middle counselor). Although not as dramatic as Michizane's exile to Dazaifu, the double-layered references to political struggle and defeat (that of Xiang Yu's and Hiromi's) surely served to resound with and reinforce the impending tragedy for Shigehira's figure.

> 灯暗数行虞氏涙
> 夜深四面楚歌声
> *tomoshibi kurō shite wa sūkō gushi no namida*
> *yo fukete wa shimen soka no koe*[46]

The poem, of course, refers to the well-known *Shiji* narrative in which Xiang Yu (232–202 BCE), the king of Chu, is on the defensive at Gaixia. He hears the sound of his native land's songs coming from all directions, and interprets this as a sign that he has been surrounded by his own soldiers who have already surrendered to the enemy Han forces led by Emperor Gaozu (Liu Bang, 256 or 247–195 BCE). He bids farewell to his beloved consort Yu (Yu meiren [The Beauty]; Gubijin in Japanese), who sheds streams of tears; the couple exchange performances of poetry each has composed. Through this allusion, then, the text suggests that Shigehira envisions himself in the role of Xiang Yu, while he designates Senju no mae as the consort Yu's double in the romantic tragedy.

The *Heike* passage proceeds to provide a detailed account of the story of the king of Chu and his consort:

> The heart of the matter of this song is this: in the past in China, Gaozu of the Han and Xiang Yu of the Chu fought for dominance seventy-two times, and every time Xiang Yu won. However, finally Xiang Yu lost a battle and faced demise. At that time, there was a horse, Zhui, that could fly through a thousand *li* in a day, so he was about to flee on it together with his consort Yu, but quite unexpectedly, the horse's legs would not budge. Xiang Yu shed tears, saying, "My power has already left me. *There is no way to escape now.* The enemy's attack is nothing compared to the sadness I feel in having to part with my consort," and grieved throughout the night. The lamplight became dim, and feeling desolate, Yu shed tears. As the night wore on, the enemy surrounded Xiang Yu and made a battle cry. Based on this Kisshōkō composed a *fu*. The third-rank middle captain [Shigehira] must have remembered this; it sounded ever so elegant.[47]

46. Kajihara and Yamashita, *Heike monogatari*, 2: 222; For the *Wakan rōeishū* citation, see Sugano, *Wakan rōeishū*, 362–63.

47. Kajihara and Yamashita, *Heike monogatari*, 2: 223; my italics.

The passage has Xiang Yu state very clearly that "there is no way to escape," explicitly blames the horse Zhui for Xiang Yu's fall at that particular moment, and trails off just as the Han forces begin their attack; all of these details together create a tragic tone that seem to imply that the king of Chu and his consort met their ends on that night. The "parting" over which Xiang Yu is distraught can be read as a parting through death, since he appears convinced that he cannot break free from the situation.

This retelling of the *Shiji* passage in this specific manner is intriguing, when we consider that in the original passage, Xiang Yu is *not* defeated on that very night. He does have a last banquet with his consort Yu, in which he composes a poem saying that his horse will not move; Yu composes a poem as well, which is not quoted. We find out, though, that the horse *does* budge and that the king successfully escapes in the middle of the night; he braves a few more battles before his ultimate defeat. Meanwhile, we hear nothing about the fate of his consort.[48] In any event, what is

48. For the narrative concerning Xiang Yu's last battles, see the "Xiang Yu *benji*" section of *Shiji*, 333–37. The exact route and timing of the Yu meiren story's transmission to Japan remains vague; it is interesting that in China, the famous narrative of her suicide seems to have been popular by the Ming dynasty, but there appears to be a large span of time between the *Shiji* and the Ming in which the contours of her legend remain amorphous. Yu's legend seems to have garnered some degree of fame in Japan already in the Heian period, as shown by this ninth-century *kanshi* by Tachibana no Hiromi. In the eleventh century, there is a poem by Su Dongpo (Su Shi, 1036–1101) titled *Yuji mu* (Consort Yu's grave):

> Under the curtains, the fair one wipes the traces of her tears;
> In front of the gate, the stalwart soldiers' energy billows.
> In this upheaval, who did not fail the king?
> Only Consort Yu and Lord Zheng.
>
> 帳下佳人拭泪痕
> 門前壮士氣如云
> 倉黄不負君王意
> 只有虞姬与鄭君

Su Dongpo enjoyed significant fame in Japan, so it is possible that this poem was known among the composers of *Heike*. The traces of the consort's tears appear in the first line of the poem; the myriad warriors who no longer obey the wishes of Xiang Yu are contrasted with Yu and a loyal minister, Zheng, who refuses to submit to the Han (he is not featured in the *Shiji* passage). See Wang, *Su Dongpo shiji*, 255. The title of the poem ominously suggests the fate of Yu meiren; although the short poem does not state that she died on that final night with her king (much less that she committed suicide), it is possible that readers, including Japanese readers in this particular case, understood this poem to mean that Yu sacrificed herself for the sake of her lord.

crucial here is that the narrator (and by implication, Shigehira) misreads Xiang Yu and his consort's fates at Gaixia.

Fantastic "misrememberings" of past texts are not uncommon throughout premodern Japanese literary history, of course, as we will see also in chapter 4; however, the remarkable juxtaposition of the *azuma kudari* portion's use of *waka* poetry tropes and the current passages' treatment of *kanshibun* suggests, I believe, that the possibility of "mere" error should not cause us to overlook an interpretive opportunity. Indeed, the quoted *Wakan rōeishū* poem, though ominous, does not state that escape was impossible; in fact, as we will see in more detail below, other versions of *Heike* mention explicitly that Xiang Yu did flee successfully on this night. Given these circumstances, it seems that a deliberate choice to emphasize inescapability is a distinct possibility in the passage above, in this particular version of *Heike*. If there were audience members familiar with less fateful versions of the story, Shigehira's poetic invocation, together with the narrator's lengthy explanation of the poem's context, must have seemed jarring and rather ironic. This irony—the discrepancy between other tellings of the Xiang Yu narrative that permit the breaking free from immobility, and this *Heike* version's interpretation that rewrites this story of freedom (albeit temporary) into its opposite, the entrapment into one's final hours—would have brought to light the textual construction of Shigehira's captive positionality quite clearly. In other words, in the realm of *kanshibun*, Shigehira's figure is situated as one who corners himself deeply into a discourse of confinement, transforming a narrative of escape into a tragedy in which being surrounded into defeat and death is accepted as fate.

Shigehira is not the only figure who becomes embroiled in a narrative of entrapment; by casting Senju no mae as the consort Yu, the female entertainer is subsumed into a framework of constrained destiny. When Yoritomo sees Senju on the morning after her banquet with Shigehira and asks her about him, she is not given a chance to answer because Yoritomo's retainers interrupt in order to speak on her behalf; the men talk about how elegant they found Shigehira, and how talented he is in the arts. The entire section ends rather abruptly after this, with the rest of Senju's actions phrased as hearsay—that she must have become a nun at Zenkōji because of her longing for Shigehira, and that people say she achieved rebirth in the Pure Land because she fervently prayed for his salvation.[49] Senju is thus literally silenced right after her night with the man whom others around her (including the man himself) claim to be the love of her life; it is as if she has no choice but to live out the remainder of her years performing this textual construction. Her figure is made to bring to life her role as the tragic Chinese consort's double so well that she cannot stray from it until her death.

The weaving of this romantic tragedy is, however, ironic, if we read "The gossamer and brocade robes" poem by Michinaga discussed earlier in yet another fashion. It is possible that in singing the poem, Senju no mae is meant to allude to her own feelings about being summoned to perform in front of a customer: just as the dancers feel forced to perform despite the robes that weigh them down, Senju no mae, too, is not particularly ecstatic about performing her role as female entertainer, but since it is her job, she does so despite her resentment for having to perform. If this were the case, the exchanges between Senju and Shigehira would acquire a different tone; the passage would be not only a commentary on Shigehira, who appears to overlook such a possibility and proceeds to weave a grand tale of love based only on what he desires, but also a testament to which the power of *kanshibun* engulfs even those around Shigehira and produces an inescapable destiny.

The embroilment of Senju's figure in the entrapped trope of the captive becomes even more striking when we consider that female entertainers were frequently associated with a mobile lifestyle. I have discussed these women in depth elsewhere, so I will not repeat the details here; in the context of Senju's figure, however, we might note that phrases such as "[they] never stay put in the misty fields of spring," "they have no fixed place," and "traveling and wandering" were routinely borrowed from Chinese poetic traditions and used to refer to various groups of female entertainers, and life spent aboard a boat had become an emblematic sign for certain categories of these professional women.[50] Thus female entertainers were tropically depicted as being thoroughly familiar with movement in life, particularly in the *kanshibun* genre. Given this context, we can see that *Heike*'s presentation of the romance between Shigehira and Senju stands out: the text, through the story of Xiang Yu and his

49. Kajihara and Yamashita, *Heike monogatari*, 2: 223–24.
50. Kawashima, *Writing Margins*, 298–301 and 43–46, respectively.

devoted consort, not only seals Shigehira's future as a captive, but also sweeps Senju no mae into a life course tied down by her devotion to him. Her entrapment, rendered even more salient because of the contrast between the expected tropes about her lifestyle and the supposed path she actually chose, in turn further emphasizes the immobilized fate of her partner Shigehira; the web of textual allusions and plot twists entangles the figure of this captive into a self-enforced inertness that leads him to accept his doomed future.[51]

Shigehira reappears for the final time in chapter 11. As the scene opens, he is still at Munemochi's residence in Izu, having spent over a year in the eastern lands. In response to the incessant demands of the Nara monks for his handover, however, the Minamoto forces seal his fate by launching him on his return journey westward—not back to the capital, but to his death in the hands of the Buddhist clergy whose temples his forces had burned. The trip itself receives no description: "With the grandson of Minamoto no Yorimasa, Yorikane, as escort, [Shigehira] is finally sent off to Nara. He did not enter the capital, but from Ōtsu via Yamashina he took the road to Daigo."[52] *Azuma kudari* is a journey eastward, and there is no comparable textual history of a return trip west; following this tradition, the story skips directly from Izu to the outskirts of the capital,

51. Compare this story with the noh play *Senju* mentioned earlier in this chapter: the play retells the story of Shigehira and Senju in a manner like *Heike*'s, but in a much more dramatic way. Both *kanshi* examined in this chapter make an appearance in the play. The presentation of "The gossamer and brocade robes" poem closely resembles that of the *Heike* version, but "The lamplight dark" poem is placed after a description of Shigehira's unfortunate capture, and it is Senju, not Shigehira, who recites the *kanshi*. In *Heike*, narration about the evening's banquet ends right after "The lamplight dark" passage translated in full; since there is little depiction of the night beyond the singing of *kanshi*, it is even a bit of a surprise to hear later on in the story that Senju felt devoted to him to the extent of becoming a nun. In contrast, the noh play provides more detail about the couple's night spent together, and ends in a heart-wrenching scene of separation as Shigehira is taken away and Senju is beside herself in tears (Nishino, *Yōkyoku hyakuban*, 114–20). These factors, together with Shigehira's assertion that he had engaged in battle and burned temples against his own will because such acts were commanded by his father, work to produce a sympathetic representation of sadly fated, blameless lovers who are victims of circumstance. The *kanshi*, particularly "The lamplight dark" poem, thus becomes proof of a female entertainer's devotion to her ill-fated lover, not a misreading of mobility/immobility as I argue is the case in *Heike*.

52. Kajihara and Yamashita, *Heike monogatari*, 2: 332.

where he bids a moving farewell to his wife, and without a pause after their meeting, the scene changes to the Nara monks in hot debate over the exact method of his execution, which is carried out swiftly. Thus ends the tale of Taira no Shigehira's life in the Kakuichibon version of *Heike*.

The Kakuichibon in Context

The story of Taira no Shigehira in the Kakuichibon *Heike* is thus powerfully told through the use of two literary genres, *waka* and *kanshibun*, that had defined the culture of the court for centuries leading up to the Genpei wars; furthermore, as I have illustrated above, the passages that are shaped through these two genres thoroughly and completely disempower the figure of Shigehira. Thus Shigehira, arguably the epitome of a late Heian courtier-warrior, is portrayed as one who acquiesces to his own death through textual strategies that he himself is shown to employ. This particular maneuver, however, is not one that is necessarily shared by other extant versions of the *Heike*. We might thus pause in order to contextualize Kakuichibon's telling of Shigehira's story amid its various other manifestations in the *Heike* oeuvre. As I noted above, *Heike* is famous for the sheer number of variants, and the text under discussion is but one of many.[53] Broadly speaking, one of the most standard taxonomic methods is to divide the versions into the two categories of *yomihon* (texts for reading) and *kataribon* (texts for recitation).[54] The

53. The categorization of *Heike* versions is a dauntingly complicated process. Criteria for division range from whether the text was written mainly for oral performance or for the purposes of "recording" events and meant to be read, to whether it is an abridged form that selects certain scenes to highlight (*ryakubon*) or a longer, more meandering version (*kōhon*). Such distinctions have been used and debated for decades, yet the fact that versions often blur the boundaries of these categories makes the task of grouping quite untidy; for instance, an "abbreviated" version may narrate a specific incident in more length than a version that otherwise seems more comprehensive in scope. The authorship of the versions remains open to debate as well; the range of possible contributors includes monks, officials, and the performers themselves, and their geographical origins span the capital region to the eastern provinces.

54. A similar classification divides the *tōdōkei* (versions recited by the *tōdōza* performers) texts from non-*tōdōkei* texts.

first group is typically characterized by its relative length, which owes to its inclusion of eastern detail—that is, narratives that focus on the Minamoto forces and their allies that hail from the Bandō plains region in eastern Japan. The *yomihon* versions are also commonly said to be more "records-oriented" in their language and interest in detail. There are also variant texts within the *yomihon* category that share their relative brevity with the recited versions; these variants mostly predate the better-known versions of the *kataribon* group. The recited texts, in contrast to the *yomihon*, tend to narrate the story from a viewpoint that prioritizes events surrounding the capital, with details about eastern warriors being omitted or abbreviated. This group can be further subdivided into two schools, the Ichikata and the Yasaka, with the Kakuichibon, which came to dominate the *heikyoku* scene, belonging to the former.[55]

In all of these numerous versions, we find that none presents the story of Shigehira in a manner that closely resembles Kakuichibon's narrative emphasis and generic delineation. Some of the *yomihon* are particularly striking in the ways that they differ from the Kakuichibon: for example, the twenty-chapter Nagatobon, dating possibly from the late thirteenth century with additional editings in later eras, presents a highly abbreviated rendition of Shigehira's eastward journey, relating it in a few short lines that refer to the tropic places of the *azuma kudari* template while featuring not a single *waka* poem.[56] This brevity is notable since Nagatobon is elsewhere much more verbose than the recited versions. This version also presents Tachibana no Hiromi's *kanshi* about Xiang Yu and Yu meiren in a markedly different manner from the one in the Kakuichibon. Nagatobon presents the poem twice: first, as with the Kakuichibon, it is recited in the scene between Shigehira and Senju, but in the Nagatobon, the poem makes a second appearance in a scene between Shigehira and his official wife that comes right before his execution. That is, the *kanshi* is first situated in a context like the one found in Kakuichibon: it is explained as a poem about Xiang Yu's feeling of

55. I have based this categorization on Yamashita Hiroaki's views in Kajihara and Yamashita, *Heike monogatari*, 1: 428–45. The debate over the chronology of the myriad *Heike* versions has been fueled by scholars such as Atsumi Kaoru and Tomikura Tokujirō as well as Yamashita, among numerous others. For a useful summary of these debates over the various versions and their dates, see Takehisa, *Heike monogatari hassei kō*.

56. Kurokawa et al., *Heike monogatari: Nagatobon*, 618.

desperation when faced with a sudden enemy attack.[57] However, the prose that explains the significance of the poem when it appears for a second time in a scene about Shigehira and his wife explicitly states that Xiang Yu, realizing his impending defeat, bids farewell to his consort *before his escape*.[58] Nagatobon's recognition of Xiang Yu's actual fate in *Shiji* thus contrasts sharply with Kakuichibon's insistent discourse of inescapability. Similarly, a later *yomihon* text, *Genpei jōsuiki*, dating most likely from the early to mid-fourteenth century, exhibits the same narrative contours as the Nagatobon: although this version tends to devote more time to each story segment as expected of a *yomihon*, the *azuma kudari* section is quite brief and completely lacks *waka* poetry citations, while the *kanshi* about Xiang Yu and his consort Yu is explained as being one that describes the scene before the king's flight.[59]

57. Ibid., 622–23.

58. Ibid., 704.

59. Though *Genpei jōsuiki* had been categorized since the Edo period as a related but separate work from *Heike*, in more recent years it has come to be considered a *Heike* variant of the *yomihon* lineage. The organization of this text is different from other versions: it consists of forty-eight chapters, Shigehira is captured in chapter 37, and the bulk of the narrative about him takes place in chapters 38 and 39. *Genpei jōsuiki* is notably more lengthy than the Kakuichibon in many scenes; for example, the scene between Shigehira and one of his lovers, commonly referred to as Dairi no nyōbō (imperial woman-in-waiting)—who is here identified as a granddaughter of Shinzei (Fujiwara no Michinori, 1106–59, scholar and political schemer who was killed in the Heiji disturbance of 1159 for siding with the Taira)—is told in much greater detail in *Genpei jōsuiki* than in the Kakuichibon (Ikebe, *Genpei jōsuiki*, pt. 2, 433–40).

Jōsuiki's lack of emphasis on *waka* composition during Shigehira's trip east is very clear: instead of a poetic *azuma kudari*, there is an insertion of an *engi* narrative that describes the origins of a temple called Chōkōji, which Shigehira visits en route and where he writes down his name upon a pillar (ibid., 443–47). In fact, the story of Jijū and the *waka* composed at Mt. Shirane are instead narrated as being events in the *azuma kudari* of Taira no Munemori, Shigehira's older half-brother, who is portrayed as a pathetic and cowardly figure in both *Jōsuiki* and the Kakuichibon (ibid., 619–26). The association of Munemori's rather comical figure with the *azuma kudari* tropes in lieu of an association with Shigehira gives the audience a very different impression of the voyage from the one told in the Kakuichibon.

Furthermore, *Jōsuiki* explicitly states that Xiang Yu fled, bidding farewell to his consort Yu (ibid., 450–57); the passage also says that Shigehira rejected intimate relations with Senju no mae at the end of the evening, and that another female entertainer, Iō, is sent but she also fails to seduce him. The two women faithfully attend to him for over a year, even though he continues to withhold sexual relations; the narrator states that after his

Other *yomihon* versions' stories of Shigehira vary from Kakuichibon's in different ways.[60] For instance, the Shibu kassenjōbon is thought to be an early *yomihon* variant that was possibly produced in the mid-thirteenth century, with revisions and additions in the following century.[61] This text does refer to tropic places along the Tōkaidō and provides the *waka* exchange between the protagonist and Jijū, yet once Shigehira arrives in Kamakura, his encounter with Senju is represented as a mere passing event. She is mentioned as a beautiful and sympathetic woman who is ordered by Yoritomo to accompany the middle captain while he is in Izu, but none of her interactions with Shigehira is provided, nor are any *kanshi* invoked.[62] Another version is the Enkyōbon, a lengthy text whose date of composition has been hotly debated in recent years, with some scholars asserting that the bulk of the text dates from the early thirteenth century with a few later editing touches, and others finding it more plausible that it took its present form sometime in the second half of the thirteenth century.[63] While this version's presentation of Shigehira's scene in Kamakura closely resembles

---

death, the women become nuns because they had become emotionally attached to the captured aristocrat.

60. Another *yomihon* variant worth mentioning is *Genpei tōjōroku*, a largely incomplete version of *Heike* with only parts of three chapters having survived. The text is abridged in form like the *kataribon*, yet incorporates narratives about events and people of the eastern provinces. Its dates, like most *Heike* versions, are controversial, but the general consensus is that it was likely completed before the Nanboku era, possibly in the late thirteenth century. Despite its fragmentary condition, *Tōjōroku* nevertheless includes a section on Shigehira in chapter 8, which covers events from his capture at Ichinotani to his *azuma kudari*. As with other *yomihon* texts, Shigehira's *azuma kudari* is much less elaborate than the one found in the Kakuichibon. Shinomiya gawara is mentioned, but Semimaru is not invoked; the only extended narrative pause on his itinerary involves his exchange with Jijū, and after this visitation, the text becomes even more succinct, listing one place-name after another but not mentioning Mt. Shirane (Yamashita Hiroaki, *Genpei tōjōroku*, 206–27). Unfortunately, the chapter that would have included his exchange with Senju no mae is no longer extant.

61. Matsumoto Ryūshin and Keiō gijuku daigaku fuzoku kenkyūjo, *Shibu kassenjōbon Heike monogatari*, 1–2 emphasizes the earlier date, whereas Shida Itaru ("Shibu kassenjōbon *Heike monogatari* no seiritsu," 65–90) and Takehisa Tsuyoshi (*Heike monogatari hassei kō*, 259–68) summarize the current debate over Shibu kassenjōbon's dating and concede to the later dating.

62. Takayama, *Kundoku Shibu kassenjōbon Heike monogatari*, 341–58.

63. For a summary of this debate, see, for example, Kobayashi Yoshikazu, "Enkyōbon *Heike monogatari* no seiritsu," 91–112.

that of Kakuichibon's, the protagonist's *azuma kudari* in the Enkyōbon is a significantly condensed narrative, similar to the telling found in the Shibu kassenjōbon.[64]

It might make sense that the *yomihon* versions of *Heike* construct a different vision of Shigehira's life story from the one presented in the Kakuichibon, since the *yomihon* and *kataribon* tend to differ significantly in their emphases otherwise. Texts in the *kataribon* category, however, also vary from the Kakuichibon when it comes to their treatment of Shigehira. An example is the Yashirobon, which is quite likely an early *kataribon* dating from the thirteenth century, possibly the first half.[65] Though the extant editions are missing chapter 9, many aspects of Shigehira's story in chapter 10 and chapter 12 differ only slightly from the narrative of the Kakuichibon.[66] However, the most striking feature of the Yashirobon is that it presents the story of Senju no mae in an appendix and not in the body of the text. Furthermore, the details of that appended narrative differ in key ways from the Kakuichibon: the focus of the passage is upon the virtually comical eagerness of Shigehira's temporary host in Izu, under Yoritomo's orders, in his attempt to cheer up the brooding captive, and most crucially, the *kanshi* about Yu's tears is identified as a poem about Xiang Yu's defeat and consequent departure (*ochiyuku toki*) from the place of his consort.[67] A later *kataribon*, the Hyakunijukkubon, is thought to have been performed by the Yasaka school, rival to the Ichikata school to which Kakuichi belonged. As the latter school gained dominance and ultimately set the standard for *heikyoku*, the Hyakunijukkubon waned in popularity; most scholars

64. Yoshizawa, *Ōei shosha Enkyōbon Heike monogatari*, 806–8.

65. The scholarly consensus is that the Yashirobon dates from the thirteenth century, though Chigira Mamoru, in his work "Yashirobon *Heike monogatari* no seiritsu," asserts that contrary to accepted theories, the Yashirobon may date from the fourteenth century (113–36).

66. There are some small differences between the Yashirobon and Kakuichibon's *azuma kudari* sections also; for example, the section about Jijū lacks a discussion of her worries over her mother and the accompanying poem; the reference to Saya no Nakayama and Saigyō's poem is missing; the *waka* on Mt. Shirane reads *kyō made ni* (instead of Kakuichibon's *kyō made zo*), which emphasizes the "it is due to the fact I have been without incident until today" interpretation of the poem over other possibilities I have outlined above. See Satō and Haruta, *Yashirobon Heike monogatari*, 365–82.

67. Ibid., 607–11.

believe that it likely predates the Kakuichibon.[68] So named because it organizes the narrative into 120 *ku* (verses) that are much smaller in unit than the chapter organizations seen in other versions, this version resembles the older Yashirobon in that although its portrayal of Shigehira's *azuma kudari* differs only slightly from the Kakuichibon's,[69] it states quite importantly that the *kanshi* by Tachibana no Hiromi is one that describes the parting between Xiang Yu and Yu meiren when the king is about to flee.[70]

This examination, albeit brief and sweeping, of some major *Heike* versions in comparison to the specific narrative about Shigehira as featured in the Kakuichibon, then, suggests that the latter is uniquely interested in the particulars of this figure, as we have seen in this chapter so far: that is, two elite literary traditions—*waka* poetry and *kanshibun*—appear to be purposefully brought together in quick succession, in order to strategically narrate the textual demise of the courtier-warrior during the times of the Genpei wars. What, then, might be the reasons for this interest? To explore this question further, we must now turn to the intersection of Kakuichibon's potential textual agendas and the era in which it was produced: the presentation of Shigehira's story turns out to be inseparable from the way this version looks back on events in the late twelfth century and retells these events by weaving discourses specific to relations of power in the fourteenth century.

The End of the Capital As We Know It

Scholars agree that the *kataribon* group, to which the Kakuichibon belongs, is generally characterized by a viewpoint that privileges the capital as a site for courtly culture: these texts speak nostalgically about the Heian capital, while tending to omit the extended narratives concern-

68. See Mizuhara, *Heike monogatari*, 3; 393–427.

69. For example, the discussion of parent-child bonds after Shigehira's meeting with the female entertainer at Ikeda (here called Yuya, not Jijū) is missing in the Hyakunijukkubon.

70. Mizuhara, *Heike monogatari*, 164.

ing warriors hailing from the eastern provinces that we find in *yomihon* versions; what portrayals of Yoritomo and his forces we do encounter are often unflattering.[71] Indeed, there is ample textual evidence in the Kakuichibon to support this view; for example, the narrator waxes hyperbolic in the following passage:

> Ah, the old [Heian] capital was a splendid capital! The divine deities that protected the royal city manifested themselves with gentle rays in all directions, and the miraculous temples were constructed north and south with their roof tiles lined up in a row. Not a person suffered, and [the capital's location] was well situated among the Five Provinces and Seven Roads.[72]

Thus the Heian capital is said to be not only most divinely august, but also most geographically suitable for ruling the country.

Consistent with the view that privileges the Heian capital, we also find criticism of warriors from the east, who are frequently portrayed as unsophisticated ruffians unsuitable for life in the refined city. Consider the following comments regarding the famed Minamoto general, Yoshitsune. When he is called upon to lead the procession for an imperial purification ritual, the narrator recalls the same event held two years before and remembers it as a wondrous sight, with Emperor Antoku flanked by smartly attired Taira aristocrats unparalleled in their appearance. The narrator then states: "Today, it is Yoshitsune who leads the guarding of the procession. Unlike Kiso no Yoshinaka, he seemed surprisingly accustomed to the capital, but still, he was not as good as even the dregs of the Taira ranks."[73] Yoshinaka is a fellow Minamoto warrior hailing from the Kiso region in Shinano Province; he is famously ridiculed in *Heike* for behaving like a country bumpkin despite his military prowess. Although Yoshitsune comes across somewhat better, he is still described as being far inferior as a powerful man-about-the-capital compared to the Taira's courtly manners and tastes.

What we often see in the Kakuichibon, then, is a standpoint that prioritizes an idealized courtly past of the Heian capital; those who offend

71. See, for instance, Kajihara and Yamashita, *Heike monogatari*, 1: 428–33.

72. Ibid., 2: 269–70. The Five Provinces are those near the capital, Yamashiro, Yamato, Kawachi, Izumi, and Settsu, and the Seven Roads are Tōkai, Tōsan, Hokuriku, San'in, San'yō, Nankai, and Saikai.

73. Ibid., 254–55.

against this sensibility are ruthlessly mocked. At one level, Shigehira's story fits well into this context; his figure is tragic, and the genres of *waka* poetry and *kanshibun* that are used to tell his tale can certainly be understood as homages to courtly literary traditions. Kakuichi's school received patronage from powerful members of the capital, as I will discuss in more detail in a moment; thus, such glorifications would likely have appealed to those patrons' tastes. In addition, the scholar Sasaki Kōichi asserts that the *biwa hōshi* themselves considered Shigehira's *azuma kudari* section as one of the highlights of *heikyoku* performance.[74] Indeed, a passage that deftly refers to an array of courtly texts as well as modes of writing would have been an impressive display of knowledge and skill for the *biwa hōshi*, and may have contributed to the elevation of their art to a more elite status.

On the other hand, the text relates a complicated stance vis-à-vis the capital; as we have seen in the above analysis of Shigehira's trip east, the capital is not merely a coveted object of nostalgia, but a place that is recognized as being contested, fraught, and at best, transformed. Indeed, the narrator suggests as much throughout the course of this lengthy text. For instance, the very beginning of chapter 10, right before the introduction of Shigehira's life as a captive, describes the scene after the decisive battle at Ichinotani, in which the Taira suffer a massive defeat. The decapitated heads of important clan members are carried into the capital, and the Minamoto argue that these Taira heads should be paraded in full view across the wide avenue Higashi no tōin and be subjected to *gokumon*, the practice of hanging heads at a prison gate after executions as an object lesson for all to see. The retired emperor Goshirakawa consults with court officials, who strongly advise against the spectacle, saying, "Since times past, there has never been an example in which the heads of those who had climbed to the rank of minister or upper aristocracy were exhibited in procession on wide avenues."[75] Goshirakawa thus denies the Minamoto request, but the latter appeals the decision vigorously by declaring that without the public ritual, their forces would be without adequate inspiration to fight against the Taira, who are enemies of the imperial court as well as of their own family. The retired emperor finally yields to this argument, and the Taira heads come to suffer the

74. Sasaki Kōichi, "'Kaidō kudari' no michiyukibun," 572–88.
75. Kajihara and Yamashita, *Heike monogatari*, 2: 196.

shameful fate described as being unprecedented for people of their social standing. The capital is thus presented as a place in which extraordinary and unusual things can now happen, where former high-ranking aristocrats can be treated like common criminals, and imperial authorities are willing to give in to the demands of military strongmen, formerly considered "barbarians" from the east. Something is amiss; the conditions of the capital, as well as those in power there, have decidedly changed in the times of the Genpei wars.

The Taira, moreover, had already fractured the foundations of national governance, even before the arrival of the eastern warriors. In the very first chapter, the narrator states: "The country and islands of Japan contain only sixty-six provinces, out of which the Taira controlled thirty and a few, which is more than half of the country,"[76] suggesting that the central government and the Taira were two competing authorities who vied for rulership of Japanese territory. It is significant that although Kiyomori and his fellow family members ostensibly worked as members of the government, the text positions them as being divisive and in clear contention with that government.[77] Another crucial feature of the Taira's challenge to the status quo comes in the form of *sento*, or the moving of the country's capital. Before the Heian period, *sento*, which will be explored in more detail in the next chapter, was a common practice, with emperors moving the location of the capital periodically according to factors such as geomancy. However, as the narrator makes a point of explaining to us, "Since the capital was moved from Nagaoka to this [Heian] capital in the thirteenth year of Enryaku [794], the second day of the tenth month, there have been thirty-two emperors, and over 380 years";[78] given this context, Kiyomori's decision to move the capital in 1180 to Fukuhara in Settsu Province (see map 4), which the Taira had established as a home base, appears as an unusual development. As a matter of fact, it did not last long, since the capital was moved back to its

76. Ibid., 1: 16.

77. Another interesting, well-known story concerning Kiyomori is presented in chap 6, "Gion nyōgo" section (ibid., 354–57): he is said to be, in fact, a publicly unrecognized son of Emperor Shirakawa (1053–1129). If this were the case, then he would be an imperial prince challenging the authority and structure of the rule of the land—a rebel internal to the system.

78. Ibid., 268.

Heian location in just under six months. Although this instance of *sento* was short-lived, its execution in the first place is provided in the narrative as proof not only of Taira arrogance and whim, but also the extent of their power with respect to the imperial structure.

Indeed, that there are two reigning emperors at the time of Shigehira's capture is striking: Antoku (1178–85, r. 1180–85), to whom Kiyomori is the maternal grandfather, escapes the capital when the entire Taira clan flees westward to avoid the advancing Minamoto forces in 1183. It is then that another emperor, Gotoba (1180–1239; r. 1183—98), is enthroned in the capital as the next legitimate ruler. However, when the Taira flee with Antoku, they also take the Three Treasures, the material proof and symbols of imperial rule. The emperorship, therefore, becomes an unsteady seat of power in which a sovereign rules without the proper possessions that prove his legitimacy, and his double exists elsewhere far westward. Matters are not secure for Antoku, either: the Taira first arrive at Dazaifu in the distant southwestern province of Chikuzen, where they attempt to base themselves and to build a palace for the emperor, but they are ousted when a local strongman decides to side with the Minamoto. The entire clan together with the emperor flees once more, this time back slightly eastward; they eventually settle off the coast of Yashima in Sanuki Province aboard boats. The imperial palace of this emperor is thus literally fluid, being adrift in the ocean with waves as the parodic double of the palace grounds that are firmly entrenched on solid ground.

The capital and its most powerful inhabitants, then, are deeply troubled throughout the late twelfth-century world narrated in the Kakuichibon *Heike*. The rapid pace with which the narrative outlines the myriad rises-and-falls of individuals and families and the rupturing of the fundamental components of Heian-period rulership—imperial presence, governance by the court, and its very location in the capital—for which *Heike* is famous, makes sense, of course, considering the mid-fourteenth-century context in which the Kakuichibon *Heike*, one of the latest versions of this text, was produced.[79] As I have already

79. The *yomihon* versions' sympathetic eye toward Yoritomo and his *bakufu* in Kamakura may be due to their temporal concurrency—that is, many *yomihon* were produced before the fall of the Kamakura *bakufu* (Yamashita Hiroaki, *Genpei tōjōroku*, 269–71). Also, another version called the Nantobon, whose classification and dating

outlined in the previous chapter, much had happened by the time of Kakuichibon's establishment in 1371: the Kamakura *bakufu* collapsed in 1331, when Emperor Godaigo rose in revolt against it in the Genkō disturbance, with the help of the Ashikaga clan. The conclusion of this conflict was, on the surface, the recentralization of power in the capital, with the new Ashikaga *bakufu* based there alongside the court. But disagreements among the victors led to the Nanboku era, mentioned in chapter 2 and to be explored in more detail in the next chapter of this book; during this time, a dual structure of power manifested itself yet again in the form of two imperial courts located in different geographic regions, the Northern Court in the capital and Godaigo's Southern Court in Yoshino (see map 4). Complicating matters even more was the development of infighting among the victorious Ashikaga; the shogun and his brother battled each other, thereby triggering further national instability.

Kakuichibon is a text that seems well aware of these dramatic developments; the events of the late twelfth century can easily be understood as being analogous to developments contemporary to the text—that is, those of the mid-fourteenth century. The two-emperor configuration of the Nanboku era obviously finds a precedent in the simultaneous emperorship of Antoku and Gotoba during the Genpei wars. Furthermore, the audience is told that among the three imperial treasures of the mirror, seal, and sword that were taken by the Taira when they fled the capital in 1183, only the first two were recovered, from the ocean, when that clan met its demise in 1185 after a fierce battle finale aboard boats in which most of the members sank into the sea, dead or alive. This suggests that the emperor contemporary to the Kakuichibon's audience is, in a way, irreparably incomplete: he is always already missing a crucial authentic emblem of power, in addition to being embroiled in a north-south

are widely open to debate, may have been produced after the Kakuichibon. Yamashita Hiroaki, in *Heike monogatari no seiritsu*, asserts that the Nantobon is a mid- to late Muromachi text, and concludes that the Nantobon represents an extensively reedited conglomeration of previous versions (246–76). Sakurai Yōko expresses a similar view, pointing out that compilations that based their selection of narratives on both *kataribon* and *yomihon* texts emerged in the fifteenth century (*Heike monogatari no keisei to juyō*, 332–87). Indeed, Nantobon's passage concerning Shigehira may have been copied from the one in Kakuichibon. See Matsumoto Ryūshin, *Nantobon Nanto ihon Heike monogatari*, 2: 729–43.

imperial divide.[80] Moreover, the conflict found in the Kakuichibon is not simply intraimperial: it is likely not an accident that the last named major incident in the main body of the text is the Jōkyū rebellion of 1221, instigated by Gotoba.[81] The failure of the retired emperor's plot to overthrow the Kamakura *bakufu* and to reconsolidate power under the imperial court is an ominous reminder that a return to a Heian-style courtier rule is likely impossible.

Indeed, the year of Kakuichibon's completion, 1371, was one in which Prince Kaneyoshi (1330?–1383), a son of Emperor Godaigo and leader of the Southern Court, was granted the title "king of Japan" by the Hongwu emperor of the Ming dynasty in China (r. 1368–98). Kaneyoshi had established a stronghold for the Southern Court in Dazaifu; his international recognition added some degree of authenticity to the Southern Court's continued claims to legitimacy. Kaneyoshi's "kingship" lasted for only a year, but it still symbolized the disunity within the imperial structure, and the sense that the outcome of the conflict between the Northern and Southern Courts was still far from certain; the ontological significance of the capital as a space that houses the pinnacle of national authority, and the very existence of such an authority itself, were being constantly called into question during this time.

How might we, then, situate the representation of Shigehira in this context? I would argue that the Kakuichibon does not present a simple vision of chaos and loss, in which the narrator is merely aggrieved over a tumultuous era. Rather, in the thorough disempowerment of the figure of the courtier-warrior of the late Heian period, the text negates

80. Gotoba took the throne with a temporary replacement sword, which becomes permanent, as all efforts to recover the original sword from the ocean result in failure. The imperial treasures become the center of controversy again during the Nanboku wars: Emperor Godaigo secretly removes the Three Treasures when he flees the capital to Yoshino, giving authority to the Southern Court that it would not otherwise have had. In the meantime, the Northern Court claims that it still has the Three Treasures in its possession; the status of these objects as fakes erupts into controversy. After investigation, they are deemed inauthentic, and handed over to the Southern Court for ritual disposal. The significance of the treasures continues to be debated, particularly by those in the Northern Court, whose emperors have been taking the throne "improperly" without the regalia. For a full discussion, see Watanabe Daimon, *Ubawareta sanshu no jingi*, particularly the first two chapters.

81. End of chap. 12, before the "Initiate's Chapter."

the possibility of a nostalgic return to that ideal, instead sweeping the slate clean and laying the groundwork for a different mode of authority. In other words, while the Kakuichibon may appear to be sympathetic to the woes of the capital's courtly elites when compared to *yomihon* versions, it is not a text that sings the praises of the city's glorious past as an end to itself. Rather, the Kakuichibon undermines the bedrock of the courtly tradition, sealing the constituent parts of this bedrock—*waka* poetry and *kanshibun*—as relics of the past that need to be fundamentally recast in order to play a useful role amidst the power plays of the post-Genpei era.

At a time when a reunified capital, in which the military and the civilian modes of governance coexisted instead of finding themselves separated by hundreds of kilometers, was a tenable yet unstable idea, the Kakuichibon powerfully conveys to its audience that such a reunification would stand not for a return to an era before the *bakufu* existed but for a forging of a new terrain that would now officially contain within itself the fractures of power. It is Shigehira's tale of movement that serves to organize the narrative as a whole around this division: by clearly mapping the literary and political parameters of authority in the late twelfth century, every retelling of the narrative becomes a reinforcement of a particular, constructed historical memory that functions, in its contemporary setting, to separate the two governing bodies, and to perform the fall of the obsolete courtier-warrior and the disintegration of his familiar environment. The text's portrayal of this fall is therefore not, I would argue, merely subversive, but constructive—in that it makes way for new states of being that signify the possession of authority. A crucial key to this new authority, as suggested by the Kakuichibon, involves one's relationships with past texts.

Around the time of Kakuichibon's completion, there appears to have been a significant shift in the patronage of the *tōdōza* and *Heike* narration itself. Scholars such as Hyōdō Hiromi have argued that the most prominent house of the Minamoto was considered the official "keepers" of *Heike*, which not only legitimized the Minamoto's rise to power, but also had pacificatory powers over the deceased and potentially dangerous spirits of the eradicated Heike clan. Hyōdo notes that up to the first half of the fourteenth century, the Nakanoin family, who were then considered the *uji no chōja*, or "clan heads" of the Minamoto, had been overseers of the *tōdōza* and thus of *heikyoku*.[82] However, after the Nanboku wars, the Ashikaga shogunal house took over the role of *uji no chōja* of the Minamoto by the time of Yoshimitsu (1358–1408; became shogun in 1368), the third shogun, thereby gaining authority over the *tōdōza* and Kakuichibon in particular.[83] At first glance, this shift may seem far from extraordinary; the Ashikaga, who claimed Minamoto ancestry, had acquired political dominance, and their attaining control over *Heike* may appear to be an incidental part of that acquisition.

However, further scrutiny suggests otherwise. The Nakanoin branch of the Minamoto functioned almost exclusively among court circles, beginning with Michikata (1189–1238), who served successive emperors during and after the Jōkyū rebellion. The Ashikaga branch, on the other hand, were based in the eastern provinces and had served the Kamakura *bakufu*, before eventually turning its back on that failing institution during the Nanboku wars and seizing power for itself. The new shogunate's possession of *Heike* thus signifies a transfer of power *within* the Minamoto clan, from the courtly to something more complicated. Kakuichibon's nuanced portrayal of the two literary genres—*waka* poetry and *kanshibun*—and their specific portrayal of the tragic fall of a courtier-warrior, therefore, acquires particular significance within this context.

The shogun Ashikaga Yoshimitsu went on to flourish in both courtly and military arenas, eventually attaining the rank of prime minister as well as shogun, and even being offered the posthumous title of *daijō hōō* (retired sovereign who has taken the tonsure).[84] He was also involved in the decision to compile the twentieth imperially commissioned *waka* anthology, *Shin goshūi wakashū* (New later collection of gleanings of *waka* poetry, ca. 1384); he was clearly interested in the traditions of courtly culture. On the military front, he is well known as a strong leader and unifier, having overseen the end of the Northern-Southern Court

82. This designation was given to the branch within a clan that held the highest rank at court. Although Yoritomo seized power as the Kamakura shogunate, his descendants failed to prosper: both his sons, Yori'ie (1182–1204) and Sanetomo (1192–1219), were likely assassinated, and the Hōjō took over the rulership of the Kamakura *bakufu*.

83. This shift represented a change in lineage dominance within the Minamoto (from the descendants of Emperor Murakami [926–67] who had wielded power in the early medieval period, back to those of Emperor Seiwa [850–80], which included the likes of Yoritomo). See Hyōdō, *Heike monogatari no rekishi to geinō*, 8–18.

84. Yoshimitsu's son declined this honor on his father's behalf. Ibid., 76–91.

divide, quelling wars in the western provinces and wresting away the title of "king of Japan" for himself in establishing official relations with Ming China. In a way, then, Yoshimitsu appears to represent the ideal of the courtier-warrior, who travels seamlessly between both arenas and flourishes as a result.

The *Heike* version he maintained, however, suggests that the figure of the fourteenth-century courtier-warrior is distinctly different from the late twelfth-century one. In the Kakuichibon, the figure of Shigehira is made to succumb to self-disempowering textual interpretations; the pen is mightier than the sword, indeed, when a formidable courtier-warrior is shown to read, allude, and compose texts in ways that seem to force his resignation regarding his ultimately tragic fate. In other words, although Shigehira's execution is something that the Kakuichibon composers obviously did not invent, the very manner in which his life story moves from point A (his capture in battle) to point B (his death) is a specific textual effect that is created through the unraveling of past literary traditions and approaches. Here, the lore of Shigehira's path to his death consists not of resistance or expressions of dissension but of acceptance built upon particular interpretations of texts. The lesson for the new courtier-warrior (or, perhaps, the warrior-courtier) gained through the negative example of Shigehira's figure, then, might be the very importance of reading: one must now not ignore texts out of fear of disempowering misinterpretations, but instead take texts into one's own hands and make them work for oneself—including the *Heike*.

Lee Butler has shown persuasively that the court was able to strategize, adapt to, and withstand challenges to its power throughout the centuries before and after the Nanboku wars, and its members regarded even the most powerful warriors with contempt when it came to matters of culture.[85] If so, taking the bull of court culture by its horns and trying to lead it to new directions would have made sense as an important item on the list of Yoshimitsu's agenda; texts and their management can be viewed as a display of cultural prowess, and the figure of Shigehira in the Kakuichibon is a powerful object lesson. Like the noh theater Yoshimitsu famously patronized, the Kakuichibon reframes the courtly literary tradition in significant ways. If noh takes familiar courtly narratives and

85. Butler, *Emperor and Aristocracy in Japan*, 11.

recasts them, often radically, into performative modes that suit the needs of contemporary audiences and patrons, then similarly, the Kakuichibon seizes well-known tropes in *waka* and *kanshibun* and transforms them into new commentaries regarding the dos and don'ts for those in charge. The specter of the captive-in-motion manifests itself only to disappear, each time teaching a lesson about the significance of textual traditions and interpretations.

FOUR

Suwa

Multiplicity, Ubiquity, and "Elsewhere" in Shrine Origin Narratives

If movements of various kinds were abundant as textual tropes in Heian and medieval Japan, perhaps one of the most extreme examples is the well-known tale of a man, Kōga no Saburō, who eventually becomes a deity at the Suwa Shrine in Shinano Province. He embarks on a journey in search of his lost wife; although this itinerary may sound unremarkable, the extensiveness of his trip, the imagined structure of the fictional countries he visits, and the manner of narration combine to generate a tale of travel that is outstanding for its grand, almost infinite scale. Thus it seems fitting to dedicate the last chapter of this book to an exploration of how and why narratives pertaining to the Suwa Shrine invoke tropes of movement, and how these stories together construct a striking new vision of power, its location, and its method of distribution.

The Suwa Shrine complex, consisting of the Upper Shrine (*kamisha*) and Lower Shrine (*shimosha*) located on separate sides of Suwa Lake, has been an organization of national prominence from at least the seventh century and remains popular to the present day.[1] Since its early days, the emperor and the court had bestowed their attention upon Suwa:

1. Today, the Suwa *taisha* (Great Shrine; so named in 1948 to indicate that it heads the myriad Suwa shrines scattered across the country, as I will explain in more detail below) is famous for the Pillar Festival (*onbashirasai*; for a thorough discussion, see Gerbert, "The Suwa Pillar Festival Revisited," 319–74) and a phenomenon called the "divine crossing" (*omiwatari*), which occurs a few days after the water freezes and a ruptured ice "path" snakes across the lake. For a classic, lengthy study of the Suwa Shrine complex, particularly its rituals and annual festivals, see Miyaji, *Hodaka jinjashi / Suwa jinja no kenkyū*, vol. 1, and *Suwa jinja no kenkyū*, vol. 2.

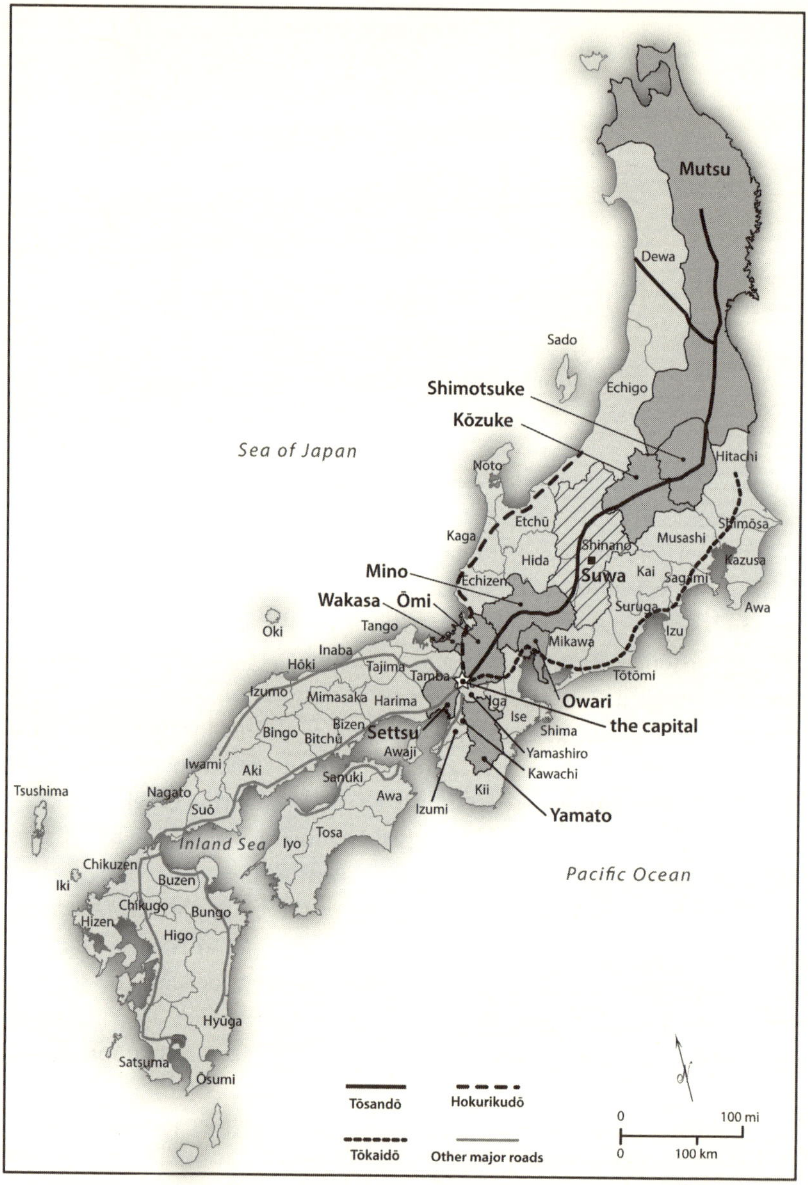

Map 6 Heian and medieval Japan: Shinano Province, where the Suwa Shrine complex is located (the striped area); and provinces that are prominently featured in *Shintōshū* Suwa stories (the shaded areas).

imperial prayers were offered at the shrine due to its capacity as a divine manager for water and rain,[2] and the main deity of the Upper Shrine, Takeminakata, was granted the rank of *juichi'i* (junior first rank).[3] Indeed, Suwa would be listed alongside such shrines as Ise, Kamo, and Kasuga in official documents by the middle of the ninth century;[4] *Engishiki* (927) ranks Suwa highest among all shrines in Shinano Province.[5] In the late Heian period, we also begin to find the enshrined deities being revered as protectors of warriors' fortunes; patronage of the shrine by those militarily capable would soon flourish.[6] During the Genpei civil wars of the late twelfth century, the Suwa establishment sided with the Minamoto in their war against the Heike, and the shrine was consequently deeply revered by the new Kamakura shogunate as housing the god of war.[7] Furthermore, the Suwa deity became renowned as a deity of hunting,

2. Empress Jitō (645–702) is said to have offered prayers at the Suwa Shrine in 691. Kojima et al., *Nihon shoki*, 3: 518–19.

3. Takeminakata was promoted to this rank in 867 (Keizai zasshisha, *Sandai jitsuroku*, 248). Furthermore, when there was a blanket promotion of shrine ranks in 893, Takeminakata would have risen to senior first rank (Keizai zasshisha, *Nihon kiryaku*, 762).

4. The late medieval compilation of documents at Enryakuji, called *Mon'yōki*, includes a text called *Shamon ichidōki*, which is said to have been composed in 867. This work provides a list of twelve venerable deities each corresponding to a sign of the Chinese zodiac; starting with Ise, the list includes the likes of well-known deities such as those at Kamo, Matsuo, and Sumiyoshi, and ends with Suwa. Fukuda, *Shintōshū setuwa no seiritsu*, 13–15.

5. Torao, *Engishiki*, 1: 611.

6. An *imayō* ("modern-style song") lyric found in the twelfth-century collection *Ryōjin hishō* lists the Suwa Shrine as housing one of the eight great deities of war in Japan (Song 248). Kobayashi Yoshinori et al., *Ryōjin hishō, Kanginshū, Kyōgen kayō*, 72.

7. Imazu, "'Suwa Daimyōjin Ekotoba' no kaisetsu," 55–56. The Suwa Shrine complex was among the *bakufu*'s list of twelve most revered shrines (Itō, *Suwa jinja no kenkyū*, 347); in particular, the Hōjō clan, which took over the Kamakura shogunate from the Minamoto soon after the establishment of the *bakufu*, regarded the Suwa Shrine as housing its clan deity (Kanai, *Suwa shinkōshi*, 14). The role of the Suwa deity as a protector of warriors can be found in *Heike monogatari*, in which the Suwa deity is named as one of the divine figures who assisted Empress Jingō in her military expedition against Silla (Kajihara and Yamashita, *Heike monogatari*, 2: 284); the same reference can be found in the *Heike* variant *Genpei jōsuiki* (Ikebe, *Genpei jōsuiki*, 565–67). *Azuma kagami* states that during the Jōkyū rebellion, a warrior from Shinano Province, Kasuga no Sadayuki, almost drowned while trying to cross the Uji River during battle, but by invoking the Suwa deity in his heart, he escaped unharmed (Kishi, *Zen'yaku Azuma kagami*, 3: 337–38).

an endeavor favored by the *bushi*; the shrine's annual festivals frequently involved ritual hunts.[8]

Indeed, the prominence of the Suwa Shrine complex in these eras is understandable; the Suwa region lay in a key strategic location near the crossroads of several major premodern thoroughfares, such as those that traversed northward to the Japan Sea and south to various points along the Pacific coast, as well as the Tōsandō, one of the *shichidō* (seven major roads) that stretched out through the national landscape (see map 6).[9] The Tōsandō radiated out from the capital and eventually reached the Ōshū region, the northeasternmost area of the country, whose relationship with the court was often dynamic and fraught, as we saw in chapter 2.[10] This road also represented an alternative transportation route to the

8. For instance, *Shasekishū* (ca. 1283) notes that the Suwa deity was known as the god of hunting (chap. 1, story 8; Watanabe Tsunaya, *Shasekishū*, 78). The Kamakura *bakufu* issued direct orders for funding the Misayama festival at Suwa, which likely included rituals, performances, and martial/hunting demonstrations. The activity of hunting had become controversial in the Heian period, together with the practice of eating meat, which was frowned upon in the Buddhist context. The Suwa deity then became the patron of hunters and meat eaters alike, and this helped in the popularization of Suwa worship across the national terrain. Indeed, in the Edo period, amulets distributed by the Suwa Shrine with the words "exempted for eating deer," supposedly enabled worshippers to engage in this practice without the fear of divine retribution. See Terada and Washio, *Suwa myōjin*, 96–97 and 106–13; Kanai, *Suwa shinkōshi*, 55–73.

9. The Suwa region was a province in itself for a brief period, from 721 to 731 (Kōgakkan daigaku shiryō hensanjo, *Shoku Nihongi shiryō*, 4: 573–74 and 6: 23–24). The reasons for the formation of the province and its rapid dissolution only a decade later remain a mystery. Emperor Tenmu (r. 673–86) first became interested in possibly constructing some type of palace in this region, as the entry for the second month, thirteenth year of Tenmu's reign suggests (Kojima et al., *Nihon shoki*, 3: 432–33). Suwa's popularity consequently surged, and a road through Mino Province into Shinano was begun in 702 and was completed in 713 (Ishikawa, *Suwa saisei no hasshō to keifu*, 53). For unknown reasons, however, Suwa was reintegrated into Shinano in 731. Even after Suwa returned to being a part of Shinano Province, the region continued to have strong ties with the central government, particularly as an important provider of horses (Yamada, *Suwa shi gaisetsu*, 44–45).

10. Kanai, *Suwa shinkōshi*, 8. Other roads that radiated out from Suwa include one that headed toward the Mikawa region near modern-day Nagoya (Ina kaidō), and another that would eventually lead to Edo in the early modern period (Kōshū kaidō); Tōsandō itself was known as an artery with particularly numerous lesser roads branching off from it (see Takeuchi Makoto, *Nihon no kaidō handobukku shinpan*, 71–73, 94–95, and 100–109).

more famous Tōkaidō when one traveled from the capital eastward.[11] It is therefore no surprise that the Suwa religious complex thrived, given the political, military, and commercial significance of its specific geography.

It is interesting, then, that in one of the earliest stories about the Suwa Shrine, its main deity Takeminakata is something of a renegade. In the *Kojiki*, he is embroiled in a tale of conflict between two competing divine lineages, represented by Amaterasu, the sun goddess and progenitor of the ruling imperial family, and Susano'o, her brother-rival who was chased away from the heavens. The narrator states that Ninigi, who is Amaterasu's descendant, tries to convince Ōkuninushi, Susano'o's heir and ruler of Ashihara no nakatsukuni (the land between the heavens and the underworld, i.e. "Japan"), to relocate elsewhere so that Ninigi may take over as ruler. A powerful pair of Ninigi's messengers arrives in Ōkuninushi's realm, demanding that he step down; Takeminakata, one of Ōkuninushi's sons, decides to put up a fight. He challenges one of the messengers to combat, but loses the duel and flees. The messengers chase after him, and Takeminakata is cornered at Suwa Lake, whereupon he begs not to be killed in exchange for his pledge that he will never leave this region.[12] In the medieval period, Takeminakata wanes in popularity as the protagonist of narratives about the Suwa Shrine.[13] Instead, we find a range of different stories all purporting to tell the origins of the shrine; none resembles the *Kojiki* story above in plot or characters, and a lineage connecting these medieval texts and the eighth-century text would be difficult to establish. Nonetheless, coincidentally or not, dissension,

11. The *ritsuryō* system of governance, established in the mid- to late seventh century, designated the *shiki shichidō*, which divided the country into the capital region (four provinces, which increased to five in 757 and was thus renamed *goki shichidō*) and regions along the seven arterial roads, one of which is the Tōsandō. This road, the longest of the seven roads, was used more frequently than the Tōkaidō until the middle of the tenth century, despite being the most mountainous and treacherous for winter travel. Kodama, *Nihon kōtsūshi*, 13–18.

12. Aoki et al., *Kojiki*, 90–93. Although *Kojiki* as a whole was not widely circulated until the Edo period, the same Takeminakata narrative also appears in *Sendai kuji hongi* (author unknown; ca. late 9th century), a historical narrative consisting of selected passages mostly from *Kojiki* and *Nihon shoki*, that was available in the medieval period. Yasumoto and Shimura, *Sendai kuji hongi*, 151–54.

13. In fact, Takeminakata does not appear at all in *Nihon shoki* (720), a text contemporary to *Kojiki*. Speculations about the reasons for Takeminakata's sparse early appearance can be found in Ishikawa, *Suwa saisei no hasshō to keifu*, 10–11, but much is conjecture.

questions of lineage, and most importantly, movement all continue to be important features of medieval narratives as defining features of the Suwa religious complex.

This chapter analyzes in detail three medieval narratives about the Suwa religious complex that belong to the genre called *engi*, or "origin narratives," that seeks to explain how something related to a particular divinity came into being—such as the account of how a shrine's annual festival began, or a detailed biography of a specific deity enshrined at a place of worship.[14] A syncretic genre, *engi* encompasses both Buddhist and Shinto concerns; for example, many texts explain how a Shinto deity is actually a manifestation of a Buddhist divinity.[15] *Engi* comprise the main type of narrative that we find in *Shintōshū*, a ten-volume collection of fifty stories; it is in this anthology that the three Suwa narratives are featured. As one might guess from the title of the collection, the stories center around Shinto matters and stories pertaining to particular shrines, yet in keeping with the *engi* genre, most are thoroughly syncretic in nature and feature Buddhist figures, usually as the true manifestations of the Shinto deities. These *engi* are thought to have been orally performed for the purpose of proselytizing and advertising the efficacies of each shrine and its deities as they are represented in the collection.

14. In Japan, *engi* began as a genre of writing that explained how things came about in a religious context. *Engi* narratives before the mid-Heian period functioned primarily as a religious establishment's justificatory document, in which the establishment's history and relationship to the court was outlined, together with a list of its material assets. Starting in the second half of the Heian period, narratives of origin became more elaborate, assuming the main role within the genre. In the Edo period, *ryaku engi* (abbreviated *engi*) came to be printed and distributed to worshipers. See Murakami, "Engi no monogatari shōshi," 382–85 and 391; Sakurai Tokutarō, "Engi no ruikei to tenkai," 445–78; and Yanase Kazuo, *Shaji engi no kenkyū*.

15. Indeed, the term *engi* is a translation of the Sanskrit Buddhist term *pratītya-samutupāda*, or dependent origination; it came to be syncretized and used in both Buddhist and Shintō contexts (see Terakawa, "Jisha engi," 156–73). *Shintōshū* itself is thought to be influenced by Tendai worldviews, in large part due to its connection with the Agui school of oral performance, as noted below; see Hashimoto, "*Shintōshū* no jōbutsu shisō," 114–26. Such syncretism is typical of religious institutions in Japan throughout the premodern era into the present day; see Teeuwen and Rambelli, *Buddhas and Kami in Japan*, particularly the editors' introduction (1–53) and the chapter "The Interaction between Buddhist and Shinto Traditions at Suwa Shrine" by Inoue Takami (187–312), which explores late Edo and Meiji-era syncretic practices at Suwa.

The circumstances surrounding the dates and authorship of *Shintōshū* are quite vague. The scholarly consensus is that the collection was first compiled in the mid-1350s,[16] but the identity of the compiler is difficult to pinpoint; the beginning of each volume states that it is "by Agui," so it is most likely that the Agui *shōdō* chanters, who performed a style of Buddhist oral storytelling that began with the Tendai priest Chōken (1126–1203) and prospered throughout the medieval era, may have played at least some role in the editing and/or compiling processes.[17] There is considerable debate over the extent of other religious performers' contributions to the production of this text, such as those who were particularly familiar with Kōzuke Province, which contains many of the shrines explicated in this collection.[18] Although much remains unknown, in the

16. The history of the collection is usually divided into two textual lines: the earliest versions of the *kohon* ("old text") line of texts are thought to have been compiled in the mid-1350s, but the earliest existing editions probably date from the first part of the fifteenth century. The *rufubon* ("standard") line, whose details at times vary significantly from those of the *kohon* texts, most likely came into being in the late fifteenth century. For the purposes of this chapter, I have based my analyses on an annotation of one of the *kohon* texts, the Akagi bunko kyūzōbon (Okami and Takahashi, *Shintōshū*). This edition lacks the first volume; thus the annotators used the first volume of another *kohon* text, the Shinpukujibon, to supplement this text; none of the Suwa narratives discussed in this chapter are from volume 1.

17. Various theories exist about the origins of *Shintōshū*; most agree that religious performers associated with shrines/deities in each of the *Shintōshū* narratives produced the *engi*, and through some process, they came to the attention of Agui chanters who compiled and possibly edited these narratives (see, for example, Nishio and Kishi, *Chūsei setsuwashū*, 276–79; Tokuda, "*Shintōshū*: kamigami no monogatari," 127–32). Kishi Shōzō provides a detailed overview of classic studies of this text, including those by Yanagita Kunio and Kondō Yoshihiro; he considers various views, including those that reject the Agui association as a mere invented legitimizing label for the collection, and reaches the conclusion that Agui probably had a light editing hand in standardizing literary styles (*Shintōshū*, 298–309).

18. For a thorough review and critique of past approaches to the Kōzuke origin theory, see Satō Kikuichirō, *Kinsei Kōzuke shinwa no sekai*. Satō argues that while past scholars, particularly those in the *minzokugaku* field, such as Kadokawa Gen'yoshi, have romanticized the possibility of a timeless eastern regionalism and/or an "original" *Shintōshū* that no longer exists, it is more productive to specifically historicize *Shintōshū* narratives that concern Kōzuke Province and its place in both the national and regional imaginaries. Fukuda Akira, on the other hand, proposes that the Agui chanters in the thirteenth century were trying aggressively to appeal to a wider audience and patrons in the eastern lands, particularly around Kamakura, so they purposefully included a large

case of the Suwa narratives, scholars are in agreement that the texts were likely composed, performed, and maintained by those associated with the Suwa Shrine complex before being compiled into *Shintōshū*.[19]

Textual figures of movement play a crucial role in the *Shintōshū*'s "Suwa engi," which stand out from other tales in the collection in their particular concern with tropes of movement as both literary techniques and physical actions of their featured characters. In my first analysis, I focus upon the story entitled "Suwa no daimyōjin no Satsuki-e no koto" (The matter of the fifth month ritual of the Great Suwa Deity), which is notable for the seemingly haphazard flow of its storyline; I suggest that these swift shifts from one scene to the next are in fact a strategy that generates strong associative equivalences between characters in different scenes. Ultimately, these equivalences, or relations of multiplicity, challenge notions of imperial legitimacy and the very idea of a single source of authority. The second story, "Shinano no kuni no chinju Suwa daimyōjin Akiyama matsuri no koto" (The matter of the autumn mountain festival of the Great Suwa Deity, guardian of Shinano Province), is concerned with movement in the form of characters traveling (or refusing to do so) from one place to another. "Akiyama matsuri" reads, on the surface, like a simple narrative of distant regional rebellion and the success of the imperial army in bringing a quick end to it, but matters turn out not to be so straightforward when we focus upon the ways in which the figure of movement works in this text. The imperial army general who leads the expedition is identified as an émigré from China, with a particular background of past allegiances that suggest dissatisfaction with the hereditary manner in which imperial legitimacy is maintained. Furthermore, the

---

number of *engi* about shrine complexes in this area, and invited chanters from these provinces to the capital to perform (Fukuda, *Shintōshū setsuwa no seiritsu*, 52–85).

19. Fukuda proposes that all extant editions of the *Shintōshū* Suwa narratives, as well as other stories about Suwa in the late medieval period, were composed, maintained, and propagated by affiliated religious performers belonging to categories such as the *yamabushi* (mountain ascetics) and *miko* (spirit mediums) in Shinano Province as well as areas closer to the capital such as Kōga and Iga; these were then edited by those who served the Suwa branch shrines in the capital region, then possibly exported back to Shinano for further editing (*Shintōshū setsuwa no seiritsu*, 238–39, 269, 300–301, 425–30, 447). Kanai Tenbi asserts that one of the *Shintōshū* narratives, titled "Suwa engi," was maintained and propagated by traveling *yamabushi* affiliated with the Suwa Shrine complex (*Suwa shinkōshi*, 16).

emperor himself comes to be rendered analogous to the rebel leader, in that both are shown to derive their powers from their concrete, stationary geographic foundations.

Third, I examine the best-known Suwa narrative in the *Shintōshū*, which is entitled simply "Suwa engi" and features a protagonist named Kōga no Saburō. As I stated at the beginning of this chapter, this particular work consists of a grand tale of one of the most extensive descriptions of travel through vast fictional geographical spaces in medieval Japan. I will show that this sweeping textual voyage represents the imagination of a new order of power dissemination: instead of a specific location from which power radiates outward, "Suwa engi" envisions an ambient sense of power, which is ubiquitous in presence and more evenly distributed throughout the national landscape. The chapter concludes with a consideration of a related trope common to all three "Suwa engi" in the *Shintōshū*: "elsewhere." Under the terms of this trope, power derives from one's identity as having come from somewhere else other than the place one is currently located. "Elsewhere," as I define it, is a form of geographic otherness that deemphasizes exact locations in favor of a more symbolic realm of "not here"; it is also a trope that works hand in hand with the strategy of ubiquity, so that the resulting effect is an everyday presence of the power-from-elsewhere. Careful attention to tropes of movement in the three texts, in other words, allows us not only to discern critiques of existing configurations of rulership up to and during the time of the *Shintōshū* but also to see that the narratives propose nuanced, alternative visions of the ways in which paradigms of power can be established.

Narrative Movement and Multiplicity in "Satsuki-e"

At first glance, "Satsuki-e," a narrative included in the fourth chapter of *Shintōshu*, seems like a random patchwork of three separate tales. First, we hear a story about a demon king, his marvelous flute, and the famous poet Ariwara no Narihira; all of the action takes place in the Heian capital. Second, we suddenly shift to the story of a military expedition to destroy the demon king, who has holed himself up in Shinano Province in a gesture of rebellion. Third, we are again abruptly transported to India, where we are told of a tale about a hideous princess who ultimately transforms into the deity at the Suwa Shrine. Although the title of the narrative might suggest that there will be an explanation of the fifth month ritual, a multiday sequence of events including ritual hunting and archery on horseback for which Suwa is famous, little attention is given to this topic; moreover, the disjointed and rapid movement among the three narrative parts has led some scholars to criticize the text as haphazard and unskillfully executed.[20] I suggest instead that, in fact, the text's apparent short attention span, typified by its seemingly arbitrary trajectory from one unrelated story to another, is precisely its most important point: characters from different segments transform into multiples of one another, connecting the once-random-seeming narrative dots into a vision of divine subversion. The three narrative segments that may appear only tangentially linked at first are actually intricately entwined through the textual strategy of multiplicity.

Let me define what I mean by multiplicity. The "double" as a literary figure is often understood through reference to the doppelgänger, a psychoanalytic term that indicates a monstrous, ghostly double of the self; in the context of nineteenth-century European literature, scholars have argued that the doppelgänger challenges the divide between the real and the phantasm, as well as the very notion of subjectivity, through narratives of displacements that involve visuality, language, sexuality, and/or time.[21] What we have are two characters that look similar on the surface, but are actually quite different in substance, thus producing an unnerving effect. The trope of multiplicity that I examine in the Suwa texts differs slightly in focus: I use the idea of doubling as a springboard to examine instances in which characters who seem radically unrelated are actually equivalents at some level; these equivalences have real potential to jar and surprise the reader. In the examples I will explore, such equivalences are not limited to pairs (as in the case of doubles), but expand out to triples and more—thus I employ the term "multiplicity" to refer to the series of equivalences between characters in a story. Ultimately, though, like the doppelgänger, the trope of multiplicity subverts the

20. For example, see Kishi, *Shintōshū*, 315.

21. See, for example, Webber, *The Doppelgänger*, 1–55.

possibility of uncontested unity, or a stable sense of singularity; in the case of "Satsuki-e," multiplicity challenges the very foundations of imperial identity and authority.

SEGMENT I: THE COURTIER AND THE DEMON KING

The first segment of "Satsuki-e" outlines the following course of events: there was a demon king named Kannara who lived in Shinano Province. He owned a marvelous, magic bamboo flute. The courtier Narihira, hearing about this flute, wishes desperately to steal the instrument away from the demon in order to make the flute a "treasure of our country."[22] The aristocrat concocts an elaborate scheme in which he goes to remote areas in the capital to play his own flute melodiously, while secretly bringing along—as if to foreshadow the importance of multiplicity to this text—one hundred decoy flutes. The demon king, lured by Narihira's expert playing, allows himself to be befriended by Narihira and lets the courtier try out his magic flute. They play together all night, and when it is almost morning, Kannara asks Narihira to give him back his flute. Narihira tries to return one of his decoy flutes instead; the demon sees through the trick, and asks for the real one, but Narihira hands him another decoy. This game is repeated until the rooster begins to cry, signaling dawn—a time of day when demons lose their powers. The demon king hurries away from the scene. Narihira, having succeeded in his trickery, presents the magic flute to Emperor Kōkō (830–87), who gladly receives it. Shortly thereafter, Kannara appears at the imperial palace to beg for the return of his flute. The emperor refuses, provoking the demon king into causing a great storm in the capital. The emperor orders Kannara to leave; the latter obeys, but not before kidnapping court attendants upon his exit. The emperor then commands one Mitsukiyo to embark on an expedition to hunt down the demon, who has fled back to Shinano Province.

One of the most striking aspects of this segment is the way in which the narrative draws a close parallel between the figures of Narihira and Kannara. This doubling is achieved through a number of textual strategies. The most obvious similarity between the two figures is their

22. Okami and Takahashi, *Shintōshū*, 98.

awe-inspiring talent in the art of the flute, but the commonalities do not stop there. The opening lines introduce Narihira as a man who is not only extraordinarily gifted in all things cultured, but as someone who has attracted much amorous interest. In referring to his adventures, the narrator uses the following specific words:

> [Narihira] is the person who had stolen away the Somedono empress. . . . He violated four imperial consorts, and the number of those who were cast aside by him, women both high and low who still clung to hopes for his affection, those who had grieved longingly for him, or those who had drowned themselves or starved themselves to death, are countless. However, Narihira had yet to be admonished by the court.[23]

There are two crucial aspects of this passage that link Narihira to Kannara. First, in describing our hero's actions with regard to imperial consorts, the text uses the term "violate" (*wokasu*). The choice of this word is crucial, since moments after the above passage, we are given the following introduction to the demon king: "During the reign of [Emperor Kōkō], there was a demon king in the province of Shinano. Nine years had passed since he had moved to that land, and he would frequently travel to the capital and *violate* people limitlessly."[24] By repeating the exact word *wokasu* to refer to the actions of both Narihira and Kannara in successive passages, the text forges a strong association between the deeds of these two figures.

Second, we must note the appearance of the Somedono empress (Fujiwara no Meishi, 826–99) in the passage referring to Narihira. The invocation of her name here is significant because she was known for having had an illicit affair with a demon.[25] The target of Narihira's imperial abduction narrative, however, is usually understood as having been

23. Ibid., 97.

24. Ibid., 97–98.

25. Kawashima, *Writing Margins*, 263–65. For the Somedono narrative, see *Konjaku monogatari*, chap. 20, story 7 (Komine, *Konjaku monogatarishū*, 4: 234–39). This story is retold in a variety of later texts, including *Kojidan* and *Uji shūi monogatari*, and interest in the contours of the story remained active in the fourteenth century as well, as we can see from examples such as *Genkō shakusho* by Kokan Shiren (ca. 1322), chap. 10, which does not specifically name Narihira, but states that Somedono was rendered ill by a demon (Fujita, *Kundoku Genkō shakusho*, 1: 213–14).

the Nijō empress (Fujiwara no Kōshi, 842–910), as related in texts such as *Ise monogatari*;[26] it is not Somedono. In the tales that cast Nijō as Narihira's love interest, we are told that the brazen paramour absconds with this empress (technically an empress-to-be), only to have her devoured by a demon. The *Shintōshū* narrative, however, switches the identity of the stolen consort from Nijō to Somedono. What could be the reason for this? In the popular cultural imagination, Nijō is a woman who falls victim to a demon *despite* the wishes of her lover; the demon and the lover are therefore two entirely separate beings. Somedono, on the other hand, is said to have engaged in a direct relationship with a demon, thus in stories about her the identity of the lover and the demon are fused into a single figure. The mention of Somedono in the biographical explanation of Narihira in the *Shintōshū* passage suggests, then, that Narihira is none other than the demon himself. Through references to talented flute playing, the repeated use of the word *wokasu*, and the intertexual implications of the Somedono empress's appearance, the first section of "Satsuki-e" collapses the identities of Kannara the demon king and Narihira the famed aristocrat, situating them as uncanny doubles of each other. The textual strategy of multiplicity—here, a doubling—thus renders what appears to be a simple story of "good" (imperial court) and "evil" (rebellious demon) into a more complex narrative that challenges facile binary distinctions.

Moreover, the text highlights the extent to which the demon king's extreme actions are taken in response to human provocation. When Kannara comes to court to beg for the return of his flute, he states that the instrument had been passed down in his family for fifty-seven generations, and makes a respectful appeal by calling the emperor honest. Despite this plea, however, the emperor refuses not only to return the flute but even to have the courtesy to provide his guest with a reply. It is then that Kannara becomes enraged and decides to take revenge. The passage thus leaves a distinct impression that the human side—the imperial court—is deceitful and disrespectful; we saw the conniving plot that Narihira had executed in order to trick the demon, and now we hear the demon begging for the rightful return of a long-time family heirloom,

26. *Ise monogatari*, story 6; Horiuchi and Akiyama, *Taketori monogatari, Ise monogatari*, 84–85.

making a trusting appeal to the emperor's sense of fairness, to which the emperor offers only devious silence as a response. Kannara seems almost sympathetic by comparison, and his anger understandable.

SEGMENT 2: THE GENERAL AND THE EMPEROR

The demon hunt comprises the second segment of "Satsuki-e"; courtly arts like the flute fade away completely here, together with Narihira, who is not heard from again for the remainder of the story. We are instead transported to the scene of a military march from the capital eastward; the narrator introduces the audience to Mitsukiyo, a general with no surname, upon whom the responsibilities of the punitive expedition are thrust. Our hero is described quite simply as a compassionate man twenty-nine years in age. On his journey to Shinano Province, he meets two warriors on horseback who want to become his travel companions. Mitsukiyo reveals his true mission to his new friends, who pledge their assistance in his battle against the demon king; the latter, in the meantime, has established his fort on Mt. Asama in Shinano. A fierce battle ensues, the newly befriended warriors succeed in binding up the demon on behalf of Mitsukiyo, and the victorious company heads home toward the capital. Before reaching their destination, however, the warriors part ways with Mitsukiyo after revealing their true identities; one of them, of course, turns out to be the deity at Suwa. The emperor is pleased, the general and the assisting deities are rewarded, and everyone seems to live happily ever after. This segment thus appears to be a straightforward representation of rightful imperial victory over the evil rebel, and of the Suwa deity as a protector of imperial interests.

Even General Mitsukiyo, however, is not entirely free from the specter of analogous figures that hint at disruptions and contestations of the distribution of power. When he is first introduced, we hear that he forbids his myriad retainers to accompany him on the demon-hunting expedition because of the dangers associated with the mission. The narrator enthusiastically commends the compassion at the root of this refusal, and compares the act to that of the mythical eleventh emperor Suinin, who is credited for terminating an imperial burial practice that required a courtier, a woman attendant, and a warrior to be killed and buried together with the emperor upon his death.[27] Suinin replaced this custom with the burial of *haniwa* clay figures that symbolized actual human beings. Mitsukiyo's consideration for the lives of his retainers is thus rendered explicitly akin to imperial generosity that ceased the practice of sacrificial burial; the figure of Emperor Suinin is invoked, it seems, as a way to exalt the general through such an association.

Indeed, the details of Suinin's alleged biography reinforce the resemblance between his figure and that of Mitsukiyo. According to *Nihon shoki* as well as *Kojiki*, Suinin is said to have quelled the rebellion of his brother-in-law, Saobiko, who had instructed his sister and empress, Saobime, to assassinate Suinin. The plot failed and Saobiko met his demise along with his sister.[28] The invocation of Suinin's name, which is strongly associated with his pacification of the revolt against the "legitimate" imperial line, foreshadows Mitsukiyo's victory over the demon king—that is, a "good" hero on the side of the privileged ruling lineage wins over a discontented member of the empire. The general and the emperor of old might, therefore, be paired as a distant double.

Suinin's victory over his rebellious relatives, however, did not mean that his life was necessarily triumphant. *Kojiki* proceeds to state that the son he had with Saobime, the renegade Saobiko's sister, was born mute because of a curse that had been put on him by Ōkuninushi, who, as we saw earlier in this chapter, was displaced by Ninigi and now has taken up residence as the Great Deity of Izumo. The narrator relates that the mute prince traveled to Izumo and paid his respects to Ōkuninushi; thereupon, the curse was finally lifted, and he was able to speak.[29] Suinin's biography can, therefore, be one that acknowledges resentful displays of power from a competing lineage of potential rulers; such competitors must be treated with reverence in order to pacify their dissatisfaction with the status quo. What is more, let us recall that the rebellious deity, Takeminakata, son of Ōkuninushi, was enshrined as the Suwa deity.

27. Okami and Takahashi, *Shintōshū*, 99–100.

28. Kojima et al., *Nihon shoki*, 1: 306–13; similarly, Aoki et al., *Kojiki*, 158–65.

29. Aoki et al., *Kojiki*, 164–71. *Nihon shoki* is less explicit about the cause of the prince's inability to speak. He is said to have recovered after seeing a swan in flight and asking about it; Suinin dispatches one of his men to go after the bird, which is finally caught in Izumo and brought back for the prince (Kojima et al., *Nihon shoki*, 1: 316–17).

This suggests that although the narrative of Mitsukiyo's victory over the demon king seems to be devoted to the task of proving the allegiance of the Suwa deity to an imperial, antirebel expedition, the appearance of Suinin's figure in the narrative, and the explicit association of Mitsukiyo to this mythical emperor, could potentially allude to an alternative story. In that parallel universe, the Suwa deity symbolizes not a powerful ally to imperial interests but a staunch resistance, albeit defeated, to the reigning imperial line.

Finally, we should also remember that Suinin's mute son is himself a product of a rebellious maternal lineage, as mentioned above; his mother, though reluctant, had been convinced by her brother to attempt to assassinate his father, the emperor. This trope of the dangerous maternal lineage will be shared with another Suwa narrative, to be discussed below. True, the immediate threats of rebellion are vanquished; thus such a family tree serves as proof, at one level, of the strength of the ultimate victors. Rebels challenging an emperor's authority is also a common theme in texts such as the *Kojiki* and *Nihon shoki*. However, my point here is that the possible, specific resonances between Mitsukiyo's and Suinin's figures, when understood in context together with the framing narrative concerning the demon king, cast a potentially complex and unsettling shadow upon what seems to be a straightforward story of the righteous defeating the defiantly wicked. The general is doubled by an imperial ancestor plagued by opposition, and it is hinted that the "good"—that is, proimperial and antidemon—Suwa deity might, in fact, be suspect in his origins and his allegiance.

Segment 3: The Princess, the Demon King, the Suwa Deity, the Emperor (Again)

The third and final segment of the text turns matters upside down by bringing everything full circle, literally: the trope of multiplicity runs wild, inverting and subverting the good and the bad, and the imperial and the demonic in practically acrobatic ways. After the successful expedition to and from Shinano Province is over, the audience is abruptly transported thousands of miles away to India, where we hear about the story of Princess Kongōnyo, a royal who had become hideous in appearance due to sins she had committed in her past life. This familiar narrative, whose versions can be found in collections such as *Konjaku monogatari*,[30] ends happily: she had been hidden away in the depths of the palace due to her repulsiveness, but hearing that the Buddha has been invited to give a sermon, she prays fervently to be able to hear the lecture in public—and, lo and behold, she is transformed into a beautiful shape by the Buddha. The narrator explains that this princess, whose true manifestation is the Thousand-armed Kannon (*Sahasra-bhuja-sahasra-netra*), is the deity housed in the lower Suwa shrine; her patient husband, the minister Gida, is the bodhisattva Fugen (*Samantabhadra*), who is the deity of the upper Suwa shrine. This revelatory scenario, in which the deities' Indian origins are traced, is a typical *engi* technique that places emphasis on the syncretic, "foreign" origin of the deity in order to ascribe extraordinary power to the divine being. There is, however, more to this segment than exoticism and the appropriation of a well-known narrative into the explanation of a shrine's origins.

The trope of multiplicity continues to operate in this segment, but in an amplified, even more subversive fashion. This is how this segment begins:

> As for the identity of this Great Deity at Suwa: in the country of Sha'e in India, King Hashinoku had a daughter named Princess Kongōnyo, who was the most beautiful woman under the heavens. However, when she reached seventeen, the color of her body changed to a golden hue, and came to take on the shape of a demon king while still alive. Scales formed, and her figure of blue, yellow, red and white swept aside those nearby, and those who saw her felt their organs jolted apart from their bodies.[31]

Note the explicit use of the term "demon king" (*kiō*) here; it is exactly the same word that was used to describe Kannara, the vilified demon king, in

30. See *Konjaku monogatari*, chap. 3, story 14 (Konno, *Konjaku monogatarishū*, 1: 233–36). In the *Konjaku* version, the princess is born hideous, whereas in the Suwa narrative, she suddenly loses her beauty as a teenager; the previous life's sins also differ (in *Konjaku*, the princess had been a kitchen maid who insulted a holy man's appearance, whereas in *Shintōshū*, she was an empress who had put to death the three hundred competing imperial consorts out of jealousy).

31. Okami and Takahashi, *Shintōshū*, 100.

the first two sections of this *engi*. Just as we saw how the word "violate" connected the demon king to Narihira at the beginning of the text, the term "demon king" here creates a strong bond between the princess and Kannara, who perished in the hands of imperial authority. Furthermore, Kannara is described as possessing a multihued body much like that of Princess Kongōnyo in an earlier passage, in which he becomes enraged upon the emperor's refusal to return the magic flute.[32] My point is that this repetition of *kiō*, like the earlier recurrence of *wokasu*, is not an accident; nor is the match in the description of their physical bodies coincidental. The final segment of "Satsuki-e" clearly situates the princess as the demon king's double.

We must now recall that the princess, in fact, is said to be none other than the Suwa deity itself; the whole purpose of the retelling of events in her life is to explain the true identity of this deity. We can therefore see that this double forms an unexpected multiple equation between the demon king Kannara and the Suwa deity through the intermediary figure of the princess: demon king = princess Kongōnyo = Suwa deity. The association between Kannara and the Suwa deity gains force when we remember that both are strongly associated with the province of Shinano.[33]

With the threefold link among the three characters established, we must now revisit the question of imperial authority. We can see that if the demon king = princess Kongōnyo = Suwa deity, then in fact, it is

32. "The demon became enraged and became its true form; its height measured two *shaku* and it shone in five colors, emitting fire from its own body" (Okami and Takahashi, *Shintōshū*, 99).

33. This is not the first time that the Suwa deity is associated with a demon king in literature. The text *Hōbutsushū* (ca. 1180s?), a collection of Buddhist tales by Taira no Yasuyori, presents the following story: Kaisei (723–81) was born an imperial prince, but had become a Buddhist monk. When he traveled to Kachio Temple in Settsu Province, he wished to copy their Prajñā-pāramitā Sutra in gold ink. However, as he was a traveling monk, he did not have any gold with him; he thus prays fervently for divine assistance. As a result, an aristocratic man appears in his dream and gives him gold; Kaisei weeps for joy, thinking that the deity Hachiman has come to his aid. He then realizes that it would be shameful to dissolve this august gold into regular water to make the ink. He thus prays fervently again, causing a *yasha* (Sanskrit: *yaksa*), a demon king, to appear with a container full of holy water in a second dream. Kaisei asks the demon king about his identity, and receives the reply that he is the deity at Suwa in Shinano Province (Koizumi et al., *Hōbutsushū, Kankyo no tomo, Hirasan kojin reitaku*, 246–47).

none other than the Suwa deity himself who pacifies his *own* double, albeit with some assistance. What appeared, then, to be a straightforward display of imperial might and an emperor's total victory over his foe is transformed into a circular system in which multiple agents act upon their own shadows. In other words, one of the most crucial disclosures made in the third section of this *engi* is that the system of multiplicity is one that leaves out the imperial institution completely in its logic of equation. We find out that there is only the illusion of the emperor's command and triumph; it turns out, in fact, that he is merely a foil, a decoy actor who does not realize the truth of his own irrelevance.

The final part of "Satsuki-e" proceeds to unravel the logic of identity and temporal progression through a now-expanded chain of identifications that extends out across time and space. The narrator, after explaining that Princess Kongōnyo eventually moved to Japan, states that Emperor Jinmu, the mythical first human emperor of Japan, is actually her child.[34] The privileged imperial line that is crystallized into the figure of Jinmu is given an astonishing origin: the womb of Princess Kongōnyo, who is the demon king's double as well as a manifestation of the Suwa deity. This assertion obviously runs contrary to the claims about Jinmu's origins that are made in texts such as *Nihon shoki* and *Kojiki*, which trace his ancestry to the deity Amaterasu. In other words, *Shintōshū* replaces the usual biography of Jinmu with one that accredits the Kannara–Kongōnyo–Suwa deity triangle with the birth of the current imperial house; this alternative genealogy turns the superiority of the imperial lineage over any point of the triangle on its head. The Japanese imperial institution thus becomes the progeny of an Indian princess; the princess, furthermore, is a "triple" of a rebellious-then-quelled demon king and the Suwa deity, all at the same time.

"Satsuki-e" carries the audience from the Heian capital and the familiar name of Narihira and his courtly musical adventure, to a sudden demon suppression expedition hundreds of miles away in Shinano, then even farther away to India and back to Japan—but this time, a defamiliarized Japan in which emperors, deities, demons, and foreign royalty morph and collide in a whirling vortex that fundamentally destabilizes the building blocks upon which power and authority are constructed.

34. Okami and Takahashi, *Shintōshū*, 103: 神武天皇此宮御子也.

The text creates a parallel narrative that undermines the surface story of a glorious and successful imperial expedition; courtiers become doubles of demons, and demons, in turn, turn out to be alter egos of deities that at first glance appeared to be earnestly serving the emperor's interests. In this way, narrative movement enables the swift and uncanny transformations of characters into equivalences of one another that form a subversive web, entrapping and nullifying claims of unhindered imperial dominance. In fact, the imperial institution is shown to be symbolic at best, as it functions as a straw figure that has only the semblance of agency.

Movement, Geography, and Lineage in "Akiyama matsuri"

The *engi* to which I turn next, "Akiyama matsuri," is found in the same chapter of *Shintōshū* and shares a number of similarities with "Satsuki-e." They both feature military expeditions by the imperial army that fights rebellious forces in the provinces, and the armies emerge victorious as a result of divine assistance. The specific tale in the case of "Akiyama matsuri" goes as follows: the story purports to explain the origins of the celebratory festival that commemorates the day on which imperial forces in the ninth century succeeded in quelling an uprising in the Ōshū region (Mutsu Province). En route from the capital to the northeast, the general of the imperial army in charge of the punitive expedition befriends two stalwart warriors who decide to accompany the troops all the way to Ōshū, where a rebel (this time human) has declared his intention to resist imperial authority over the region. The two warriors proceed to play a vital role in assisting the general's forces in reaching victory. It is then revealed that the pair are manifestations of deities, one of whom hails from Suwa, and all is well again as the general and the deities' home shrines are amply rewarded for their mission well accomplished. Upon first glance, then, "Akiyama matsuri" appears to be an even more straightforward story about good triumphing over evil, narrated in a consistent and linear fashion. Just as in the case of "Satsuki-e," however, a closer reading suggests that this *engi* is far more complicated than it first seems. This time, the distinguishing trait of the narrative is not a frantic flow from one segment to another, but the ways in which its featured characters are marked by their relationship to physical movement from one place to another, *and* to the symbolic movement of power from one authority to the next. Exploring these tropic nodes will show that this story, in fact, revolves around an incisive critique of the hereditary manner in which imperial power is transferred from one ruler to the next.

THE ÉMIGRÉ FROM CHINA

The general who is chosen to lead the imperial army is provided with a full name this time, Inase no Gorō Tamuramaru, and is identified as an émigré from China. We are not given his Chinese name, but it is explained that upon his arrival in Japan he was adopted by a Japanese family and is given a Japanese name, Tamuramaru, by which he is called for the entire length of the text. The name Tamuramaru clearly references the famous historical figure who is credited for the successful expedition against the Emishi in the early ninth century, Sakanoue no Tamuramaro (758–811). Indeed, Sakanoue no Tamuramaro's standard biography states that his ancestors came from China; however, casting him as a first-generation émigré is an invention particular to this text;[35] *Shintōshū* spends a significant amount of time dwelling on Tamuramaru's diasporic character. Assigning a foreign origin to a figure is an obvious way to mark him as extraordinary. However, the *specific* details of Tamuramaru's supposed

35. Tamuramaro's father, Katsutamaro (728–86), is said to have submitted a lineage chart indicating his ancestry to the emperors he served; in the document, he states that his family descended from Liu Azhi, great-grandson of Emperor Ling (r. 168–89) of the Eastern Han dynasty. Liu Azhi is said to have emigrated from China to Japan during the reign of Emperor Ōjin (r. ca. late 4th–early 5th century). For more on the controversies over Tamuramaro's origins, see Takahashi Takashi, *Sakanoue no Tamuramaro.* Legends about the brave deeds of Sakanoue no Tamuramaro are many, including those that name him as a demon-slaying founder of Kiyomizu Temple in the capital (for details about Kiyomizu's own branch temples in Shinano Province and their worship by warriors who revered Tamuramaro, see Ushiyama, "Tamuramaro densetsu to Kiyomizudera shinkō," 125–61); others, like "Tamura no sōshi," a Muromachi-era popular narrative in the genre of *otogi zōshi*, claim that Tamuramaro's mother was a serpent (Yokoyama and Matsumoto, *Muromachi jidai monogatari taisei*, 9: 80–109).

Chinese origins suggest that, as in the case of the Indian origin of the Suwa deity in "Satsuki-e," there is more than exoticism here; the events leading up to Tamuramaru's move to Japan unsettle claims to imperial legitimacy, the very thing his Japanese army is supposed to be protecting against the villainous rebel forces.

When Tamuramaru is first introduced, significant attention is given to an explanation of the Chinese figure Zhao Gao (?–207 BCE), whom Tamuramaru supposedly served as a warrior. According to the Chinese historical narrative *Shiji*, as well as subsequent works such as the *Yiwen leiju* (A categorized collection of literary writing, edited by Ouyang Xun [557–641])[36] and Japanese texts such as *Heike monogatari*, which is contemporary to the *Shintōshū*,[37] Zhao Gao was an infamous eunuch who served the first emperor of Qin. Upon the emperor's death, he is said to have forced the suicide of the heir apparent (Fu Su, ?–210 BCE), installed another prince as the second Qin emperor Hu Hai (229?–207), only to drive him to suicide as well, and put to death numerous others in order to secure his powers at court. A famous anecdote that is said to illustrate his scheming character is one that involves a horse and a deer: when he was still serving the second emperor Hu Hai, he sought to test his political influence and to discern his allies and his enemies by bringing some deer to the palace. He then claimed that the deer were actually horses, and those who went along with the obvious lie were spared, whereas those who disagreed were systematically murdered. Zhao Gao was finally killed by Ziying, the short-lived third and last emperor of Qin.[38]

"Akiyama matsuri," however, presents a decidedly different version of Zhao Gao's biography. The *engi* claims that he served in the court of Gaozu, first emperor of the Han and conqueror of the Qin. In sources such as the *Shiji*, Gaozu is depicted as a powerful emperor who won followers for his magnanimous rule and successfully defeated his foes,

36. *Yiwen leiju*, vols. 82 (under "cattails" [*Typha latifolia*]) and 95 (under "deer") contain passages about Zhao Gao's evil deeds.

37. The opening lines of the Kakuichibon *Heike* compare Taira no Kiyomori to Zhao Gao and other Chinese tyrants who, because they ignored their loyalties to their former sovereigns, behaved selfishly, caused disorder in the world and dissatisfaction among the populace, faced destruction before long. See Kajihara and Yamashita, *Heike monogatari*, 1: 5. Before *Heike*, *Jikkinshō* refers to the deer/horse incident as an example of deceit (Asami, *Jikkinshō*, 333).

38. See "Qin shihuang *benji*," in Sima Qian, *Shiji*, 264–76.

including the mighty Xiang Yu mentioned in chapter 3.[39] In striking contrast to the generally accepted narrative, however, the *Shintōshū* text not only reassigns Zhao Gao to Gaozu's court, but further claims that Gaozu himself was afraid of Zhao Gao's powers. The narrator features the anecdote involving the deer-as-horse not just as evidence of Zhao Gao's dominance among his colleagues, but actually as proof of Emperor Gaozu's subservience to Zhao Gao.[40]

It is obvious that the *engi* misrepresents the usual understandings of Chinese history: there is great discrepancy between the time of Gaozu and the early ninth century when Tamuramaru is said to have moved to Japan to serve the reigning emperor there, making it impossible for this émigré to have served both emperors within a normal human lifespan; the second Qin emperor, Hu Hai, is mistakenly identified as Gaozu; Zhao Gao's name is written with characters that are different from his actual ones; and the details of the incident concerning the deer and the horse that supposedly gave Zhao Gao excessive confidence in his own powers is told with the identities of the animals in question reversed.[41] Such fanciful reimaginations of events in China are far from uncommon in Japanese narratives, and one could explain Tamuramaru's life story provided here simply as an attempt to bolster his power through his association with Chinese men of power. However, rather than dismissing these impossibilities as merely whimsical details or sheer ignorance, I choose to interpret these "mistakes" as a sign that the author considered it very important that Tamuramaru be given this *particular* background, regardless of any logistical problems that might arise.

While texts ranging from the *Shiji* to *Heike* cast Zhao Gao as thoroughly villainous, *Shintōshū* refers to him simply as a powerful man full of wisdom, and says nothing judgmental about his later demise nor mentions any specific act of evildoing. In contrast, *Shintōshū*'s Gaozu

39. See "Gaozu *benji*," in Sima Qian, *Shiji*, 341–94. Gaozu's magnanimity does begin to waver after he becomes emperor, but he is credited as the founder of a stable and strong dynasty (Nienhauser, *The Grand Scribe's Records*, 2: 93–101).

40. Okami and Takahashi, *Shintōshū*, 92.

41. *Shintōshū* uses the characters 朝廣 instead of his actual characters 趙高. In the "Qin shihuang *benji*" chapter of the *Shiji*, Zhao Gao tests his influence over other ministers by claiming that the two deer he presented to the emperor were actually horses, but in *Shintōshū*, Zhao Gao is said to have pointed at horses and claimed them to be deer.

comes across as a neutral figure at best, with a streak of weakness that makes him submit easily to Zhao Gao's influence at court. The passage that narrates Zhao Gao's eventual defeat highlights these points effectively: "The person called Gaozu had recently become a commoner, but was of royal lineage in the past. It had been merely five generations since his family had been ousted from court. And the changing of the emperorship is not a matter simply of this world; the king [Gaozu] became strong and Zhao Gao lost."[42] There are a number of crucial points in this passage. First, Gaozu's eventual victory is justified by the claim that his family was of royal lineage generations ago. The argument thus might appear to be that he had the right qualifications for reclaiming the throne because of his family heritage. However, the narrator then states that dynastic change is "not a matter simply of this world"—that is, it is something karmic and subject to divine intervention, beyond the complete control of human beings. This statement provides an explanation for a turn of events the narrator seems to feel the text's audience might otherwise struggle to understand. Gaozu, who is clearly depicted as an average ruler at best, was able to triumph over the powerful retainer Zhao Gao; this could happen because Gaozu was of royal descent, but also because matters of dynastic transition are beyond ordinary human comprehension.

On the flip side of this excuse lies a critique: the ascension to the throne of a vaguely ineffective emperor whose sole claim to the imperial position is his ancestral lineage, and the defeat of a wise competitor. Zhao Gao's failure to seize power is not blamed upon flaws in his character or evil deeds he committed, nor is there a suggestion that he should not have dared to compete for the throne in the first place; he was an imperial contender who lost due to forces he could not be expected to manage. Perhaps the wrong deities had been mistakenly addressed, or perhaps it was an unlucky turn of karmic events that brought about these results. Tamuramaru is said to have fled to Japan because Zhao Gao's side had lost to the resurgent imperial forces of Gaozu; the text explicitly states that because Tamuramaru was not a retainer on the winning imperial side, he could no longer reside in China. Tamuramaru is therefore cast as an ethical, purposeful refugee headed for Japan, and there is no hint that he was a former employee of a wicked insurgent.

42. Okami and Takahashi, *Shintōshū*, 92.

The implications of the passage's commentary are significant: to begin with, the method of imperial succession—that is, the movement of power from one emperor to the next—and even the privileging of a single imperial lineage are subtly but, I would argue, firmly questioned. Ambiguity over succession possibilities makes room for readings that undercut the very source of imperial authority: arguments over who can claim rightful possession of the position of emperor, and the means by which such claims are secured. The portrayals of Zhao Gao and Gaozu leave a strong impression: factions that fight over the imperial throne are given a balanced treatment, the reigning emperor can be depicted as ineffective, and competition for the throne is viewed neutrally or at worst with resignation, with the understanding that victory or defeat may depend on deeds in previous lives that are beyond the control of an individual, and even divine intervention (which, of course, makes sense in an *engi*, which served as advertisements for divine powers). Thus we see that on the one hand, the phenomenon of Chinese dynastic change is not viewed in a negative light but is portrayed in a sympathetic manner; on the other hand, the narrator refuses to necessarily place the so-called unbroken lineage of the Japanese imperial family in a position of privilege. The textual effects generated by these representations create instability at the core of the imperial institution.

LAND AND LINEAGE

The Japanese emperor whom Tamuramaru serves is Kanmu (r. 781–806). Emperor Kanmu is routinely heralded as an august figure most famous for founding the Heian capital in 794, thus ending the practice of *sento*, in which the capital was moved from place to place with each reign, sometimes more often.[43] Kanmu first became engaged in the project of an enduring *sento* early in his reign: he moved the capital from its location in Heijō (est. 710; present-day city of Nara) to a new capital at Nagaoka (est. in 784 in the outskirts of present-day Kyoto to the southwest); however, when Nagaoka became unsatisfactory due to factors ranging from its location in a terrain excessively prone to flooding to ominous

43. See Ōishi, "Nihon sento no keifu," 31–41.

natural disasters and vengeful spirits, Kanmu moved further northeast.[44] The second attempt of his reign to establish a long-lasting capital proves successful: the new Heian capital represented the grounding of the country's capital in a single geographical location that was to last, with a few interruptions, for nearly eleven centuries.[45] Kanmu, therefore, is an emperor fabled for his interest in the relationship between geography and governing authority; in particular, he chose to halt the tradition of frequent movement in order to anchor national power in a single and immobile seat. He might thus be easily compared to his Chinese counterpart, Gaozu: both established strong and lasting rulership, basing their power in newly founded capitals (Gaozu's Han capital, Chang'an, of course being the model for the Heian capital) from which they sought to command authority.

The figure of Kanmu, however, undergoes a series of identifications in "Akiyama matsuri" that compromise such well-known hallmarks of his reign. First, if we draw an analogy between the *specific* invocations of Gaozu and Kanmu's figures that we find in this text, the resulting implications cast a shadow on the latter's rulership. I have already suggested above that Gaozu is represented in this tale as a weak ruler who luckily managed to triumph over his foe, and that the struggle between him and Zhao Gao shows that power derived solely from lineage is questionable at best. Similarly, this story portrays Kanmu as someone who also owes the securing of his power to deities' assistance; no mention is made of

44. The practice of *sento* and the construction of new palace grounds generated alliances and patronage relationships between the emperor and the aristocrats overseeing the project, and often resulted in political consequences. A good example is the transition from the Nagaoka capital to the Heian capital; Fujiwara no Tanetsugu (737–85) was a close advisor to Kanmu and the central figure behind the *sento* to this location, but he was assassinated shortly after the move to that capital; those blamed included the crown prince, Sawara, who was deposed, exiled, and died resentfully while denying the charges of his involvement. It is then Sawara's vengeful spirit that is blamed for a string of deaths and disasters in the capital; he is posthumously pardoned and given an imperial title. See Kawajiri, *Heiankyō sento*, 18–24.

45. The longevity of the Heian capital, however, was not a given; after Kanmu's death, the famous Kusuko Incident in 810 raised the specter of *sento*. Fujiwara no Kusuko (d. 810) is said to have colluded with the retired emperor Heizei (r. 806–9) and ordered a *sento* back to the Heijō capital, ignoring the authority of the reigning emperor Saga (r. 809–23) and the will of Kanmu for a permanent place for the capital. Kusuko's order failed, she committed suicide, and the capital remained at its Heian location.

his own direct agency in the project of pacification (in fact, his army was struggling greatly against rebel forces before divine intervention).[46] The destabilization of Kanmu's source of legitimacy, his implied comparison to an unimpressive Gaozu, who is here portrayed as less than almighty, coupled with the neutral, if not sympathetic, depiction of Zhao Gao, a man with imperial ambitions of his own, renders Emperor Kanmu as less than invincible.[47]

Kanmu is equally famous for having ordered a successful quelling of the northeastern Emishi uprisings in 802 that are discussed in more detail in chapter 2. This *engi* blames these uprisings upon a single character, an insurgent in the Ōshū region by the name of Akuji no Takamaru. He is clearly called an "enemy of the imperial court" (*chōteki*) who must be punished; his surname literally means "bad deed/matter," further emphasizing the wickedness of his character. Takamaru is said to have "sealed off the province, made people suffer, and became an enemy to the imperial court."[48]

What is interesting about the depiction of Takamaru's uprising in "Akiyama matsuri" is that the text locates this rebel's source of strength directly in the physical territory in which he has chosen to establish his

46. Requests for divine assistance are far more prominent in this story, compared to "Satsuki-e." In "Akiyama matsuri," Tamuramaru travels to Kiyomizu and Kurama temples to pray for help before setting off for his expedition; he receives advice and a sword from the gods as a result (Okami and Takahashi, *Shintōshū*, 93). This is thus additional to the help of two deity-warriors who appear en route to the northeast.

47. Indeed, we might remember that Kanmu's path to the throne was not, in fact, straightforward. His enthronement represented the usurping of one imperial lineage over another: his father, Emperor Kōnin (r. 770–81), became emperor at the age of sixty-two, when there were no more heirs to the line of descendants from Emperor Tenmu (r. 673–86). Kōnin was a grandson of Emperor Tenchi (r. 668–72), from whose lineage Tenmu had wrested away the emperorship; Kōnin's unlikely reign thus represented a return of power to the Tenchi line. Moreover, his son, Prince Yamabe, who will later become Kanmu, was not born of a consort of the highest rank and thus was not a top contender in the game of succession; originally, the position of crown prince had belonged to a different prince. However, due most probably to political machinations, the crown prince was ousted after being accused of colluding with his mother in laying a curse on his father, and Yamabe took the spotlight. Thus Kanmu had a lot to prove when he took the throne, and his obsession with *sento* can be understood within this context; asserting his Tenchi lineage by abandoning the Heijō capital, which was built by those in the competing Tenmu line, was likely one way for him to demarcate a new era of rulership lineage. Kawajiri, *Heiankyō sento*, 2–14.

48. Okami and Takahashi, *Shintōshū*, 92.

stronghold. The landscape remains anonymous, as no specific place-names within Ōshū are cited in the text. Nonetheless, the terrain is described as an extraordinary place:

> Surrounding the fort, there is a wall that is made entirely of stone. The ocean lies to the east, and one can see tall waves reaching a thousand *jō*;[49] to the south, they have lined up huge boulders that almost reach the clouds. In the west, rocky mountains create a natural fortress wall, and a great river flows to the north. It is a scene unimaginable by the human mind. But within the fortress walls surrounded by the ocean and the rocks, the four seasons materialize in splendor beyond words; might this be the Pure Land?—one wonders, and one loses the will to battle.[50]

It is this unspecified wonderland, compared favorably to the Pure Land of the Amida Buddha, that makes Takamaru invincible: its splendor makes opposing soldiers weak in the knees, and it protects those within it through its extreme geographical advantage. Indeed, the imperial forces experience a great deal of difficulty in the face of the potency of Takamaru and his extraordinary land.

We have, then, a clear association between Kanmu and his archenemy, Takamaru: both are portrayed as being deeply committed to the importance of a stationary, land-based source of power with which to govern and control a bounded territory. Kanmu, the head of his court, appears to be the "rightful" possessor of this power, whereas Takamaru, a rebel, seems to be cast as an evil twin because he threatens the territorial integrity of what Kanmu and his court considered to rightfully belong to Japan.[51] The relative strengths of such claims become murky,

49. About three thousand meters.

50. Okami and Takahashi, *Shintōshū*, 94.

51. It is interesting that at least by the early medieval period, the position of *ōhōri*, or great ritualist, who lay at the core the Suwa religious establishment's Upper Shrine, was hereditary and involved the ceremonious installation of the Miwa family's male heir at age eight into the role of a "living deity." The doubling of the human agent and the deity in this very world can be viewed as being analogous to the emperor system, and possibly represented a form of doppelgänger-like resistance to monolithic authority (Terada and Washio, *Suwa myōjin*, 89–95). Since the villain Takamaru is situated as a key ancestral figure in the Suwa lineage, as we will see momentarily, it seems that the potentially competitive nature of the *ōhōri* vis-à-vis the emperor is not impossible.

however, when we remember that the story of the Chinese émigré has already added nuance to the process of succession and the emperor's right to power.

The identity of the villain, Takamaru, adds another dimension to the story. The historical Sakanoue no Tamuramaro rose to fame due to his successful military campaign against the Emishi in 802, forcing its leader, Aterui, to surrender, as I outlined in chapter 2. In the ensuing centuries, the name and identity of the rebel leader undergoes a number of transformations; for example, in the Kamakura period, we find that he is called Akuro-ō instead of Aterui. The name Takamaru is thus another one of these aliases for the rebel leader; the text *Genkō shakusho* (History of Buddhism to the Genkō era, ca. 1322), a medieval Buddhist history of Japan, is one of the earliest texts to call the northeastern villain by this name.[52] *Shintōshū*'s choice in naming the enemy of the court may, on the one hand, be part of this trend; however, in light of the powerful presence of doubles and multiples in the Suwa texts, we note as well an uncanny relationship between the rebel Takamaru and the general in charge of the imperial army sent to quell him, Tamuramaru. The very similarity of the names Takamaru and Tamuramaru aurally and visually hints at a pairing.[53] Both characters, indeed, were or are "outsiders" with respect to the central government: the "good" incarnation is a former foreigner who had fought against the now-reigning Chinese emperor, then became naturalized into fighting on behalf of the Japanese imperial

52. Fujita, *Kundoku Genkō shakusho*, 1: 195. *Azuma kagami* (ca. early 14th century) calls Aterui's counterpart Akuro-ō (Kishi, *Zen'yaku Azuma kagami*, 2: 123). The well-known *gunki* narrative about the life of Minamoto no Yoshitsune, *Gikeiki* (ca. mid- to late 14th century), also invokes the name of Takamaru as the villain (Kajihara, *Gikeiki*, 81 and 138).

53. *Shintōshū* inscribes Tamuramaru's name as 田村丸, in which the character 丸 could be read as either "maru" or "maro." In earlier texts, however, Sakanoue no Tamuramaro's first name is written as 田村麻呂; the characters 麻呂 are unequivocal in their reading, "maro." The doubling between the conqueror and the conquered, in fact, is not far-fetched when we consider that it occurs already in a text from the late Heian period, *Mutsu waki*, mentioned in chapter 2. The narrative states that a certain Sakanomote Moremaro was involved in the pacification of the northeast. The characters for the first name, Moremaro, are written 母礼麻呂: "More" is none other than the name of one of the two Emishi rebels quelled by Tamuramaro in 802. Thus there is a precedent for the confusion between and conflation of the imperial general who quelled the rebellion and those that led it. Yanase et al., *Shōmonki, Mutsu waki, Hogen monogatari, Heiji monogatari*, 155 and 180–81.

cause, whereas the "bad" half is trying to legitimize a territory in which the powers of the central state cannot reach. It seems, then, that the nomenclature "Takamaru" is here used for a purpose, quite possibly due to its similarity to Tamuramaru, the "good" hero. If the rebel and his conqueror overlap in identity, the dynamic between the winner and loser of the battle becomes noticeably nuanced.

Lastly, the question of lineage returns in "Akiyama matsuri" as a form of subversive, ironic commentary. The narrator states that after the death of the rebel Takamaru, his daughter is captured and brought to Suwa, where she becomes pregnant with the Suwa deity's child and gives birth to the line of shrine priests (*kannushi*).[54] In this way, the religious institution of Suwa keeps very much alive the heritage of Takamaru the rebel. We might understand this development as a cooptation of a rebellious force into sexual and procreative submission by a powerful divine institution that aligned itself with the imperial cause; on the other hand, we might also read it as the shrine's maintenance of the seeds of defiance against the ruling powers. In other words, the daughter might be viewed as a war trophy, but the narrative situates her as playing an important progenital role within the matrix of the Suwa religious complex: she is clearly located as the source of a lineage that governs the Suwa Shrine. In this way, Takamaru's daughter embeds the bloodline of the rebel into the fabric of the Suwa establishment in a way that resists totalizing claims to its wholehearted participation in the imperial agenda. If the invocation of the conflict between Gaozu and Zhao Gao challenged the paradigm of continued hereditary rule, the case of Takamaru's daughter shows that while heredity may be a means by which rights to power are transmitted, it can also be a method through which subversive genetics are passed down.

"Akiyama matsuri" thus presents its audience with a slippery terrain, populated by characters who appear to play key roles in a clichéd drama of rightful conquest, but in fact point to one another's subversive possibilities concerning the legitimacy of the Japanese imperial line. The background story of a Chinese émigré now working for the Japanese emperor turns out to challenge blood lineage as a justification of transferring power from one ruler to the next; on the other hand, the potential for dissent within a single blood lineage is highlighted by the incorporation

54. Okami and Takahashi, *Shintōshū*, 96.

of rebel genes into the Suwa religious complex. Furthermore, we find the trope of multiplicity in this text as well: the emperor himself draws on geographical location and physical terrain in a manner that is similar to his enemy's, and the conquering army's general becomes, at one level, a double of the rebel. This *engi* employs tropes of movement both physical and symbolic to weave a chain of associations that together recast existing structures of power.

Movement and Presence in "Suwa engi"

We now arrive at the third and final *engi* about Suwa found in *Shintōshū*. It is the longest of the Suwa narratives and the most famous, and it presents one of the most extensive journeys in Japanese medieval textual history. "Suwa engi," like "Satsuki-e," claims to tell the tale of the former, human life of the Suwa deity. It is a version that is completely different from the explanation we heard in that previous *engi*, but such contradictions are common among this genre, in which a deity often has a number of different originary narratives associated with it.[55]

55. In fact, there is a second lineage of narratives that feature the same protagonist, Kōga no Saburō. The *Shintōshū* narrative belongs to the Yorikata line, while another line of texts, called the Kaneie line, has two sublines of its own, the Kōgabon and Igabon (Saburō's differing first names account for the names of the two main lines). Various differences exist between these two textual traditions, but most important, none of the Kaneie line texts exhibits a concern for the particular and striking configuration of movement that is found in the Yorikata line texts, and the *Shintōshū* text in particular. In the Kōgabon texts, Saburō either falls into a single underground country, Yuiman, and returns to Japan directly ("Yoshidabon Kōga Saburō Kaneie," in Kanai, *Suwa shinkōshi*, 341–73), or has a highly abbreviated itinerary (Fukuda, "Shiryōhen," 59–76). The Igabon is thought to have borrowed elements from the Kōga and Yorikata lines; its most notable feature is the casting of the protagonist's travels underground as an abbreviated one-way tour through various hells. Shiraishi Kazumi suggests that this emphasis on the narration of hell is Igabon's most distinctive feature compared with the Kōga and Yorikata lines ("Suwa honji 'Shinano no Suwa no shinden' ni tsuite," 52–56). The Yorikata line itself has textual variants; one later version that greatly abbreviates Saburō's underground travels is included in Matsumoto, *Otogi zōshi*, 249–87. For further detailed comparisons of these textual lineages, see Matsumoto, "Chūsei ni okeru honjimono no kenkyū 3," 300–323.

This complex *engi*, which comes at the very end of the entire *Shintōshū* volume, presents a new relationship between the movement and multiplicity that have so far been the hallmark of stories about Suwa. "Suwa engi" is marked by its abundance of narrative arcs with characters moving across immense spaces; it is a tale that features virtually limitless, kinetic narrative repetition about a character who is constantly on the move. The protagonist of this story travels through a vast terrain numerous times; what is more, the story of his voyages themselves becomes a series of much-told tales. At first glance, it may be tempting to explain such repetitions simply as a technique characteristic of oral storytelling; we might think that when telling a long story, chanters felt a need to constantly refresh the audience's memory about events that have transpired, particularly when dealing with a plot as intricate as that of "Suwa engi."[56] However, I read these repetitions not as mere memory-enhancement aids typical of a performative mode of narration, but as a purposeful, metaphorical imagining of how power is distributed throughout a realm.

I will argue that it is the insistence on relentless multiplicity of narrative that generates the textual effect of what I call ubiquitous presence: this textual strategy resists and rejects the possibility of one-timeness, of a figure who simply enters the scene and is then gone again—such as a fleeting tourist who passes through a distant locale. What we have instead are comings-and-goings so plentiful in number that a figure comes to

---

The temporal relationship between the Kaneie and Yorikata lines has been a topic for considerable speculation; Shiraishi Kazumi, in "Suwa honji no shomondai," suggests that there may have been special connections between Suwa and the Kōga region (located in present-day Shiga Prefecture) before the *Shintōshū* era, such as Suwa branch shrines in this region, but admits that such connections are difficult to prove (49). Matsumoto Ryūshin and Yokoyama Shigeru assert that the Kaneie line came first, and that the Yorikata line represents a rewriting of it (Yokoyama and Matsumoto, *Muromachi jidai monogatari taisei*, 8: 112), while Shiraishi takes the stance that the Yorikata line is, after all, older, based on comparative internal evidence of the two lineages ("Suwa honji no shomondai"); Fukuda Akira imagines that the two narrative lineages were originally separate, with the Kaneie line emerging first; however, the lines intermingled as travelers from Suwa, particularly those responsible for bringing tributary horses to the capital, met up with those in regions closer to the capital—such as Kōga—that had a similar tradition of snake worship, but separated again (*Shintōshū setsuwa no seiritsu*, 368–458 passim).

56. Shiraishi claims that such repetitions are hallmarks of oral storytelling, and that the multiplicity in this specific text surely bored the audience, but that they dared not interrupt because it was a divine narrative ("Suwa honji no shomondai," 49–51).

acquire a sense of *presence* in a space; the hero narratively traverses various worlds so many times in the copious repetitions of his life journey that he becomes a figure who is always moving through a place, so much so and so often that he transforms into a constant existence in that place. In this way, he is able to ubiquitously inhabit—literally or symbolically—a vast number of places, all at once.[57] Ironically, then, movement here indicates not motion in the sense of the nomadic or a wandering state of being, but a constant presence that curiously resembles movement's opposite.

"Suwa engi" begins as a story of three brothers. A man named Kōga no Yoritane prospered as the head of security (*sōtsuibushi*) for the provinces traversed by the thoroughfares Tōkaidō, Tōsandō, and Hokurikudō and had three sons. Before passing away in old age, Yoritane names his youngest son, Saburō Yorikata, as the head of his household, and commands this son to inherit his position as the head of security for the fifteen provinces along the Tōkaidō. In contrast, the oldest son, Tarō Yorimune, is entrusted with the eight provinces of the Tōsandō, and the second son, Jirō Yoritada, is made responsible for the seven provinces along the Hokurikudō. Saburō, on a roll of good fortune, is also made the provincial governor of Yamato Province by the emperor; when he arrives there, he meets a beautiful granddaughter of the vice governor, Kasuga, whom he marries right away.

Everything seems to be going well for Saburō until one day, Kasuga is mysteriously abducted during an outing. He searches for her all over Japan, to no avail; he then finally finds a giant camphor tree on Mt. Tateshina in Shinano Province, and at the foot of it, a hole big enough to fit a person—and Kasuga's robe and a tuft of her hair. He enters the hole after constructing an elaborate lifeline system, and fortunately finds Kasuga after a search of the underground land. The pair joyously makes their escape, but at the very last moment, Kasuga realizes that she

57. Interestingly, the Upper Shrine's head priest, the *ōhōri*, was never supposed to leave Suwa for any significant length of time. The one exception occurred in 1087, when the then *ōhōri*, Tameie, broke this taboo by deciding to leave for the capital accompanying the famed warrior Minamoto no Yoshi'ie (1039–1106), who was on his way home from a successful northeastern expedition. As if to prove the powers of the divine prohibition, shortly after leaving Suwa, Tameie was forced to commit suicide to take responsibility for the casualties that resulted from a drunken brawl started by his men; he did not make it out of Shinano Province alive (Fujimori, *Suwa jinja*, 79).

has forgotten her treasured mirror at the place of her captivity. Saburō thus sends her out of the hole to freedom first, and runs back to fetch his wife's mirror. In the meantime, we find out that the second of the three brothers, Jirō, had always envied Saburō for having been named their father's successor despite his being the youngest. Jirō thus seizes this opportunity to destroy Saburō's lifeline, murder his retainers, and abscond with Kasuga. When Saburō rushes to the underworld's exit with Kasuga's mirror, he finds no way to return to the "normal" world above ground. In grief, he embarks on a journey in search of a different exit. Thus begins Saburō's long trip through a total of seventy-three countries (*kuni*) in the underground world; the bulk of "Suwa engi" relates the details of this journey.

The narrative of Saburō's underground voyage enters into a striking cycle of repetition soon after it begins. First, the descriptions of his travel through these lands follow a distinct pattern: upon entering a new country, he briefly notes a few landscape features, and a specific time of year. He then usually meets the head of the community and explains his predicament; the latter expresses sympathetic support for Saburō's search for an exit, and plays host quite generously for a number of days. When Saburō is about to depart, the host tells him the name of the country, and the two exchange parting *waka* as Saburō sets off to the next country. This pattern, though not repeated all seventy-three times, is nevertheless told eleven times before he reaches the last country, and thus comes to constitute a distinct narrative rhythm. While such repetition may seem tedious, I read the very predictability of that rhythm into which our hero's various visits fall as performative proof of his having traveled through all of these spaces. These repetitions are analogous to the filmic technique of a montage sequence, in which elliptical editing alludes to a progression of events. Just as the montage often uses repetitive daily practices as markers of the passage of time, or exhibits tropes of travel to suggest movement from place to place, the narrator of "Suwa engi" sculpts the contours of Saburō's visits in specific, recurring patterns in order to synecdochically establish the protagonist's passage through all seventy-three countries.

When Saburō finally reaches the last underground country, named Yuiman, he is taken into the ruler's residence and provided with a bride named Yuima, the youngest daughter of that ruler. Saburō seems to forget all about his troubles and lives in this paradise for thirteen years, until one day he is reminded of his first wife, Kasuga. He dreams that she is crying at his sleeve, thus he decides to reembark on his mission to head home. Though regretful, Saburō's father-in-law grants his permission for our protagonist's departure, but he decides to take him on a tour of the "secret places" of his land as a parting gift. This marks the beginning of the next cycle of narrative repetition: the tour is told as if it were a condensed, miniature version of Saburō's journey through the seventy-two countries that he had experienced prior to his arrival in Yuiman. The traveling party passes through field after field, a journey that is punctuated by wondrous palaces that welcome them and hold banquets, in a manner distinctly analogous to (though more lavish than) the way in which Saburō was welcomed at each country. The father-in-law then shows Saburō the Four Seasons Gates: the East Gate is abloom with spring flowers, the South Gate is full of fresh summer greenery, the Fall Gate is cool with autumn winds, and the North Gate is desolate with frost. In a single sweep of the eye, Saburō is able to cycle through all of the seasons of a year; this act again clearly refers to his travels through the seventy-three countries, each of which is described as being caught in a specific seasonal moment when he arrives onto the scene. What we have, then, is the first retelling of Saburō's travels outward from his original point of entry into the underground world to Yuiman.

After completing this excursion, Saburō is finally ready to venture on his return trip to Japan. To the audience's surprise, we are told that our hero will not be retracing the steps he took on his outbound trip; rather, the itinerary involves a thousand-day expedition through a wholly different landscape full of dangerous beings determined to prevent his safe arrival. What is even more striking, however, is that the narration of this return trip itself occurs not once, but twice; the telling of the return trip thus also splits into a pair of narrative iterations. First, the ruler of Yuiman provides a highly detailed, anticipatory forecast of Saburō's upcoming adventure home, as he equips his son-in-law with multiple magic implements and good advice designed to lead him out of trouble. The return journey, therefore, is first related as a predicted series of events that have yet to happen but are about to occur. Second, the narrator then gives us the actual experiences of Saburō as he embarks on his return journey; the details are somewhat condensed compared to the version given by the ruler of Yuiman, but the narrative is augmented by the inclusion of *waka* poetry exchanged between Saburō and the various beings who first threaten him but are tamed into submission by the methods the protagonist has learned from his father-in-law. What we find, then, is that each of the legs of Saburō's trip is narrated twice: in the outbound trip, (1) we are told about his travels through the seventy-three countries via a recurring mode of narration that molds each of his experiences in a country into a particular arrangement of events, and (2) we are given a condensed, metaphorical retelling of this trip when he takes a tour around the "secret places" of the seventy-third country with his in-laws. On his return, (1) Saburō's father-in-law narrates the journey in detail as a series of predictions, and (2) we are provided with the details of the actual trip back to Japan as these predictions come true one by one.

This whirl of narrative iteration may seem complex enough; however, "Suwa engi" is a pièce de résistance of sorts, and does not let us catch our breath. When Saburō finally reaches Japan, he emerges from Mt. Asama (incidentally, the same mountain on which the demon king in "Satsuki-e" had established his fort after escaping the capital), and makes his way home to Kōga in Ōmi Province, to a temple hall that had been built as an offering for his deceased father. Saburō, however, has emerged from the underground in the shape of a giant snake, and realizing this, he hides himself under the hall in shame. Coincidentally, it is there that a group of Buddhist monks have gathered for a session of Lotus Sutra chanting that day. One of the monks asks another for the telling of an "old story," to which the latter replies with the entire life tale of Saburō: his ancestry, his father's dying wishes, his marriage to Kasuga, Jirō's evil schemes, his wanderings under the ground, his time in Yuiman, and his reemergence in Mt. Asama, to name a few highlights. In other words, the monk recapitulates all of the events that have been told to the audience so far. The audience, therefore, has now been exposed to Saburō's *entire* life story twice: once as an unfolding linear narrative that has led them to this point in time, and again as a flashback by the monk.

The monk (who turns out to be a manifestation of Saburō's clan guardian deity from Ōmi) then grants instructions for a purification ritual so that our protagonist may regain his human appearance; the transformed hero then rushes to Kasuga's side. It is here that a final retelling is performed in abbreviated form: the narrator states that Kasuga described her ordeals with Jirō (about which the audience was told in detail earlier in the text), and Saburō related to his beloved about his journey underground, the seventy-three *kuni*, and his thousand-day return trip home—these narratives, we are told, occurred "over and over" as husband and wife retold of his or her trials and tribulations repeatedly to each other. The act of storytelling is therefore expanded out to virtually infinite reproduction; Saburō comes to narratively move through these many places practically ad infinitum. Such numerous traversings, I would argue, come to anchor his figure as a de facto presence in any of those places; he is around so often that he might as well be a member of that community. In this way, Saburō is able to establish his presence ubiquitously; he is everywhere all at once, all the time.

After Saburō and Kasuga are reunited, the *engi* enters into a more linear mode of narration in which stories are related only once; however, this shift in storytelling actually marks the start of the second strategy of ubiquitous presence. What we encounter is not the end of multiplicity, but rather, a more explicit illustration of this trope: the narrator establishes a detailed, networked distribution of divine power across a large part of the Japanese landscape. We are told that Saburō materialized in Shinano Province as the Great Suwa Deity of the Upper Shrine, and Kasuga as the deity of the Lower Shrine. Yuima, Saburō's wife in the underground world, missed her husband so much that she travels to Japan. There she is reunited with her beloved, but also meets his other wife, Kasuga, with whom she becomes close friends. It is explained that she therefore became the deity at Asama, close to Suwa and also in Shinano Province. We then hear about the fates of Saburō's other family members: the formerly evil second brother Jirō deeply repents his past crimes and is allowed to become the deity at Tanaka in Wakasa, the province closest to the western starting point of the Hokurikudō. Tarō, who had disagreed with Jirō's rebellion against Saburō and had severed ties with him, becomes the Great Jigen Deity at Utsunomiya in Shimotsuke Province, located along the Tōsandō. As for the parents of the three Kōga brothers, the father appears as the Great Sekizan Deity, whose home lies in the northeastern part of the capital, and the mother as the deity at Nikkō, located in Shimotsuke Province. We then hear about a beautiful Indian princess who refuses a bad marriage prospect and eventually flees to Japan, whereupon she becomes acquainted with the Great Suwa Deity (né Saburō) and falls into an affair with him. Kasuga is not pleased by this turn of events, so the princess decides to appear as the Great Nukisaki Deity in the neighboring Kōzuke Province, instead of being within the boundaries of Shinano in which Kasuga and Saburō reside.

When we map out all of the above locations, what we have is a wide-ranging geographical network of those associated with Saburō, and the Kōga clan more generally, as shown in map 6. By identifying divine presences that have close ties to the Suwa establishment at crucial geographical junctures in a significant area of medieval Japan, the narrative establishes a far-reaching network of religious authorities that are associated with the Suwa Shrine complex. "Suwa engi" is a work that makes its concern with geographical mappings of power quite evident, right from the beginning of the text: the narrator starts by dividing Japan into two, with the capital in the middle, and proceeds to outline the three roads east (Tōkaidō, Tōsandō, and Hokurikudō) and the four roads west. When we superimpose this framework of medieval Japanese geography with the careful spatial situatings of the divine figures we find at the end of this *engi*, what emerges is a map of the eastern half of Japan in which those associated with Saburō strongly assert their supernatural powers: Tōsandō is littered with his kin, Hokurikudō is anchored by his brother, his wife hails from Yamato Province, his father is enshrined in the capital, and the Kōga clan is said to have control of the Tōkaidō in the role of head of security. Just as the narrative arc spirals into repetitions that produce the effect of ubiquitous presence, divine powers are similarly divided and distributed to key locational points across a large part of Japan to establish an extensive—if not quite ubiquitous—Kōga (and therefore Suwa) presence across a significant part of Japan. The explicit linking of various deities across the country to the Suwa religious complex through familial relations makes the Suwa establishment a presence in areas far and wide.

This trope of ubiquitous presence proposes a particular, alternative system for the display and distribution of power in place of what we typically think of as the center-region paradigm. This alternative system replaces the model of governance in which power is anchored in a location that becomes a charismatic center, such as the capital; "Suwa engi" instead conceptualizes a matrix of power in which centers of authority matter far less than an all-encompassing sense of presence. In other words, the Suwa narrative rejects the configuration in which command radiates outward from one or even multiple centers of power. This *engi* instead envisions a new method for emanating power that relies far less on the cultural, social, and political capital of locations in which the ruling authorities are situated, than upon an ambient sense of presence across the many corners of the country.

In fact, the strategy of ubiquitous presence that we find in "Suwa engi" has its concrete counterpart. The Suwa establishment is known for its numerous "branch shrines"; already a notable phenomenon in the thirteenth century, they are today said to number over five thousand across all of modern Japan.[58] The essence of the deity was thought of as being infinitely divisible, and through the process of *kanjō*, or the welcoming of a deity from somewhere else, this divisible and portable divine presence could be franchised into a national network.[59] The Suwa religious complex is, therefore, one that seeks to be everywhere as much as possible: just as Saburō's repeated crossings produce the effect of his being in myriad places simultaneously, the material presence of Suwa branch shrines in communities in so many corners of the nation renders the religious institution, whose powers reach across a vast quantity of space, an immediate and local existence.

A question might still remain at this point in the analysis of the "Suwa engi": how does the trope of ubiquitous presence ultimately differ from the more familiar model of the dissemination of power—that is, if all of the branch shrines as well as Saburō himself obtain their charisma

58. Kanai, *Suwa shinkōshi*, 27. Although there are other religious complexes that have more branch shrines, such as those dedicated to better-known figures for worship like Inari (fox), Hachiman (the mythical Emperor Ōjin), or Tenjin (Sugawara no Michizane), Suwa still counts as one of the most extensive branch shrine networks in Japan (Terada and Washio, *Suwa myōjin*, 25). One of the reasons why the Suwa religious establishment was able to create so many branch shrines might be that warrior clans who worshiped the Suwa deity, including the Hōjō who headed the Kamakura shogunate, possessed a vast network of land parcels scattered across the nation in the thirteenth and fourteenth centuries; branch shrines were constructed on such sites (Kanai, *Suwa shinkōshi*, 16).

59. The earliest example of *kanjō* is said to have taken place in 860 CE, when the deity Hachiman, whose home base was in Buzen Province in northern Kyushu, was received in the capital. In the case of Suwa, less formal methods of dissemination may have existed as well, such as the establishment of shrines by those who originally hailed from Suwa but had moved elsewhere (Miwa, *Suwa taisha*, 167–73).

from the Suwa Shrine complex in Shinano Province, what distinguishes Suwa's strategy from the mode of governance that is anchored in one or two places and emanates power outward to the regions through ruling apparatuses such as provincial governor's offices? The answer to this question lies in part in the structure of the trope of ubiquitous presence I have outlined above, in which presence is evenly established through numerous places simultaneously, and in part in the analysis to follow. I will argue that the final trope, prominently featured in all three *Shintōshū engi* about the Suwa Shrine, is key in understanding the location and ontology of power in these narratives. It is a trope that I will term "elsewhere."

I'm Not from Around Here: The Powers of "Elsewhere"

All three of the "Suwa engi" that I analyzed above are vitally concerned with a logic of "elsewhere." By the powers of "elsewhere," I refer to the charisma understood to belong to beings that come from a place other than one's own. I locate this term as a form of identifying geographical otherness, but the emphasis is on one's *being from another place,* rather than on the exact identity of that other place. In other words, it is the status of "being from elsewhere" that is more important than the specific attributes associated with the precise place from which one hails.[60] Furthermore, "elsewhere" as

60. "Elsewhereness," as I have defined it here, represents a specific institutional development analogous to two terms articulated by Orikuchi Shinobu. One is *marebito*, or "visiting deities," who ordinarily reside in the divine realm but visit human communities during specific events such as annual rituals and festivals (Ariyama et al., *Chōkū Orikuchi Shinobu jiten*, 93–94); the other is *hokaibito*, the nomadic performing artists who visit communities to tell stories about deities who were defeated by divinities of the reigning imperial court (Kimura, *Saihakken Nihon no tetsugaku*, 104). However, my conceptualization of "elsewhere" in the Suwa narratives differs from these terms in some important ways. For example, Orikuchi's divine *marebito* is a decidedly periodic, temporary presence in this world, whereas in the Suwa case a deity from "elsewhere," because of this trope's particular association with ambient ubiquity, is much more present in the daily sense. *Hokaibito*, on the other hand, are human agents in the romanticized role of singing songs on behalf of subjugated deities; although the disseminated narratives concerning Suwa do share aspects and resound with the *hokaibito* paradigm, I see the

a trope does not operate alone in the Suwa texts; its significance is brought to the fore when it crucially dovetails with another trope, that of ambient ubiquity, to generate with it a presence of power from somewhere else that is nonetheless very much a part of the daily landscape.

Let us begin by revisiting "Satsuki-e" and "Akiyama matsuri," this time through a more detailed examination of the divine figures that assist the military leaders of the imperial army in their triumph against the rebels. As noted above, both texts feature a pair of deities who "happen" to appear in front of the hero and eventually help lead him to victory. In each of these stories, the two deities present themselves to the general at very specific geographical locations. My argument is that this focus on what appears to be trivial minutia is, in fact, a vital part of the narrative; it is these details that illustrate the importance of elsewhereness as an empowering attribute. First, let us turn to the case of "Satsuki-e." In this work, the pair of deities first materializes in front of the general, Mitsukiyo, at points *outside* of Shinano Province, the expedition's destination; the passage is quite precise in pinpointing the exact locations at which each deity first encounters our human hero. The question is, what is the relationship between the location where Mitsukiyo meets the two deities—the home territories in which each deity's shrine is located—and the place at which the target of the punitive military expedition has set up defense?

The first of the two warrior-deities who present themselves is the Atsuta deity. He presides over the famous shrine situated in Owari Province, in the southern part of the present-day city of Nagoya, and is cast as the more junior of the divine pair.[61] The narrator states that this deity approached Mitsukiyo on the banks of the Sunomata River, which

strategy of "elsewhere" as being more systematic, aggressive, and pervasive on a national scale. Furthermore, Orikuchi's terms tend to be timeless and thus less useful as a tool for examining specific historical configurations. Terada and Washio give another explanation for the geographical reach of the Suwa deity, arguing that it was the deity's permissive stance concerning the practice of hunting that made it popular across the country (*Suwa myōjin*, 111–13), which is certainly one convincing explanation; what I wish to emphasize here, though, is less the particulars of the deity's efficacy, but the overall, paradigmatic approach to disseminating influence and religious power.

61. The narrator states: "The Great Deity of Atsuta is a retainer [of the Suwa deity] and a nephew; he is the son of the Utsunomiya deity, a younger brother of the Suwa deity" (Okami and Takahashi, *Shintōshū*, 103).

flows along the border of Mino and Owari Provinces; the text specifies that the meeting took place on the eastern bank, meaning that Mitsukiyo was greeted in Owari Province by this divine figure. This means that the Atsuta deity greets the general from the capital at a place on the borders of, but still within, the deity's home province. However, in contrast, we are told that the second divine figure, the Suwa deity, first steps forward at a place called Fuseya in Mino Province, which is located to the south of present-day Gifu city, on the northern banks of the Kiso River. The Suwa deity, therefore, appears in front of Mitsukiyo in a province that is *not his own*—an adjacent province and a place "elsewhere" from his home territory. This is clearly different from the case of the Atsuta deity described above.

What might be the possible implications of these seemingly minor geographic details that the narrator provides? Let us recall that in "Satsuki-e," the rebellious demon king and the Suwa deity *both* call Shinano Province their home. I propose that in order for the deity to be fully empowered, it was necessary for the Suwa deity to materialize at a place outside of Shinano first, so that he can then enter his home province *as a figure from elsewhere*. The Atsuta deity's itinerary reinforces this theory: since his home is in Owari Province, he is a priori a foreign presence in Shinano; therefore, there is no particular need for him to first step outside of Owari in order to mobilize his powers of elsewhere vis-à-vis Shinano Province.

"Akiyama matsuri" presents us with a narrative of double deities that is similar to "Satsuki-e" but varies in crucial ways that further support the argument above. This time, the Suwa deity is paired with the deity from Sumiyoshi, whose shrine is located in Settsu Province; they appear one after another in front of the general Tamuramaru at a place called Ina in Shinano Province when he is on his way northeast to quell the rebellion, and offer their assistance. In this case, the two divine figures hail from locations that are elsewhere vis-à-vis the Ōshū region, where the insurgent Takamaru has set up fort. This means that the deities could *both* appear in front of the general in Ina, which was the home base of the Suwa shrines. In "Akiyama matsuri," unlike in "Satsuki-e," it is possible for the Suwa deity to materialize within the boundaries of his provincial turf because Tamuramaru's expedition was headed *elsewhere*—that is, the enemy lay in a distant province hundreds of miles to the northeast of Suwa. The powers of "elsewhere" could therefore operate during the crucial battles that bring victory for the imperial forces.

The longer "Suwa engi" is, if anything, even more committed to this discourse, privileging elsewhereness throughout. As I have noted above, when Kasuga is kidnapped, the narrator relates that Saburō first frantically looks for her high and low throughout the many mountains across the provinces of Japan. Still unsuccessful, he enters the hole in the ground at Mt. Tateshina in Shinano Province, where he is finally reunited with his wife, only to be separated from her again due to the machinations of his jealous brother Jirō. Quite interestingly, it is at the point when our hero discovers that his lifeline has been cut and he is trapped in the underground world that he makes the following plea to the Amida Buddha: "I pray that I may maintain my current form and see Kasuga once more in this life; please *transport me to another country* [*kuni*] so that I may obtain a way to return to Japan."[62]

This is a fascinating wish; what he asks is that the Buddha transport him first to a land elsewhere before he is able to see his wife. In other words, although we might expect Saburō to make a wish to return directly to his homeland and be reunited with his wife immediately, particularly given his extensive above-ground search, that is not what he prays for; instead, he expresses a desire to journey to yet another land somewhere else, so that he then may plot his return to Japan. Why would Saburō ask to be carried first to a different space from the place to which he longs to go back? I believe that the answer to this riddle lies in the narrative that follows: he must first go elsewhere—in fact, many, many elsewheres in the form of seventy-three underground countries—in order to accrue enough powers to reappear in his home country in a state superior to his former mere humanity.

The precise characteristics of this underground world also warrant further exploration in our discussion of elsewhereness. I will maintain my focus upon the outbound trip to Yuiman, since this route provides the most salient examples of elsewhereness. First, the number of countries in this alternative universe is only a few in excess of the number of provinces in Japan at the time of *Shintōshū*'s compilation.[63] Moreover, although this

62. Ibid., 288. The exact phrase is 今生春日姫今一度合、*別國移*、日本返便令得.
63. The narrator states that there are "sixty-plus provinces" (ibid., 277).

world is clearly described as a place that is distinctly separate from Japan, the glimpses of the underground countries we are given on Saburo's travels reveal these communities to nevertheless resemble Japan fairly closely.[64] For example, the seasonal cycles remain the same, and the activities performed at each seasonal moment, such as farming and harvesting, sound familiar. The topography is often explicitly noted as being strikingly similar as well,[65] and Saburō has no linguistic barriers in communicating with the residents of the lands he visits. The exchange of *waka* poetry serves as another important reinforcement of similitude: thinking back to chapters 1 and 2, it is clear that this commonality in cultural practice between underground countries and Japan is not an insignificant matter.

What distinguishes the underground world from that above ground, then, is a single crucial factor: the way in which Saburō is viewed by others around him. For instance, the narrative makes a point of discussing the reactions of an underground country's residents upon first encountering Saburō: they are usually described as being frightened or surprised, or as talking about Saburō as a "person who does not resemble a person."[66] In other words, the underground world, which appears to be quite similar to Japan in many respects, is a place in which Saburō becomes a from-elsewhere-being, vis-à-vis his surroundings; it is the constant, perplexed reactions of the myriad underground beings that produce Saburō's "from elsewhere" subjectivity. The culminating moment of this production occurs when he finally reappears in Japan in the form of a snake; yet again, he does not realize his own radical transformation until others shun him as a beast. Saburō's epic travels thus have a cumulative effect of rendering him as a from-elsewhere-being in his own world; he is now a marked existence even in his homeland.

In contrast, however, Saburō never expresses a reciprocal feeling of being surprised or frightened by the shape of those he meets on his long

64. The word "Japan" appears multiple times; for example, the narrator says, "this is what was happening in Japan, so leaving that aside for now [*kore wa nihon no koto nareba sate okinu*] . . . " (ibid., 288), when segueing from Kasuga's plights when she is abducted by Jirō to Saburō's adventures underground; also, when Saburō emerges after his travels in the form of a snake, the monk explains: "Although he is Japanese, simply by wearing the clothing of Yuiman, he looks like a snake" (ibid., 310–11).

65. E.g., ibid., 289: "The light of the sun, moon, and stars [of this country] closely resembled that of this country [= Japan]."

66. Ibid.

journey underground. These residents of foreign lands are not noted as having extraordinary appearances or behaviors, aside from their initial distress at seeing Saburō. It is, then, as if each time he enters an underground country, he is morphed into an alien being unbeknownst to his own self, while those around him remain more or less constant categorically, even though they inhabit different lands. In other words, the underground is a space of defamiliarization—not of place, but of the subject who comes to bear the mark of elsewhereness. In the logic of movement, both the moving subject and those who are visited by that subject are, in essence, from elsewhere in regard to each other—that is, Saburō is always explicitly viewed as being from elsewhere by residents of an underground country, just as each underground country is a new "elsewhere" for Saburō. What this narrative stresses, however, is the way in which the protagonist is invariably positioned as a foreign being, while indigenous communities remain curiously interchangeable and conceptually static. This paradigm permits the ascription of elsewhere-based empowerment solely to the traveling subject; he takes with him all of the credit for elsewhereness that the various underground countries create on his behalf.

If the trope of elsewhereness stands for the construction of the defamiliarized subject and, in stark contrast, the maintained normalcy of the various lands the subject visits, the trope also casts a nuanced light upon the question of geographical origin. For example, "Suwa engi" delivers one final punch of "elsewhere" when Saburō emerges from his underground voyage. Ritual purifications cure him of his serpentine appearance, and reunited with his beloved Kasuga, the two together travel to a country in the south of China, where they master divine powers, and return to Japan to settle as the deities of the upper and lower Suwa shrines as explained above. That the pair travel to China in particular is, I would argue, less important than their crossing to a space elsewhere before finally resting as divinities of Suwa. In other words, their Chinese trip is less about the specific divine powers available in China than about its being the icing on the cake of the enormous arc of elsewhereness that marks Saburō's life: his life course, which began in the Kaga region of Ōmi Province, takes him across Japan, through numerous underground countries, and then to China before ultimately settling down at Suwa. Similarly, Tamuramaru's Chinese origin in "Akiyama matsuri" is, on the one hand, vital in its analogous critique of imperial lineage, as delineated above. On the other hand, however, the narrator is equally emphatic that it was Tamuramaru's move to Japan that allowed his military talents to mature fully.[67] Being an "elsewhere" person, then, is what gives Tamuramaru powers that would not have been realized had he stayed in one place.

What, then, can we make of these specific attentions to arrivals from elsewhere in the *Shintōshū* Suwa narratives? Let us recall that the Suwa complex relied on ubiquitous presence as its strategy for disseminating power; that is, the numerous branch shrines found across Japan articulate its national ambition and its conceptualization of how authority functions at each locale. The worshiping of a deity not indigenous to a particular place necessitates an extra public relations "hook": it is in this context that elsewhereness may be usefully promoted as that which marks a deity as being special, more efficacious, and ubiquitously preferred. The discourse of elsewhereness grounds the power of Suwa divinities as beings who have come from somewhere else as they manifest themselves in locations near and far. At the same time, the Suwa establishment, which sought out believers elsewhere and everywhere outside of its home territory deep in the mountains of Shinano, chose to do so by deemphasizing its specific point of origin. That is, instead of courting pilgrims inward toward its center, as did institutions like the Ise shrine, Suwa's vector pointed outward to the establishment of points of worship in other communities; it sought to exhibit power not through a beckoning, but through attempts at ambient omnipresence.

Suwa's approach to establishing authority thus differs significantly from a structuring of power that renders visible its origin in a single identifiable location, from which representatives descend upon the regions to put into action (at least theoretically) the desires of those back at the center. Michele Marra has convincingly argued that the *Shintōshū* represents a Buddhist attempt to coopt local Shinto deities into a national, Buddhist-centric paradigm through syncretic explanations of deities' "true" origins;[68] at one level, we can certainly see such an agenda in operation in the collection as a whole. There are, though, also other aspects of the texts to be explored: specifically in the case of the Suwa

67. Ibid., 92.

68. Marra, *Representations of Power*, esp. chap. 3 (115–35).

narratives, we see a firm commitment to a vision of power distribution that is fundamentally different from previous imaginings.

One final, crucial conceptualization of elsewhereness reinforces this point. In "Suwa engi," we find that the network of the seventy-three countries underground is not visualized according to a conventional paradigm of space. Instead of a two-dimensional mapping, in which these countries would border one another in a manner similar to the way that territories are divided and arranged in the "real" world above ground, what we find is that each of the underground countries is envisioned as being *inside* another. In other words, it is not the case that Saburō travels from one underground country to another by crossing a two-dimensional border, as one would if the countries lay next to each other; rather, in each country that Saburō visits, he finds a hole in the ground big enough to fit a person, and he enters this hole to emerge in the next country. The underground spaces are thus conceptualized as nesting inside one another, very much like a matryoshka doll. This geometric architecture, I would argue, creates a space that is three-dimensional as well as centerless: there is no single point that houses the seat of power, and therefore no diminishing of influence proportional to the distances from that seat. The recursive structure of space in this *engi* implodes the center-region dichotomy; the Suwa model instead presents an array of infinitely subdividable, from-elsewhere divine agents who are less servants of the "real" deity hundreds of miles away than nonhierarchical, potent beings that are capable of granting wishes and protection to a vast populace simultaneously.

Suwa Slippages

In the era of the Nanbokuchō, in which a radical fragmentation of power was rampant, a thoroughly fractured view of power and of alternative modes of its dissemination makes sense. As mentioned previously, in rapid succession, the Kamakura *bakufu* falls in 1333, Emperor Godaigo flees to Yoshino to establish the Southern Court in 1336, and the main supporter of the Northern Court, Ashikaga Takauji, takes the title of *sei'i taishōgun* in 1338; power struggles continue for the next few decades. In 1351 Takauji "surrenders" to the Southern Court and scraps the Northern Court during the Shōhei unification, but mainly as a measure to obtain the authority of an imperial command to disempower his rival and brother Tadayoshi; the Northern Court is reestablished only a year later, and matters do not officially come to a resolution until 1392.

Meanwhile, the Suwa establishment experienced turbulence of its own in the first half of the fourteenth century: it sided with the Kamakura *bakufu* at the start of the Nanboku wars in 1333, which ended in defeat. However, even after that *bakufu* was eradicated, those at Suwa continued to undermine the powers of the victors by first taking in and offering protection to the heir of the Kamakura shogunate, Hōjō Tokiyuki (?–1353), with whom they instigated the Nakasendai rebellion in 1335 against the new regime.[69] Furthermore, after suffering defeat in that rebellion, some factions based in Suwa continued to resist the status quo by then siding with the Southern Court once Takauji broke relations with Godaigo: they granted safe harbor to Godaigo's son, Prince Muneyoshi (1311–85), and supported his rebellious activities, much to the chagrin of the new shogunate.[70] The time of *Shintōshū* was thus highly uncertain for all concerned, in which divided and competing loci of authority each battled furiously to try to claim its own singular dominance; within this context, the ways in which the *engi* about Suwa challenge conventional paradigms of power can be read not only as a narrative that refers to the times in which it appears but also as a strategic attempt to stake out a place for Suwa's own claims to legitimacy amid the rapidly changing political disarray at a national level. Thus multiplicity, ubiquity, and elsewhereness all suggest alternative ways in which authority might be disseminated through a fraught landscape in which monolithic claims to power were perilously difficult to sustain.

However, even though I have delineated the ways in which *Shintōshū*'s "Suwa engi" can be understood as bold reconceptualizations of the workings of power, my aim is not to romantically herald the Suwa religious institution as irreverently renegade, fundamentally antiauthor-

69. Sakurai Yoshio, *Nanbokuchō nairan to tōgoku*, 28–35.

70. Imazu, "'Suwa Daimyōjin Ekotoba' no kaisetsu," 56; and Yamada, *Suwa shi gaisetsu*, 62–70.

itarian, or necessarily egalitarian. Indeed, when we examine a contemporaneous text called *Suwa daimyōjin ekotoba* (The illustrated text of the Great Suwa Deity, ca. 1356), we find little in the way of the tropes I have outlined above as being crucial to the *Shintōshū* narratives. This document purports to outline the history of the Suwa deity in an illustrated format, even though the visual material is now unfortunately completely missing. It was submitted for review by the highest echelons of power, including Emperor Gokōgon of the Northern Court (r. 1352–71) and the shogun Ashikaga Takauji.[71] It is attributed to Suwa Enchū (1295–1364), a member of the Upper Shrine's priestly lineage who began his career as part of the Hōjō regime in Kamakura, but after civil strife, managed to climb to a position of power under Takauji's new Muromachi *bakufu*.[72]

The first third of *Ekotoba* is dedicated to establishing how the Suwa deity has been devoted to the task of vitally assisting and protecting the Japanese nation throughout the ages. This divinity is credited as having contributed significantly to the advancement of imperial causes, ranging from Empress Jingō's mythical expedition to Silla to the warding off of the Mongolian invasion in the early thirteenth century. Interestingly, the defiant Takeminakata is mentioned at the very beginning, but his rebelliousness is greatly underplayed.[73] The rest of the document is dedicated to the descriptions of Suwa's annual festivals and rituals, and there is little overlap between *Ekotoba* and any of the three *Shintōshū* narratives. Clearly, *Ekotoba* aims to situate the Suwa religious institution as an important and unwavering supporter of the causes promoted by the ruling powers, whether or not that was actually the case. In light of events

71. Tanigawa et al., *Jisha engi*, 53. The analysis of the *Ekotoba* is based on the edition in this volume, 55–78, and the one in *Shintō taikei* (Takeuchi, *Suwa*, 3–57). For a thorough discussion of the various extant editions of this text, see Imazu, "'Suwa Daimyōjin Ekotoba' no kaisetsu," 55–80 and Kanai, *Suwa shinkōshi*, 192–217.

72. Enchū was likely born and raised in Kamakura and had served the *bakufu* before its fall as an official and a falconry expert. He managed to gain the favor of Ashikaga Takauji, maintaining official positions in the new *bakufu* and assuring the continued reverence for Suwa despite notable disasters like the Nakasendai rebellion. For a thorough discussion of Enchū, see Itō, *Itō Tomio chosakushū*, 1: 344–457.

73. Takeminakata challenges the divine messengers to a contest of strength, but the outcome is not provided; it then simply states: "When he reached the waters of Suwa in the province of Shinano, the deity Takeminakata said, 'I will not go anywhere else but here'" (Tanigawa, *Jisha engi*, 55.)

such as the Nakasendai rebellion mentioned above, those affiliated with the Suwa Shrine complex were likely to have been regarded with wary caution by the Northern Court and Takauji, even in the 1350s; it therefore makes sense that Enchū wanted to produce a document that clears the name of Suwa in the eyes of the powers that be, and firmly reestablish the Suwa Shrine complex as an august and efficacious institution worthy of powerful patronage. *Ekotoba* shows that the promotion of Suwa's prosperity was certainly not limited to efforts by those who propagated narratives with new visions of power structures; those like Enchū sought to ensure the survival and thriving of the shrine through a more ingratiating yet practical and direct method of appealing to existing powers.

Last but not least: if the *Shintōshū* texts strongly challenge the vision of a singular imperial, governing authority, they do so through the construction of just such a singular authority somewhere else. We are not surprised that *Ekotoba* suppresses the multiplicity of the Suwa religious institution itself, but similarly motivated erasures occur in the *Shintōshū* narratives as well. The Suwa establishment has a complicated structure: as stated earlier, the Upper Shrine and Lower Shrine are located on opposite sides of Suwa Lake and are separated by a distance of over twelve kilometers (see map 7); each of these shrines is further subdivided into separate subshrine units.[74] The structure of management differs notably between the two shrines: at the Upper Shrine, the head priest, who is called the *ōhōri*, is deemed a divinity who takes this position while he is still a child and is thereafter forbidden to leave the district of Suwa; at the Lower Shrine, the priest is thought to occupy a more standard role of human servant to the gods.[75]

This divided structure of the Suwa complex led to conflicts and competition between the two shrines, which were no secret. Disputes

74. The Upper Shrine houses a front shrine (*maemiya*) and a main shrine (*honmiya*), whereas the Lower Shrine contains a spring shrine (*harumiya*) and an autumn shrine (*akimiya*). In today's terms, road maps indicate that Shimosha is in Shimosuwa-machi, whereas Kamisha straddles Suwa-shi and Chino-shi.

75. Miwa, *Suwa taisha*, 126–38. For a thorough discussion of the role of *ōhōri* and its potentially subversive role as a second nexus of divine, kingly authority, see Shimada Kiyoshi, "Chūsei Suwa kamisha no *ōhōri* to shokuishiki," 1–36, and Itō, *Itō Tomio chosakusū*, 6: 443–51.

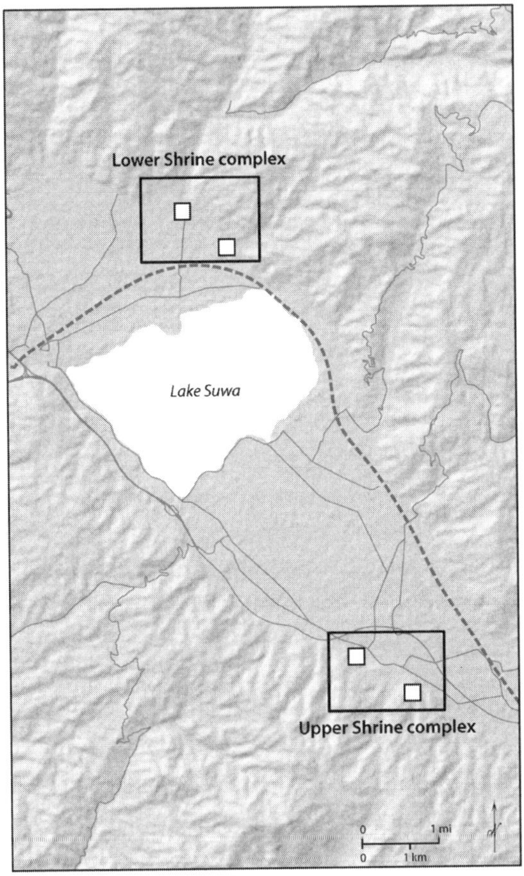

Map 7 The Suwa Shrine complex and the surrounding area.

concerning the relative importance of the two shrines were common: the Miwa clan, whose descendants managed the Upper Shrine as the *ōhōri*, and the Kanasashi clan, who oversaw matters of the Lower Shrine, each made claims that their shrine was established before the other.[76] A

76. See Terada and Washio, *Suwa myōjin*, 20–24, for specifics concerning how a postwar debate over which of the two shrines represents the "original" authority of the Suwa religious complex has raged on: after the discovery in Kyushu of a lineage chart claiming that the Lower Shrine was established as early as the sixth century CE, possibly long before the Upper Shrine, which did not rise to prominence until the eighth-century Kanmu era, some have argued that the Lower Shrine's authority trumps that of the Upper

document dating from 1249, signed by the *ōhōri* Nobushige, explains to the Kamakura *bakufu* the superiority of the Upper Shrine as the original and thus more important of the two shrines; the document seems to have been submitted as an attempt to resolve a dispute with the Lower Shrine.[77] On the other hand, *Azuma kagami* relates an incident in which miraculous powers righted the wrong of an unequal distribution of land reward that had originally given more to the Upper Shrine than to the Lower Shrine.[78] The deities that are revered in each shrine have been a point of controversy as well; the Upper Shrine claimed that, since it enshrined Takeminakata, it wielded more prestige than the Lower Shrine, which housed Takeminakata's divine wife, Yasakatome; indeed, when Takeminakata was granted junior first rank in 867, Yasakatome was provided with a lower, senior second rank.[79]

The two shrines often took different sides in times of civil strife: for example, during the twelfth-century Genpei wars, the Upper Shrine sided with Minamoto no Yoritomo, whereas the Lower Shrine at first took the side of Kiso no Yoshinaka, who was Yoritomo's kin and soon-to-be rival, even though both shrines eventually sided with Yoritomo against the Taira forces.[80] Up to and during the Nanbokuchō era, the Upper Shrine was most prominently responsible for political resistance,

---

Shrine; others, meanwhile, have challenged the authenticity of this lineage chart and its details. On the other hand, Itō Tomio asserts that the Upper Shrine was superior at least through the early medieval period, as important festivals were hosted there, and the latter seems to have paid taxes to the former, thus suggesting a hierarchy (*Itō Tomio chosakushū*, 5: 41–53).

77. The document, "Suwa Nobushige *gejō*," is one of the oldest surviving documents to address possible strife between the two shrines. Suwa shiryō sōsho kankōkai, *Suwa shiryō sōsho*, 15: 5–9.

78. Kishi, *Zen'yaku Azuka kagami*, 1: 68–69. Kobayashi Kei'ichirō suggests that such a narrative was likely concocted by members of the Lower Shrine who were struggling to claim equal footing with the Upper Shrine (*Shinano chuseishi ko*, 162–63).

79. Keizai zasshisha, *Sandai jitsuroku*, 248. Matsumoto Ryūshin suggests that, in fact, the "Satsuki-e" narrative, which features the story of Princess Kongōnyo and her husband, Minister Gida, as the true divine deities of the Suwa Shrine complex, might represent the Lower Shrine's *engi* alternative to those of the Upper Shrine. In "Satsuki-e," Kongōnyo is said to be enshrined in the Lower Shrine, and she is clearly cast as the main deity of the pair. This stands in contrast to the Kōga no Saburō story in "Suwa engi," which strongly emphasizes the Upper Shrine's male divinity. Matsumoto, "Chūsei ni okeru honjimono no kenkyū 3," 323–26.

80. Miwa, *Suwa taisha*, 54–56.

as outlined above, first by siding with the losing Hōjō regime, then by fighting against the new shogunal forces of Ashikaga Takauji as an ally of the above-mentioned Prince Muneyoshi. Suwa Enchū of the "Illustrated Text" hails from the Upper Shrine lineage, and thus was saddled with the heavy burden of reviving his clan under these difficult circumstances. In the meantime, the Lower Shrine remained less visible in these involvements, although they did support the Upper Shrine's ambitions in a number of battles.[81]

Matters deteriorated significantly starting in the mid-fourteenth century, however, when the two shrines went to war on opposing sides in a skirmish involving the provincial lord.[82] Throughout the fifteenth and sixteenth centuries, the two shrines became even more obvious enemies: the Upper Shrine forces burned down the Lower Shrine grounds in 1449, to which the Lower Shrine retaliated with an attack and arson on the Upper Shrine during a festival in 1480. The Lower Shrine attacked the Upper Shrine again in 1483 but was defeated, and the Upper Shrine's forces conquered the Lower Shrine in 1518, which marked the de facto defeat of the Lower Shrine and the burning of most of their records. Furthermore, within each shrine order, strife took place; most notably, power struggles among the families that administered the Upper Shrine resulted in the massacre of some by others in 1483, and a cycle of revenge that followed.[83]

What the *engi* narratives present us with, however, is either a *single* "Suwa deity" who appears in front of imperial generals such as Mitsukiyo or Tamuramaru to help them win wars, or, at most, either a harmonious husband-and-wife team in the form of Princess Kongōnyo and her devoted minister husband, or a tightly knit network of familial relations centering around Kōga no Saburō. These narratives erase the ruptures that make the very term "Suwa deity" in singular form an oxymoron, as we

81. Itō, *Itō Tomio chosakushū*, 5: 253–56.

82. The Lower Shrine sided with the forces of the Ogasawara, the provincial lord (*shugo*) of the region, against the Upper Shrine. Terada and Washio, *Suwa myōjin*, 119.

83. For details of the struggles between the two shrines in this period, see Itō, *Itō Tomio chosakushū*, 5: 269–83; see also Miyasaka and Asakawa, *Zusetsu Suwa no rekishi*, 1: 79–81; Yamada, *Suwa shi gaisetsu*, 80–81. Also, Kanai Tenbi suggests that the two textual lineages involving Kōga no Saburō, the Yorikata line and the Kaneie line, each correspond to versions upheld by the Upper Shrine and the Lower Shrine respectively (*Suwa shinkōshi*, 19).

can see from the multiple structure of the Suwa complex. The insistence upon singularity or harmony suggests that the narrators viewed a divided Suwa as not being as powerful as a unified one. It is an ironic full circle of these *engi*: the narratives subvert the singularity of Japanese imperial authority through tropes such as doubles, multiplicity, and ubiquity, but they also resort to a discourse of singular power when advertising the efficacy of the Suwa establishment. Here might be the ultimate double in the text: political subversion coexists with its opposite, and we find ourselves reminded of the complexity and difficulty of transcending the parameters of existing power structures without reproducing the hierarchies and suppressions that characterize those structures at another level.

EPILOGUE

Thus we come to the end of our investigation of how various tropes of movement work to illuminate the ways in which systems of power are imagined in different texts in tenth to fourteenth-century Japan. A curious thought might arise at this point: it seems that in looking at movement, we discover that stops and sojourns can also provide equally important moments for reflection, ranging from the strategic vision of stability characteristic of women attendants at court to a captive's literary containment in Kamakura. What of the textual moments that highlight various states of stillness as nevertheless productive or meaningful?

After the analytical journey we have just concluded, it should be evident that at one level, stasis is an illusory effect that is both generated and dismantled by tropes of movement: movement, in its contrast with stasis, enables one to conceptualize a positionality that is stable, immobile, and permanent (sometimes negatively so), even as the same trope constantly pulls the rug out from under the feet of such a positionality by pointing to the untenability of nonmotion. However, we might also think of stasis not as a state that is merely the opposite of movement—thus being different and separate from it—but rather as one that is more inherently and paradigmatically enmeshed with the state of motion. Perhaps it would be more useful to think not of an enduring fixedness as a condition of power, but of *pauses*—that is, rests that assume the resumption of movement at some point in the future.

Here we are reminded of the term *chinza*, which refers to the enshrinement of a deity at a particular religious structure or institution, as in the case of the Suwa deity, whose divisible self came to be situated in myriad shrines across many provinces. This term is routinely used to indicate the presence of a divinity at a particular location, but its implications resonate with the discussion at hand: *chin* literally means to apply physical pressure upon or to pacify, to render quiet something that was not previously so, whereas *za* indicates the condition of being positioned, or seated, in a location. Thus *chinza* implies that a deity is restrained into enshrinement; the term contains within itself a dynamism, and hints at a condition that is temporary as well as possibly fraught. These connotations may seem jarring, since a visit to a shrine nowadays provides little hint that the physical architecture and the reigning divinity together form anything less than a solid institutional partnership that is the object of long-time veneration; however, the discourse of *chinza* strongly hints at the fragility of such a partnership by pointing to uncertainties that could endanger the fundamentals of a particular economy of worship.

Perhaps not wholly coincidentally, an early example of the term's usage depicts the challenges involved in rendering a spirit into the state of *chinza*. One of the most fabled figures of early mythical-historical narratives is the imperial prince Yamato Takeru; whether romanticized as a tragic hero in the *Kojiki* or glorified as a bold imperial warrior in the *Nihon shoki*, he is portrayed as having journeyed west and east, subjugating opponents on behalf of the emperor, but eventually offending a deity and dying on the road. Both texts claim that upon his death, Yamato Takeru was initially buried, but he rose from the shackles of the earth by transforming himself into a swan and flying away. His consorts and children chase after him, catch up with him, construct a tomb again, and respectfully *chinza* him there. However, the swan takes off once more, flying away high into the sky.[1] Although these eighth-century accounts significantly predate the figures discussed in this book, it is nonetheless striking to find the very predicament of *chinza* in these examples: a mythical prince's spirit in divine ornithological form can be tamed only briefly into stillness; his escape only highlights the fleeting capacity of *chinza*, as he is able to break its bonds with ease. Yamato Takeru is a quintes-

1. The *Kojiki* passage: Aoki, *Kojiki*, 187–91. In *Nihon shoki*, the swan flies away not once, but twice, necessitating three burial mounds; also, this passage does not actually use the term *chinza* (Kojima et al., *Nihon shoki*, 1: 381–87).

sential figure-in-motion, who travels across the country on his military expeditions, and exits the human realm in flight; although today, numerous shrines across Japan worship him as their patron deity, his elusive proclivity for movement lurks at the root of his legendary biography. Thus *chinza*, as a snapshot of a given moment, can appear successful, but its seeming stability is one that always contains unpredictable capacities for motion. Analogously, authority—lay or religious, civilian or military, local or national—might also be effectively thought of as occupying the state of *chinza*, whenever there is a semblance of intransience.

We might here meditate on the character *chin* in *chinza* a bit further; it appears also, in fact, in the term *chinjufu*, the military headquarters in the northeast mentioned in the discussion of Fujiwara no Sanekata in chapter 2. *Chinju* is an interesting concept: in the combination *chinjufu* (with *fu* indicating a government agency), it clearly points to the human task of "pacifying," protecting, and advancing the imperial court's territorial interests in the northeast. When *chinju* is invoked more generally, it tends to refer to the divine realm: for instance, the *chinjugami*, or *chinju* deity, remains a popular religious figure today as a deity native to a place, who offers protection to locales ranging from a whole village to a smaller, specific unit of land. Rituals honoring these deities when constructing a home or a building are still common. However, this definition of a *chinju* deity turns out to be a relatively recent usage, appearing only in the Edo period (1600–1868); in previous eras, the term had a more complex register of meanings.[2] In the Heian period, *chinjugami* were designated as such by the court when a deity was deemed to provide special protection over matters of national security; thus *chinjugami* in this context refers not to a general group of local deities-next-door, but to a title given for the purpose of defending imperial rulership.[3] In the medieval period, *chinjugami* referred not necessarily to a deity "native" to a place, but to one who is invited or assigned, from elsewhere, to *chinza* at a particular location—as in the case of the spread of the Suwa deity.[4] This configuration

2. Nihonshi kōjiten henshū iinkai, *Nihonshi kōjiten*, 1435.

3. Yokoi, "Chinjugami to ōken."

4. Indeed, the emphasis on syncretism in the *Shintōshū* renders all deities "foreign," in that they have Buddhist roots; furthermore, stories assign the manifestations of such deities in the form of *chinjugami* to a variety of locations across the premodern Japanese landscape (see Kikuchi, "*Shintōshū* ni okeru shōdō setsuwa no keisei").

establishes a competitive, hierarchical relationship between any preexisting deities and those that are later assigned to *chinju* a place; the mission of "pacification" for the *chinju* deity, therefore, included not only the taming of generic, unknown spiritual dangers that threatened a community, but also the controlling of the native deity, whose powers would be usurped or at least mitigated by the arriving divinity. The condition of those assigned the task of *chinju* can thus be understood as an *uncomfortable* one: whether it is a *chinjufu* shogun who must constantly be on guard against uprisings, conflicts with the provincial governor, or the prospect of being called back to the capital to be replaced, or a *chinjugami* who must keep the native divinity in line while protecting a village from various evils, the term is restless at the core. *Chinju* is also a term that constantly alerts us to relations of power, whether it operates in national, regional, and/or religious realms: "Who is *chinju*-ing whom (or attempting to do so), and for what reasons?" are questions that easily arise when one considers the multifaceted, often volatile project of *chinju.*

Another compound term that includes the character *chin* sheds further light on the intricacies of movement and its containment: *chinkon.* Literally meaning the appeasing (*chin*) of spirits (*kon*), the term has been a popular keyword for scholars of premodern Japan in the past few decades. For instance, certain Heian-era texts have been reinterpreted as strategies for appeasing constrained, gendered souls by giving them a voice; female authors are cast as appeasing their own unsettled spirits through the release of literary expression.[5] The performing arts have also been reexamined through the *chinkon* rubric. For example, as mentioned in chapter 3, *Heike monogatari* can be viewed as a textual performance of pacification, an attempt to placate the vengeful spirits of those defeated in the Genpei wars by telling their stories; this reading is one of many that situate a primary function of the performing arts as protection of specific groups (the victors of war, the populace, etc.) from supernatural forces that linger and wish them harm.[6] Like *chinju, chinkon* is thus also a term that points to the intricate negotiations of containment and release in Heian and medieval Japan.

One of the most fascinating aspects of *chinkon* in the context of tropes of movement, though, is its appearance in the name of a ritual

5. See, for example, Takahashi Bunji, *Monogatari chinkonron.*
6. See, among others, Moriya, *Geinō to chinkon.*

held at the imperial palace: *chinkonsai* (*chinkon* festival). Conducted on the day before the *ni'inamesai*, the annual harvest festival held in the eleventh month of the lunar year, its exact significance has been a topic of some debate. *Ryō no gige* (Commentary on *ryō* codes), an exposition of administrative codes dating from 833, includes a definition of *chinkon* that reads as follows: "*Chin* is to render secure [*anzuru*]. People's positive forces [*yōki*] are called *kon*. *Kon* are in motion. It is said that [one] invites the wandering *kon* to be secured [*chin*] at the core of the body. Thus it is called *chinkon*."[7] Here, the passage clearly situates one's spirit as something whose nature is to be always on the move; in order for it to be snatched out of this natural state, one needs to anchor it into one's body—like a helium balloon caught and morphed into an internalizable object. Based on this passage, the imperial *chinkonsai* has been interpreted as a rite in which the otherwise wandering spirit of the emperor is properly secured to his body, thus ensuring his continued health and long rule.[8] That the emperor's *kon* could be, by definition, something that drifts away unless rituals are periodically performed to contain it within his corporeal materiality is a striking testament to how movement and stasis are conceived. In this paradigm, being still is the opposite of inertia. What we have is not an object at rest because rest is its default state; rather, "rest" is a state achieved only through substantial efforts to tame motion into submission. Kinetic energy has been transformed into potential energy, but this transformation may reverse at any moment. This vision of the emperor's *kon* allows us to imagine, by extension, any state of seeming stability or permanence as something that is carefully produced through exertion, and always containing within itself the energy of unraveling into motion unexpectedly. Indeed, we might think of emperorship itself as a form of *chinza*: it is a position that embodies temporariness, restlessness, and the prospect of departure (that is, abdication) from the very start.

Finally, we might also consider *chinza* as being analogous to the other type of movement explored in this book: that of literary motion,

7. Ritsuryō kenkyūkai, *Ryō no gige yakuchūhen*, 2: 7.

8. Matsumae, *Kodai denshō to kyūtei saishi*, 103–50. There are other scholars who contest this interpretation of *chinkonsai*, and want to understand the term *chinkon* more straightforwardly as an appeasement of harmful spirits (see Watanabe Katsuyoshi, *Chinkonsai no kenkyū*).

in which seemingly unexpected textual registers, genres, plotlines, tropes, and repetitions are often abruptly incorporated into the flow of an existing narrative. In the works we have studied, such disruptions have indicated a transporting of a text "from elsewhere"—that is, one that does not appear to naturally belong to a narrative's trajectory—and harnessing it into the story being told. The resulting effect of this embedding, in fact, also resembles a deity's containment into unfamiliar territory—that is, we can imagine the literary ruptures as being rendered into *chinza* by their surrounding text; the discordant prose or poetry brought into the scene is caught into place by the words that frame it. Our attention to literary movement, therefore, is one that allows us to focus in on these textual *chinza* moments as those that have something particularly important to say. In a case such as the *utamakura*, it may seem as if there is little dissonance between the literary device and the surrounding words; as an integral part of how a great number of *waka* signify, an *utamakura* seems hardly like a jarring presence in the flow of a poem. We might here, though, recall the project of *chinkon*—that is, the necessity of pressing into place an object that we might have thought would naturally belong there. Similarly, approaching *utamakura* as a presence that is the result of a purposeful harnessing allows us to heighten our awareness of its complex signification and capacity for slippages.

Thus both texts and figures in motion intersect and are entangled together in a heavy but permeable net; as such, this concurrence of movements-temporarily-captured, too, becomes a beacon indicating moments of meaning. Itineraries, whether in motion or in between states of motion, trace a text's stance on the powers that be, and the powers that could become.

List of Characters

Abutsuni 阿仏尼
Agui 安居院
Akuji no Takamaru 悪事高丸
Akuro-ō 悪路王
Amaterasu 天照
Anrakuji 安楽寺
Aridōshi myōjin 蟻通明神
Ariwara no Narihira 在原業平
Ariwara no Shigeharu 在原滋春
Ashikaga Tadayoshi 足利直義
Ashikaga Takauji 足利尊氏
Ashikaga Yoshimitsu 足利義満
asobi 遊女
Aterui 阿弖流為
Atsuta 熱田
Atsuyoshi, Prince 敦慶親王
aware あはれ
azuma 吾妻/東
azuma kudari 東下り
bakufu 幕府
biwa hōshi 琵琶法師
chihō 地方
chinjufu 鎮守府
chinjugami 鎮守神
chinkon 鎮魂
chinkonsai 鎮魂祭

Chinu 血沼
chinza 鎮座
Chōken 澄憲
chōteki 朝敵
daijō daijin 太政大臣
daijō hō'ō 太上法皇
dōsojin 道祖神
Eiga monogatari 栄華物語
Emishi 蝦夷
engi 縁起
Engishiki 延喜式
Enkyōbon 延慶本
Fujiwara no Kanesuke 藤原兼輔
Fujiwara no Kintō 藤原公任
Fujiwara no Michikane 藤原道兼
Fujiwara no Michinaga 藤原道長
Fujiwara no Michitaka 藤原道隆
Fujiwara no Morosuke 藤原師輔
Fujiwara no Morotada 藤原師尹
Fujiwara no Morotō 藤原諸任
Fujiwara no Mototsune 藤原基経
Fujiwara no Narichika 藤原成親
Fujiwara no Naritoki 藤原済時
Fujiwara no Naritsune 藤原成経
Fujiwara no Onshi 藤原温子
Fujiwara no Sadanaka 藤原貞仲
Fujiwara no Sanekata 藤原実方
Fujiwara no Saneyori 藤原実頼
Fujiwara no Senshi 藤原詮子
Fujiwara no Sumitomo 藤原純友
Fujiwara no Tadahira 藤原忠平
Fujiwara no Takaie 藤原隆家
Fujiwara no Tametsune 藤原為経
Fujiwara no Tokihira 藤原時平
Fujiwara no Yukinari 藤原行成
Genji monogatari 源氏物語
Genkō disturbance 元弘の乱

Genkō shakusho 元亨釈書
Genpei jōsuiki 源平盛衰記
Gida 祇陀
gokumon 獄門
Gosen wakashū 後撰和歌集
gunki 軍記
Hamana Bridge 浜名の橋
haniwa 埴輪
Haruizumi no Amaneiko 春澄洽子
Haruizumi no Yoshitada 春澄善縄
Hasedera 長谷 (初瀬) 寺
Hashinoku, King 波斯匿王
Heike kindachi zōshi 平家公達草紙
Heike monogatari 平家物語
heikyoku 平曲
hito no kuni 人の国
Hōjō Tokiyuki 北条時行
hototogisu ほととぎす
Hyakunijukkubon 百二十句本
hyōhaku 漂白
Ichikata 一方
Ikuta River 生田川
Imakagami 今鏡
imayō 今様
inaka 田舎
Inase no Gorō Tamuramaru 稲瀬五郎田村丸
Isawa Fort 胆沢城
Ise (poet) 伊勢
Ise monogatari 伊勢物語
Ise Shrine 伊勢神宮
Izayoi nikki 十六夜日記
Jigen (deity) 示現
Jijū 侍従
jō (unit of measure) 杖 (丈)
Jōkyū rebellion 承久の乱
juichi'i 従一位
Kagerō nikki 蜻蛉日記

Kaidōki 海道記
Kakuichi 覚一
Kakuichibon 覚一本
kamisha 上社
Kamo Shrine 賀茂神社
Kanasashi 金刺
Kaneyoshi, Prince 懐良親王
kanjō 勧請
Kannara 官那羅
kannushi 神主
Kano no suke Munemochi 狩野介宗茂
kanpaku 関白
kanshibun 漢詩文
Kasuga (Saburō's wife) 春日
Kasuga Shrine 春日大社
kataribon 語り本
Kazan (temple) 花山
Kenrei moni'in ukyō no daibu shū 建礼門院右京大夫集
Ki no Tsurayuki 紀貫之
kiō 鬼王
kishu ryūritan 貴種流離譚
Kiso no Yoshinaka 木曾義仲
Kitabatake Aki'ie 北畠顕家
Kitabatake Chikafusa 北畠親房
Kitano tenjin 北野天神
Kōfukuji 興福寺
Kōga no Jirō Yoritada 甲賀次郎諏任
Kōga no Saburō Yorikata 甲賀三郎諏方
Kōga no Tarō Yorimune 甲賀太郎諏致
Kōga no Yoritane 甲賀諏胤
Koichijō 小一条
Kojiki 古事記
Kokin wakashū 古今和歌集
kokufu 国府
Kongōnyo, Princess 金剛女宮
Konjaku monogatari 今昔物語
Konparu Zenchiku 金春禅竹

kotokuni こと国
kuji 公事
kuni 国（國）
Makura no sōshi 枕草子
Man'yōshū 万葉集
matsubi setsudan keishiki 末尾切断形式
michiyuki 道行
Minamoto no Michikata (Nakanoin Michikata) 源通方（中院通方）
Minamoto no Taka'akira 源高明
Minamoto no Yorikane 源頼兼
Minamoto no Yorimasa 源頼政
Minamoto no Yoritomo 源頼朝
Minamoto no Yoshitsune 源義経
minzokugaku 民俗学
Mitsukiyo 満清
Miwa 神
Miyoshi no Yoshimune 三善善宗
More 母礼
Motomezuka 求塚
Mt. Asama 浅間山
Mt. Kibune 貴船山
Mt. Kurama 鞍馬山
Mt. Shirane 白根山
Mt. Tateshina 蓼科山
Muneyoshi, Prince 宗良親王
Mutsu waki 陸奥話記
Nagatobon 長門本
Nakanoin family 中院家
Nakasendai rebellion 中先代の乱
Nakatsukasa 中務
Nakoso Barrier 勿来の関
ni'inamesai 新嘗祭
Nijō, Empress (Fujiwara no Kōshi) 二条后（藤原高子）
Nikkō (deity) 日光
Ninigi 邇邇芸
Noriyoshi, Prince 憲良/義良親王
Nukisaki (deity) 抜鉾

Ōe no Masahira 大江匡衡
ōhōri 大祝
Ōkagami 大鏡
Ōkuninushi 大国主
Orikuchi Shinobu 折口信夫
Ōsaka 逢坂/相坂
Ouyang Xun 歐陽詢
Pine of Akoya 阿古屋の松
rokkasen 六歌仙
Ryō no gige 令義解
Saigyō 西行
Sakanoue no Tamuramaro 坂上田村麻呂
Sandai jitsuroku 三代実録
Sanekatashū 実方集
sanjūrokkasen 三十六歌仙
Saobiko 狭穂彦
Saobime 狭穂姫
Saya no Nakayama 佐夜の中山
sei'i taishōgun 征夷大将軍
Sei Shōnagon 清少納言
Sekizan (deity) 赤山
sekkan 摂関
Semimaru 蟬丸
Senju no mae 千手前
sento 遷都
sesshō 摂政
Sha'e 舎衛
shaku 笏
Shibu kassenjōbon 四部合戦状本
shichidō 七道
Shiji 史記
shikashū 私家集
shimosha 下社
"Shinano no kuni no chinju Suwa daimyōjin Akiyama matsuri no koto" 信濃國鎮守諏訪大明神秋山祭事
Shin goshūi wakashū 新後拾遺和歌集
Shin kokinshū 新古今集

Shinshō hōshi shū 信生法師集
Shintōshū 神道集
Shiogama Shrine 塩竈神社
Shioya no Tomonari 塩谷朝業
Shishigatani conspiracy 鹿ヶ谷の謀議
shōdō 唱導
Shōhei unification 正平一統
Sima Qian 司馬遷
Somedono, Empress (Fujiwara no Meishi) 染殿后 (藤原明子)
sōtsuibushi 総追捕使
Sugawara no Michizane 菅原道真
Sumiyoshi 住吉
Sunomata River 洲俣河
Susano'o 須佐之男
Suwa daimyōjin ekotoba 諏訪大明神絵詞
Suwa Enchū 諏訪円忠
"Suwa engi" 諏訪縁起
Suwa Lake 諏訪湖
Suwa Nobushige 諏訪信重
"Suwa no daimyōjin no Satsukie no koto" 諏訪大明神五月會事
Suwa Shrine 諏訪大社
Tachibana no Hiromi 橘広相
Tachibana no Tamenaka 橘為仲
Tachibana no Yoshitoshi 橘良利
Taga Fort 多賀城
Taira no Kiyomori 平清盛
Taira no Koremochi 平維茂
Taira no Koreyoshi 平維吉 (維良)
Taira no Masakado 平将門
Taira no Munemori 平宗盛
Taira no Shigehira 平重衡
Taira no Tokushi (Kenrei mon'in) 平徳子 (建礼門院)
Takeminakata 建御名方
Tanaka (deity) 田中
Tendai 天台
Tōdaiji 東大寺
tōdōza 当道座

Tōkan kikō 東関紀行
Tosa nikki 土佐日記
tsuchi wokasu 土犯す
Tsurezuregusa 徒然草
Ubara 菟原
uji no chōja 氏長者
utamakura 歌枕
uta monogatari 歌物語
waka 和歌
Wakan rōeishū 和漢朗詠集
wokasu 犯す
Xiang Yu 項羽
Yamato monogatari 大和物語
Yamato Takeru, Prince 倭建命/日本武尊
Yanagita Kunio 柳田国男
Yasaka 八坂
Yasakatome 八坂刀売
Yashirobon 屋代本
Yiwen leiju 藝文類聚
yomihon 読み本
Yoshimine no Munesada (Henjō) 良岑宗貞 (遍照)
Yuima 維摩
Yuiman 維縵
Yu meiren 虞美人
Yuya 熊野
Zeami 世阿弥
Zenkōji 善光寺
Zenkunen disturbance 前九年の役
Zhao Gao 趙高
Zhui 騅

Bibliography

Abe Toshiko. *Henjōshū zenshaku.* Vol. 15 of *Shikashū zenshaku sōsho.* Tokyo: Kazama shobō, 1994.

———. *Kōhon Yamato monogatari to sono kenkyū.* Tokyo: Sanseidō, 1954.

Adolphson, Mikael, Edward Kamens, and Stacie Matsumoto, eds. *Heian Japan: Centers and Peripheries.* Honolulu: University of Hawai'i Press, 2007.

Akasaka Norio. *Hyōhaku no seishinshi: Yanagita Kunio no hassei.* Tokyo: Shōgakkan, 1994.

Amino Yoshihiko, ed. *Hyōhaku to teichaku: Teijū shakai e no michi.* Vol. 6 of *Nihon minzoku bunka taikei.* Tokyo: Shōgakkan, 1984.

———. *Muen, kugai, raku: Nihon chūsei no jiyū to heiwa.* Tokyo: Heibonsha, 1978.

———. *Umi to rettō no chūsei.* Tokyo: Nihon editā sukūru, 1992.

Aoki Kazuo et al., annots. *Kojiki.* Vol. 1 of *Nihon shisō taikei.* Tokyo: Iwanami shoten, 1982.

Appadurai, Arjun. *Modernity at Large: Cultural Dimensions of Globalization.* Minneapolis: University of Minnesota Press, 1996.

Ariyama Daigo et al., eds. *Chōkū Orikuchi Shinobu jiten.* Tokyo: Bensei shuppan, 2000.

Arntzen, Sonja. *The Kagero Diary: A Woman's Autobiographical Text from Tenth-Century Japan.* Ann Arbor: Center for Japanese Studies, University of Michigan, 1997.

Asami Kazuhiko. *Jikkinshō.* Vol. 51 of *Shinpen Nihon koten bungaku zenshū.* Tokyo: Shōgakkan, 1997.

Batten, Bruce. *To the Ends of Japan: Premodern Frontiers, Boundaries, and Interactions.* Honolulu: University of Hawai'i Press, 2003.

Bhabha, Homi. *The Location of Culture.* New York: Routledge, 1994.

Bialock, David T. *Eccentric Spaces, Hidden Histories: Narrative, Ritual, and Royal Authority from* The Chronicles of Japan *to* The Tale of Heike. Stanford: Stanford University Press, 2007.

Bowring, Richard. *Murasaki Shikibu: The Tale of Genji.* Cambridge: Cambridge University Press, 1988.

Butler, Lee. *Emperor and Aristocracy in Japan, 1467–1680: Resilience and Renewal.* Cambridge, MA: Harvard University Asia Center, 2002.

Cadzyn, Eric, ed. *Trespasses: Masao Miyoshi / Selected Writings.* Durham, NC: Duke University Press, 2010.

Chigira Mamoru. "Yashirobon *Heike monogatari* no seiritsu—Yashirobon no kotaisei no kenshō, kan san 'Kogō no tsubone no koto' wo chūshin to shite." In *Heike monoga-*

tari no seiritsu, ed. Tochigi Yoshitada et al., 113–36. Tokyo: Yūseidō shuppan kabushiki kaisha, 1993.

Chow, Rey. *Writing Diaspora: Tactics of Intervention in Contemporary Cultural Studies.* Bloomington: Indiana University Press, 1993.

Farris, William Wayne. *Heavenly Warriors: The Evolution of Japan's Military, 500–1300.* Cambridge, MA: Council on East Asian Studies at Harvard University, 1992.

Friday, Karl. *Samurai, Warfare, and the State in Medieval Japan.* New York: Routledge, 2004.

Fujimori Ei'ichi. *Suwa jinja.* Tokyo: Gakuseisha, 1986.

Fujita Takuji, ed. *Kundoku Genkō shakusho.* Vol. 1. Kyoto: Zen bunka kenkyūjo, 2011.

Fukuda Akira. *Shintōshū setsuwa no seiritsu.* Tokyo: Miyai shoten, 1984.

———. "Shiryōhen: Mochizuki Yoshikichishi shozō 'Suwa no honji.'" *Denshō bungaku kenkyū* 2 (April 1962): 59–76.

Gerbert, Elaine. "The Suwa Pillar Festival Revisited." *Harvard Journal of Asiatic Studies* 56, no. 2 (December 1996): 319–74.

Haga Yaichi, and Sasaki Nobutsuna, eds. *Kōchū yōkyoku sōsho.* Vol. 2. Tokyo: Hakubunkan, 1914.

Hasegawa Masaharu. *Kyōkai kara no hassō: Tabi no bungaku, koi no bungaku.* Tokyo: Shintensha, 1989.

Hasegawa Masaharu et al., eds. *Tosa nikki, Kagerō nikki, Murasaki Shikibu nikki, Sarashina nikki.* Vol. 24 of *Shin Nihon koten bungaku taikei.* Tokyo: Iwanami shoten, 1989.

Hashimoto Akihiko. "*Shintōshū* no jōbutsu shisō: Dewa Haguro gongen no koto." In vol. 1 of *Shōdō bungaku kenkyū*, ed. Fukuda Akira and Hirota Tetsumichi, 114–26. Tokyo: Miyai shoten, 1996.

Hashimoto Fumio et al., annots. and eds. *Karonshū.* Vol. 50 of *Nihon koten bungaku zenshū.* Tokyo: Shōgakkan, 1975.

Heldt, Gustav. *The Pursuit of Harmony: Poetry and Power in Early Heian Japan.* Ithaca, NY: Cornell East Asia Series, 2008.

Henmi Jun. "Kōga no Saburō no hyōhaku." In *Chūsei setsuwashū.* Vol. 23 of *Kanshō: Nihon koten bungaku*, ed. Nishio Kōichi and Kishi Shōzō, 451–56. Tokyo: Kadokawa shoten, 1977.

Hisamatsu Sen'ichi, and Kubota Jun, annots. *Kenreimon'in ukyō no daibu shū.* Tokyo: Iwanami shoten, 1978.

Honma Yōichi, ed. and annot. *Honchō mudaishi zenchūshaku.* Vol. 1. Tokyo: Shintensha, 1992.

Horiuchi Hideaki, and Akiyama Ken, annots. *Taketori monogatari, Ise monogatari.* Vol. 17 of *Shin Nihon koten bungaku taikei.* Tokyo: Iwanami shoten, 1997.

Hosoi Kazuyu et al. *Iwateken no rekishi.* Tokyo: Yamakawa shuppansha, 1999.

Hotta Shōzō. *Yakubun Azuma kagami hyōchū.* Vol. 1. Tokyo: Tōyōdō, 1943.

Hyōdō Hiromi. *Heike monogatari: "katari" no tekusuto.* Tokyo: Chikuma shobō, 1998.

———. *Heike monogatari no rekishi to geinō.* Tokyo: Yoshikawa kōbunkan, 2000.

Ichiko Teiji, ed. and annot. *Heike monogatari*, vol. 2. Vol. 46 of *Shinpen Nihon koten bungaku zenshū.* Tokyo: Shōgakkan, 1994.

Ikebe Yoshikata, annot. *Genpei jōsuiki,* part 2. Vol. 8 of *Kokubun sōsho.* Tokyo: Hakubunkan, 1926.

Imai Gen'e. *Yamato monogatari hyōshaku.* Vols. 1 and 2. Tokyo: Kasama shoin, 1999 and 2000.

Imazeki Toshiko. *Shinshō hōshi shū shin yakuchū.* Tokyo: Kazama shobō, 2002.

Imazu Takahiro. "'Suwa Daimyōjin Ekotoba' no kaisetsu." *Shintōshi kenkyū* 42, no. 3 (July 1994): 55–80.

Ishikawa Katsuyoshi. *Suwa saisei no hasshō to keifu.* Tokyo: Hōritsu jōhō shuppan kabushiki kaisha, 2005.

Itō Tomio. *Itō Tomio chosakushū.* Vols. 1, 5, and 6. Tokyo: Nagai shuppan kikaku, 1977 (vol. 1) and 1978 (vols. 5 and 6).

Itoga Kimie, annot. *Kenrei mon'in ukyō no daibu shū.* Vol. 28 of *Shinchō Nihon koten shūsei.* Tokyo: Shinchōsha, 1979.

Kajihara Masa'aki, annot. and ed. *Gikeiki.* Vol. 62 of *Shinpen Nihon koten bungaku zenshū.* Tokyo: Shōgakkan, 2000.

Kajihara Masa'aki, and Yamashita Hiroaki, annots. *Heike monogatari,* vols. 1 and 2. Vols. 44 and 45 of *Shin Nihon koten bungaku taikei.* Tokyo: Iwanami shoten, 1991 and 1993.

Kakimoto Tsutomu. *Yamato monogatari no chūshaku to kenkyū.* Tokyo: Musashino shoin, 1981.

Kamens, Edward. Utamakura, *Allusion, and Intertextuality in Traditional Japanese Poetry.* New Haven: Yale University Press, 1997.

Kanai Tenbi. *Suwa shinkōshi.* Tokyo: Meicho shuppan, 1982.

Katagiri Yōichi, annot. *Gosen wakashū.* Vol. 6 of *Shin Nihon koten bungaku taikei.* Tokyo: Iwanami shoten, 1990.

Katagiri Yōichi et al., eds. and annots. *Taketori monogatari, Ise monogatari, Yamato monogatari, Heichū monogatari.* Vol. 12 of *Shinpen Nihon koten bungaku zenshū.* Tokyo: Shōgakkan, 1994.

Kawaguchi Hisao, annot. *Kanke bunsō, Kanke goshū.* Vol. 72 of *Nihon koten bungaku taikei.* Tokyo: Iwanami shoten, 1966.

Kawai Yasushi. *Genpei no nairan to kōbu seiken.* Vol. 3 of *Nihon chūsei no rekishi.* Tokyo: Yoshikawa kōbunkan, 2009.

Kawajiri Akio. *Heiankyō sento.* Vol. 5 of *Shirīzu Nihon kodaishi.* Tokyo: Iwanami shoten, 2011.

———. *Taira no Masakado no ran.* Vol. 4 of *Sensō no Nihonshi.* Tokyo: Yoshikawa kōbunkan, 2007.

Kawanishi Hidemichi. *Tōhoku: tsukurareta ikyō.* Tokyo: Chūōkōron shinsha, 2001.

Kawashima, Terry. *Writing Margins: The Textual Construction of Gender in Heian and Kamakura Japan.* Cambridge, MA: Harvard Asia Center Publications, 2001.

Keizai zasshisha, eds. *Nihon kiryaku.* Vol. 5 of *Kokushi taikei.* Tokyo: Keizai zasshisha, 1897.

———, eds. *Sandai jitsuroku.* Vol. 4 of *Kokushi taikei.* Tokyo: Keizai zasshisha, 1897.

Kidō Saizō, annot. *Tsurezuregusa.* Vol. 10 of *Shinchō Nihon koten shūsei.* Tokyo: Shinchōsha, 1977.

Kikuchi Ryōichi. "*Shintōshū* ni okeru shōdō setsuwa no keisei—chinjugami no shinkannen." *Komazawa kokubun* no. 26 (February 1989): 57–75.

Kimura Junji. *Saihakken Nihon no tetsugaku: Orikuchi Shinobu—ikidohoru kokoro.* Tokyo: Kōdansha, 2008.

Kishi Shōzō. *Shintōshū*. Vol. 94 of *Tōyō bunko*. Tokyo: Heibonsha, 1967.

———, annot. *Zen'yaku Azuma kagami*. Vols. 1, 2, and 3. Tokyo: Shinjinbutsu Ōraisha, 1976 (vols. 1 and 2) and 1977 (vol. 3).

Kobayashi Kei'ichirō. *Shinano chūseishi kō*. Tokyo: Yoshikawa kōbunkan, 1982.

Kobayashi Yasuharu, annot. *Kojidan*. Vol. 1. Tokyo: Gendai shichōsha, 1981.

Kobayashi Yoshikazu. "Enkyōbon *Heike monogatari* no seiritsu." In *Heike monogatari no seiritsu*, ed. Tochigi Yoshitada et al., 91–112. Tokyo: Yūseidō shuppan kabushiki kaisha, 1993.

———. *Heike monogatari no seiritsu*. Osaka: Izumi shoin, 2000.

Kobayashi Yoshinori et al., annots. *Ryōjin hishō, Kanginshū, Kyōgen kayō*. Vol. 56 of *Shin Nihon koten bungaku taikei*. Tokyo: Iwanami shoten, 1993.

Kodama Kōta. *Nihon kōtsūshi*. Tokyo: Yoshikawa Kōbunkan, 1992.

Kōgakkan daigaku shiryō hensanjo, eds. *Shoku Nihongi shiryō*. Vols. 4 and 6. Ise: Kōgakkan daigaku shuppanbu, 2001 and 2004.

Koizumi Hiroshi et al., annots. *Hōbutsushū, Kankyo no tomo, Hirasan kojin reitaku*. Vol. 40 of *Shin Nihon koten bungaku taikei*. Tokyo: Iwanami shoten, 1993.

Kojima Noriyuki et al., eds. and annots. *Nihon shoki*, vols. 1, 2, and 3. Vols. 1, 2 and 3 of *Shinpen Nihon koten bungaku zenshū*. Tokyo: Shōgakkan, 1994, 1996, and 1998.

Komine Kazuaki, annot. *Konjaku monogatarishū*, vol. 4. Vol. 46 of *Shin Nihon koten bungaku taikei*. Tokyo: Iwanami shoten, 1994.

Konno Tōru, annot. *Konjaku monogatarishū*, vol. 1. Vol. 33 of *Shin Nihon koten bungaku taikei*. Tokyo: Iwanami shoten, 1999.

Koyama Hiroshi et al., eds. and annots. *Yōkyokushū*, vol. 2. Vol. 34 of *Nihon koten bungaku zenshū*. Tokyo: Shōgakkan, 1975.

Koyamachi Teruhiko, annot. *Shūi wakashū*. Vol. 7 of *Shin Nihon koten bungaku taikei*. Tokyo: Iwanami shoten, 1990.

Kubota Jun, and Baba Akiko, eds. *Utakotoba utamakura daijiten*. Tokyo: Kadokawa shoten, 1999.

Kubota Jun, and Hirata Yoshinobu, annots. *Goshūi wakashū*. Vol. 8 of *Shin Nihon koten bungaku taikei*. Tokyo: Iwanami shoten, 1994.

Kudō Shigenori. *Heianchō ritsuryō shakai no bungaku*. Tokyo: Perikansha, 1993.

Kurokawa Masamichi et al., annots. *Heike monogatari: Nagatobon*. Tokyo: Kokusho kankōkai, 1906.

Kusaka Tsutomu. *Heike monogatari no tanjō*. Tokyo: Iwanami shoten, 2001.

Lamarre, Thomas. *Uncovering Heian Japan: An Archeology of Sensation and Inscription*. Durham, NC: Duke University Press, 2000.

Marra, Michele. *Representations of Power: The Literary Politics of Medieval Japan*. Honolulu: University of Hawai'i Press, 1993.

Matisoff, Susan. *The Legend of Semimaru: Blind Musician of Japan*. New York: Columbia University Press, 1978.

Matsumae Ken. *Kodai denshō to kyūtei saishi: Nihon shinwa no shūhen*. Tokyo: Haniwa shobō, 1974.

Matsumoto Ryūshin. "Chūsei ni okeru honjimono no kenkyū 3." *Shidō bunko ronshū* 13 (July 1976): 300–323.

———, annot. *Nantobon Nanto ihon Heike monogatari*. Vol. 2. Tokyo: Kyūko shoin, 1972.

———, annot. *Otogi zōshi*. Vol. 34 of *Shinchō Nihon koten shūsei*. Tokyo: Shinchōsha, 1980.

Matsumoto Ryūshin, annot., and Keiō gijuku daigaku fuzoku kenkyūjo Shidō bunko, eds. *Shibu kassenjōbon Heike monogatari*. Tokyo: Dai'an, 1967.

Matsumura Hiroji. *Eiga monogatari zenchūshaku*. Vol. 4. Tokyo: Kadokawa shoten, 1974.

Matsuo Ashie, annot. *Genpei seisuiki*. Vol. 2. Tokyo: Miyai shoten, 1993.

Matsuo Satoshi, annot. *Tsutsumi chūnagon monogatari zenshaku*. Tokyo: Kasama shoin, 1971.

Mezaki Tokue. *Hyōhaku: Nihon shisōshi no teiryū*. Tokyo: Kadokawa shoten, 1975.

Minemura Fumito, annot. and ed. *Shin kokin wakashū*. Vol. 43 of *Shinpen Nihon koten bungaku zenshū*. Tokyo: Shōgakkan, 1995.

Mitani Eiichi. *Monogatari shi no kenkyū*. Tokyo: Yūseidō shuppan kabushiki kaisha, 1967.

Miwa Iwane. *Suwa taisha*. Tokyo: Gakuseisha, 1988.

Miyaji Naokazu. *Hodaka jinjashi/Suwa jinja no kenkyū*, vol. 1. Vol. 1 of *Miyaji Naokazu ronshū*. Tokyo: Sōyōsha, 1984.

———. *Suwa jinja no kenkyū*, vol. 2. Vol. 2 of *Miyaji Naokazu ronshū*. Tokyo: Sōyōsha, 1984.

Miyasaka Mitsuaki, and Asakawa Kiyomasa. *Zusetsu Suwa no rekishi*. Vol. 1. Matsumoto, Nagano: Kyōdo shuppansha, 1983.

Mizuhara Hajime, annot. *Heike monogatari*, vol. 3. Vol. 47 of *Shinchō Nihon koten shūsei*. Tokyo: Shinchōsha, 1981.

Morimoto Shigeru. *Yamato monogatari no kōshōteki kenkyū*. Osaka: Izumi shoin, 1990.

Moriya Takeshi, ed. *Geinō to chinkon*. Vol. 7 of *Taikei bukkyō to Nihonjin*. Tokyo: Shunshūsha, 1988.

Murakami Manabu. "Engi no monogatari shōshi." In *Chūsei setsuwashū*. Vol. 23 of *Kanshō Nihon koten bungaku*, ed. Nishio Kōichi and Kishi Shōzō, 382–92. Tokyo: Kadokawa shoten, 1977.

Naficy, Hamid, ed. *Home, Exile, Homeland: Film, Media, and the Politics of Place*. New York: Routledge, 1999.

Nagasaki Ken et al., annots. *Chūsei nikki kikōshū*. Vol. 48 of *Shinpen Nihon koten bungaku zenshū*. Tokyo: Shōgakkan, 1994.

Nakajima Etsuji. *Gukanshō zenchūkai*. Tokyo: Yūseidō shuppan, 1969.

Nakamura Sachihiko et al., eds. *Kadokawa kogo daijiten*. Vol. 5. Tokyo: Kadokawa shoten, 1999.

Nienhauser, William H., Jr, ed. *The Grand Scribe's Records*. Vol. 2. Bloomington: Indiana University Press, 2002.

Nihonshi kōjiten henshū iinkai, eds. *Nihonshi kōjiten*. Tokyo: Yamakawa shuppansha, 1997.

Ni'ino Naoyoshi. *Tamuramaro to Aterui: Kodai kokka to tōhoku*. Tokyo: Yoshikawa kōbunkan, 2007.

Nio Masanobu. "Sanekata no setsuwa—Michinoku sasen setsuwa no hassei gen'in okusoku." In *Chūko bungaku no keisei to tenkai—ōchō bungaku zengo*, ed. Inaga Keiji and Masuda Motomu, 125–50. Osaka: Izumi shoin, 1995.

Nishino Haruo, annot. and ed. *Yōkyoku hyakuban*. Vol. 57 of *Shin Nihon koten bungaku taikei*. Tokyo: Iwanami shoten, 1998.

Nishio Kōichi, and Kishi Shōzō, eds. *Chūsei setsuwashū.* Vol. 23 of *Kanshō Nihon koten bungaku.* Tokyo: Kadokawa shoten, 1977.

Oboroya Hisashi. *Fujiwarashi sennen.* Tokyo: Kōdansha, 1996.

Ōishi Shinzaburō. "Nihon sento no keifu." *Gakushūin daigaku keizai ronshū* 28, no. 78 (October 1991): 31–41.

Okada, Richard H. "Displacements of Conquest, or Exile, *The Tale of Genji,* and Post-Cold War Learning." In *Reading* The Tale of Genji: *Its Picture-Scrolls, Texts, and Romance,* ed. Richard Stanley-Baker et al., 63–79. Folkestone, UK: Global Oriental, 2009.

——— [Okada, H. Richard]. *Figures of Resistance: Language, Poetry, and Narrating in* The Tale of Genji *and Other Mid-Heian Texts.* Durham, NC: Duke University Press, 1991.

Okada Sei'ichi. *Kamakura bakufu to tōgoku.* Tokyo: Zoku gunsho ruijū kanseikai, 2006.

Okami Masao, and Takahashi Ki'ichi, annots., and Shintō taikei hensankai, eds. *Shintōshū.* Vol. 1 of *Shintō taikei: bungaku hen.* Tokyo: Shintō taikei hensankai, 1988.

Okano Tomohiko. *Kitabatake Chikafusa: "Dainihonkoku wa shinkoku nari."* Tokyo: Mineruva shobō, 2009.

Okayama Miki. *Yamato monogatari no kenkyū.* Tokyo: Ōfūsha, 1993.

Ong, Aihwa. *Flexible Citizenship: The Cultural Logics of Transnationality.* Durham, NC: Duke University Press, 1999.

Ouyang Xun. *Yiwen leiju.* Vols. 887–88 of *Yingyin Wenyuange Siku quanshu.* Taipei: Taiwan shangwu yinshuguan, 1983.

Oyler, Elizabeth. *Swords, Oaths, and Prophetic Visions: Authoring Warrior Rule in Medieval Japan.* Honolulu: University of Hawai'i Press, 2006.

Ritsuryō kenkyūkai, eds. *Ryō no gige yakuchūhen,* vol. 2. Vol. 10 of *Yakuchū Nihon ritsuryō.* Tokyo: Tōkyōdō shuppan, 1989.

Saeki Shin'ichi. *Heike monogatari sogen.* Vol. 3 of *Chūsei bungaku kenkyū sōsho.* Tokyo: Wakakusa shobō, 1996.

Said, Edward. *Culture and Imperialism.* New York: Vintage Books, 1993.

Sakaue Yasutoshi. *Ritsuryō kokka no tenkan to "Nihon."* Vol. 5 of *Nihon no rekishi.* Tokyo: Kōdansha, 2009.

Sakurai Tokutarō. "Engi no ruikei to tenkai." In *Jisha engi.* Vol. 20 of *Nihon shisō taikei,* ed. Sakurai Tokutarō et al., 445–78. Tokyo: Iwanami shoten, 1975.

Sakurai Yōko. *Heike monogatari no keisei to juyō.* Tokyo: Kyūko shoin, 2001.

Sakurai Yoshio. *Nanbokuchō nairan to tōgoku.* Vol. 4 of *Dōran no tōgokushi.* Tokyo: Yoshikawa kōbunkan, 2012.

Sanari Kentarō. *Yōkyoku taikan.* Vol. 2. Tokyo: Meiji shoin, 1930.

Sasaki Kōichi. "'Kaidō kudari' no michiyukibun." In *Nihon bungaku no dentō to rekishi,* ed. Usuda Jingorō hakushi kanreki kinen ronbunshū henshū iinkai, 572–88. Tokyo: Ōfūsha, 1975.

Sasaki Nobutsuna, ed. *Nihon kagaku taikei.* Vol. 1. Tokyo: Kazama shobō, 1953.

Satake Akihiro et al., annots. *Man'yōshū,* vols. 2 and 4. Vol. 2 of *Shin Nihon koten bungaku taikei.* Tokyo: Iwanami shoten, 2000 and 2003.

Satō Kenzō, and Haruta Noboru, eds. *Yashirobon Heike monogatari.* Tokyo: Ōfūsha, 1973.

Satō Kikuichirō. *Kinsei Kōzuke shinwa no sekai: zaichi engi to denshōsha.* Tokyo: Iwata shoten, 2007.

Scott, James C. *The Art of Not Being Governed: An Anarchist History of Upland Southeast Asia.* New Haven: Yale University Press, 2009.

Seki Yukihiko. *Setsuwa no kataru Nihon no chūsei.* Tokyo: Soshiete, 1992.

———. *Tōhoku no sōran to Ōshū kassen—"Nihonkoku" no seiritsu.* Vol. 5 of *Sensō no Nihonshi.* Tokyo: Yoshikawa kōbunkan, 2006.

Selinger, Vyjayanthi R. *Authorizing the Shogunate: Ritual and Material Symbolism in the Literary Construction of Warrior Order.* Leiden: Brill, 2013.

Seno'o Yoshinobu. *Heianchō uta monogatari no kenkyū—Yamato monogatari hen.* Tokyo: Kasama shoin, 2000.

Shida Itaru. "Shibu kassenjōbon *Heike monogatari* no seiritsu—Ikuta no mori, Ichinotani kassendan wo yomu." In *Heike monogatari no seiritsu*, ed. Tochigi Yoshitada et al., 65–90. Tokyo: Yūseidō shuppan kabushiki kaisha, 1993.

Shih, Shu-mei. *Visuality and Identity: Sinophone Articulations across the Pacific.* Berkeley: University of California Press, 2007.

Shimada Kiyoshi. "Chūsei Suwa kamisha no *ōhōri* to shokuishiki: sokui girei no kōsei to imi." *Kokugakuin daigaku Nihon bunka kenkyūjo kiyō* 77 (March 1996): 1–36.

Shimomukai Tatsuhiko. *Bushi no seichō to insei.* Vol. 7 of *Nihon no rekishi.* Tokyo: Kōdansha, 2009.

Shiraishi Kazumi. "Suwa honji no shomondai." *Miyazaki daigaku kyōiku gakubu kiyō / jinbun kagaku* 70 (September 1991): 47–66.

———. "Suwa honji 'Shinano no Suwa no shinden' ni tsuite." *Miyazaki daigaku kyōiku gakubu kiyō* 73 (March 1993): 47–62.

Sima Qian. *Shiji.* Beijing: Zhonghua shuju, 1959.

Spivak, Gayatri. *A Critique of Postcolonial Reason: Toward a History of the Vanishing Present.* Cambridge, MA: Harvard University Press, 1999.

Stockdale, Jonathan. *Imagining Exile in Heian Japan: Banishment in Law, Literature, and Cult.* Honolulu: University of Hawai'i Press, 2015.

Sugano Hiroyuki, annot. and ed. *Wakan rōeishū.* Vol. 19 of *Shinpen Nihon koten bungaku zenshū.* Tokyo: Shōgakkan, 1999.

Suwa shiryō sōsho kankōkai, eds. *Suwa shiryō sōsho.* Vol. 15. Kawagishi, Nagano: Ayusawa shōten insatsujo, 1931.

Suzuki Takuya. *Emishi to tōhoku sensō.* Vol. 3 of *Sensō no Nihonshi.* Tokyo: Yoshikawa kōbunkan, 2008.

Tachibana Kenji, and Katō Shizuko, annot. and eds. *Ōkagami.* Vol. 34 of *Shinpen Nihon koten bungaku zenshū.* Tokyo: Shōgakkan, 1996.

Tahara, Mildred. *Tales of Yamato: A Tenth-Century Poem-Tale.* Honolulu: University of Hawai'i Press, 1980.

———. "Yamato Monogatari." *Monumenta Nipponica* 27, no. 1 (Spring 1972): 1–37.

Takahashi Bunji. *Monogatari chinkonron.* Tokyo: Ōfūsha, 1990.

Takahashi Sadaichi. *Kundoku Gyokuyō.* Vols. 4 and 5. Tokyo: Takashina shoten, 1989.

Takahashi Takashi. *Sakanoue no Tamuramaro.* Tokyo: Yoshikawa kōbunkan, 1959.

Takahashi Tōru. "Kishu ryūritan no kōzō." *Kokubungaku: kaishaku to kanshō* 56, no. 10 (October 1991): 123–28.

Takayama Toshihiro, ed. *Kundoku Shibu kassenjōbon Heike monogatari.* Tokyo: Yūseidō shuppan kabushiki kaisha, 1995.

Takeda Kō, annot. *Kaidōki zenshaku.* Tokyo: Kasama shoin, 1990.
Takehana Isao. *Sanekatashū chūshaku.* Vol. 5 of *Shikashū chūshaku sōkan.* Tokyo: Kichōhon kankōkai, 1993.
Takehisa Tsuyoshi. *Heike monogatari hassei kō.* Tokyo: Ōfūsha, 1999.
Takeuchi Hideo, annot. *Suwa.* Vol. 30 of *Shintō taikei jinjahen.* Tokyo: Shintō taikei hensankai, 1982.
Takeuchi Makoto. *Nihon no kaidō handobukku shinpan.* Tokyo: Sanseidō, 2006.
Tanaka Kimiharu, Hirasawa Ryūsuke, and Kikuchi Yasuhiko. *Tsurayukishū, Mitsuneshū, Tomonorishū, Tadamineshū.* Vol. 19 of *Waka bungaku taikei.* Tokyo: Meiji shoin, 1997.
Tanaka Makoto, annot. *Mikan yōkyokushū*, vol. 6. Vol. 227 of *Koten bunko.* Tokyo: Koten bunko, 1966.
Tanaka Yutaka, and Akase Shingo, annots. and eds. *Shin kokin wakashū.* Vol. 11 of *Shin Nihon koten bungaku taikei.* Tokyo: Iwanami shoten, 1992.
Tanigawa Ken'ichi et al., eds. *Jisha engi.* Vol. 26 of *Nihon shomin seikatsu shiryō shūsei.* Tokyo: San'ichi shobō, 1983.
Teeuwen, Mark, and Fabio Rambelli, eds. *Buddhas and Kami in Japan: Honji Suijaku as a Combinatory Paradigm.* London: Routledge Curzon, 2003.
Terada Shizuko, and Washio Tetsuta. *Suwa myōjin: kami shinkō no genzō.* Tokyo: Iwata shoin, 2010.
Terakawa Machio. "Jisha engi." In *Ryōiki, ujibumi, engi.* Vol. 11 of *Kodai bungaku kōza*, ed. Furuhashi Nobutaka et al., 156–73. Tokyo: Benseisha, 1995.
Tokuda Kazuo. "*Shintōshū*: kamigami no monogatari." *Kokubungaku: kaishaku to kanshō* 58, no. 12 (December 1993): 127–32.
Tokumitsu Sumio. "Fujiwara Sanekata kashū no kenkyū—miyakobito matsu tomo shirade (hachibanka)." *Nihon bungaku kenkyū* 29 (April 1992): 39–59.
Tomikura Tokujirō. *Heike monogatari zenchūshaku.* Vol. 3, pt. 1. Tokyo: Kadokawa shoten, 1966.
Torao Toshiya, ed. *Engishiki.* Vol. 1. Tokyo: Shūeisha, 2000.
Unno Yasuo. *Imakagami zenshaku.* Vol. 2. Tokyo: Fukutake shoten, 1983.
Ushiyama Yoshiyuki. "Tamuramaro densetsu to Kiyomizudera shinkō: tokuni Shinano ni okeru seiritsu jiki to sono haikei." In *Nihon shakai ni okeru hotoke to kami*, ed. Hayami Tasuku, 125–61. Tokyo: Yoshikawa kōbunkan, 2006.
Wakashi kenkyūkai, eds. *Shikashū taisei.* Vol. 1. Tokyo: Meiji shoin, 1973.
Wakita Haruko. *Josei geinō no genryū: Kugutsu, kusemai, shirabyōshi.* Tokyo: Kadokawa shoten, 2001.
Wang Wenhao, annot. *Su Dongpo shiji.* Beijing: Zhuhai chubanshe, 1996.
Watanabe Daimon. *Ubawareta sanshu no jingi: kōi keishō no chūseishi.* Tokyo: Kōdansha, 2009.
Watanabe Katsuyoshi. *Chinkonsai no kenkyū.* Tokyo: Meicho shuppan, 1994.
Watanabe Tamotsu, ed. *Saigyō Sankashū zenchūkai.* Tokyo: Kazama shobō, 1971.
Watanabe Tsunaya, annot. *Shasekishū.* Vol. 85 of *Nihon koten bungaku taikei.* Tokyo: Iwanami shoten, 1966.
Webber, Andrew J. *The Doppelgänger: Double Visions in German Literature.* Oxford: Clarendon Press, 1996.
Yamada Shigeyasu. *Suwa shi gaisetsu—bunkashi wo chūshin to shite.* Tokyo: Okaya shoten, 1989.

Yamaori Tetsuo, and Miyata Noboru, eds. *Hyōhaku no minzoku bunka.* Vol. 8 of *Nihon rekishi minzoku ronshū.* Tokyo: Yoshikawa kōbunkan, 1994.

Yamashita Hiroaki, ed. *Genpei tōjōroku.* Toyohashi: Mikan kokubun shiryō kankai, 1963.

———. *Heike monogatari no seiritsu.* Nagoya: Nagoya daigaku shuppankai, 1993.

———. *Katari to shite no Heike monogatari.* Tokyo: Iwanami shoten, 1994.

Yamashita Michiyo. *Ōchō kajin Ise.* Tokyo: Chikuma shobō, 1990.

———. *Utagatari no jidai—Yamato monogatari no hitobito.* Tokyo: Chikuma shobō, 1993.

Yamazaki Masanobu. "*Yamato monogatari* shodan no shijitsuteki waka kaishaku to shodan no imisuru mono." *Nishō gakusha daigaku tōyōgaku kenkyūjo shūkan* 29 (1999): 25–41.

Yanagita Kunio. *Tōno monogatari.* Tokyo: Kyōdo kenkyūsha, 1935.

Yanagita Yoshinori. *Yamato monogatari no kenkyū.* Tokyo: Kanrin shobō, 1994.

Yanase Kazuo. *Shaji engi no kenkyū.* Tokyo: Benseisha, 1998.

Yanase Kazuo, and Takei Kazuto, annots. *Izayoi nikki, Yoru no tsuru chūshaku.* Osaka: Izumi shoin, 1986.

Yanase Kiyoshi et al., eds. and annots. *Shōmonki, Mutsu waki, Hogen monogatari, Heiji monogatari.* Vol. 42 of *Shinpen Nihon koten bungaku zenshū.* Tokyo: Shōgakkan, 2002.

Yasumoto Biten, ed., and Shimura Yuko, trans. *Sendai kuji hongi gendaigo yaku.* Tokyo: Hihyōsha, 2013.

Yiengpruksawan, Mimi Hall. *Hiraizumi: Buddhist Art and Regional Politics in Twelfth-Century Japan.* Cambridge, MA: Harvard Asia Center Publications, 1998.

Yoda, Tomiko. *Gender and National Literature: Heian Texts in the Construction of Japanese Modernity.* Durham, NC: Duke University Press, 2004.

Yokoi Yasuhito. "Chinjugami to ōken—chūseiteki shingi taikei no kijiku wo megutte." In *Chūsei ichinomiyasei no rekishiteki tenkai,* vol. 2: *Sōgō kenkyū hen,* ed. Ichinomiya kenkyūkai, 93–42. Tokyo: Iwata shoin, 2004.

Yokomichi Mario, and Omote Akira, annots. *Yōkyokushū,* vols. 1 and 2. Vols. 40 and 41 of *Nihon koten bungaku taikei.* Tokyo: Iwanami shoten, 1960 and 1963.

Yokoyama Shigeru, and Matsumoto Ryūshin, eds. *Muromachi jidai monogatari taisei.* Vols. 8 and 9. Tokyo: Kadokawa shoten, 1980 and 1981.

Yoshizawa Yoshinori, annot. *Ōei shosha Enkyōbon Heike monogatari.* Tokyo: Hakuteisha, 1961.

Index

Harvard East Asian Monographs
(most recent titles)

250. Wilt L. Idema, Wai-yee Li, and Ellen Widmer, eds., *Trauma and Transcendence in Early Qing Literature*
251. Barbara Molony and Kathleen Uno, eds., *Gendering Modern Japanese History*
252. Hiroshi Aoyagi, *Islands of Eight Million Smiles: Idol Performance and Symbolic Production in Contemporary Japan*
253. Wai-yee Li, *The Readability of the Past in Early Chinese Historiography*
254. William C. Kirby, Robert S. Ross, and Gong Li, eds., *Normalization of U.S.-China Relations: An International History*
255. Ellen Gardner Nakamura, *Practical Pursuits: Takano Chōei, Takahashi Keisaku, and Western Medicine in Nineteenth-Century Japan*
256. Jonathan W. Best, *A History of the Early Korean Kingdom of Paekche, together with an annotated translation of* The Paekche Annals *of the* Samguk sagi
257. Liang Pan, *The United Nations in Japan's Foreign and Security Policymaking, 1945–1992: National Security, Party Politics, and International Status*
258. Richard Belsky, *Localities at the Center: Native Place, Space, and Power in Late Imperial Beijing*
259. Zwia Lipkin, *"Useless to the State": "Social Problems" and Social Engineering in Nationalist Nanjing, 1927–1937*
260. William O. Gardner, *Advertising Tower: Japanese Modernism and Modernity in the 1920s*
261. Stephen Owen, *The Making of Early Chinese Classical Poetry*
262. Martin J. Powers, *Pattern and Person: Ornament, Society, and Self in Classical China*
263. Anna M. Shields, *Crafting a Collection: The Cultural Contexts and Poetic Practice of the* Huajian ji 花間集 *(Collection from among the Flowers)*
264. Stephen Owen, *The Late Tang: Chinese Poetry of the Mid-Ninth Century (827–860)*
265. Sara L. Friedman, *Intimate Politics: Marriage, the Market, and State Power in Southeastern China*
266. Patricia Buckley Ebrey and Maggie Bickford, *Emperor Huizong and Late Northern Song China: The Politics of Culture and the Culture of Politics*
267. Sophie Volpp, *Worldly Stage: Theatricality in Seventeenth-Century China*

268. Ellen Widmer, *The Beauty and the Book: Women and Fiction in Nineteenth-Century China*
269. Steven B. Miles, *The Sea of Learning: Mobility and Identity in Nineteenth-Century Guangzhou*
270. Man-houng Lin, *China Upside Down: Currency, Society, and Ideologies, 1808–1856*
271. Ronald Egan, *The Problem of Beauty: Aesthetic Thought and Pursuits in Northern Song Dynasty China*
272. Mark Halperin, *Out of the Cloister: Literati Perspectives on Buddhism in Sung China, 960–1279*
273. Helen Dunstan, *State or Merchant? Political Economy and Political Process in 1740s China*
274. Sabina Knight, *The Heart of Time: Moral Agency in Twentieth-Century Chinese Fiction*
275. Timothy J. Van Compernolle, *The Uses of Memory: The Critique of Modernity in the Fiction of Higuchi Ichiyō*
276. Paul Rouzer, *A New Practical Primer of Literary Chinese*
277. Jonathan Zwicker, *Practices of the Sentimental Imagination: Melodrama, the Novel, and the Social Imaginary in Nineteenth-Century Japan*
278. Franziska Seraphim, *War Memory and Social Politics in Japan, 1945–2005*
280. Cynthia J. Brokaw, *Commerce in Culture: The Sibao Book Trade in the Qing and Republican Periods*
281. Eugene Y. Park, *Between Dreams and Reality: The Military Examination in Late Chosŏn Korea, 1600–1894*
282. Nam-lin Hur, *Death and Social Order in Tokugawa Japan: Buddhism, Anti-Christianity, and the* Danka *System*
283. Patricia M. Thornton, *Disciplining the State: Virtue, Violence, and State-Making in Modern China*
284. Vincent Goossaert, *The Taoists of Peking, 1800–1949: A Social History of Urban Clerics*
286. Charo B. D'Etcheverry, *Love after* The Tale of Genji*: Rewriting the World of the Shining Prince*
287. Michael G. Chang, *A Court on Horseback: Imperial Touring & the Construction of Qing Rule, 1680–1785*
288. Carol Richmond Tsang, *War and Faith:* Ikkō Ikki *in Late Muromachi Japan*
289. Hilde De Weerdt, *Competition over Content: Negotiating Standards for the Civil Service Examinations in Imperial China (1127–1279)*
290. Eve Zimmerman, *Out of the Alleyway: Nakagami Kenji and the Poetics of Outcaste Fiction*
291. Robert Culp, *Articulating Citizenship: Civic Education and Student Politics in Southeastern China, 1912–1940*
292. Richard J. Smethurst, *From Foot Soldier to Finance Minister: Takahashi Korekiyo, Japan's Keynes*
293. John E. Herman, *Amid the Clouds and Mist: China's Colonization of Guizhou, 1200–1700*

294. Tomoko Shiroyama, *China during the Great Depression: Market, State, and the World Economy, 1929–1937*
295. Kirk W. Larsen, *Tradition, Treaties, and Trade: Qing Imperialism and Chosŏn Korea, 1850–1910*
296. Gregory Golley, *When Our Eyes No Longer See: Realism, Science, and Ecology in Japanese Literary Modernism*
297. Barbara Ambros, *Emplacing a Pilgrimage: The Ōyama Cult and Regional Religion in Early Modern Japan*
298. Rebecca Suter, *The Japanization of Modernity: Murakami Haruki between Japan and the United States*
299. Yuma Totani, *The Tokyo War Crimes Trial: The Pursuit of Justice in the Wake of World War II*
301. David M. Robinson, ed., *Culture, Courtiers, and Competition: The Ming Court (1368–1644)*
302. Calvin Chen, *Some Assembly Required: Work, Community, and Politics in China's Rural Enterprises*
303. Sem Vermeersch, *The Power of the Buddhas: The Politics of Buddhism During the Koryŏ Dynasty* (918–1392)
304. Tina Lu, *Accidental Incest, Filial Cannibalism, and Other Peculiar Encounters in Late Imperial Chinese Literature*
305. Chang Woei Ong, *Men of Letters Within the Passes: Guanzhong Literati in Chinese History, 907–1911*
306. Wendy Swartz, *Reading Tao Yuanming: Shifting Paradigms of Historical Reception (427–1900)*
307. Peter K. Bol, *Neo-Confucianism in History*
308. Carlos Rojas, *The Naked Gaze: Reflections on Chinese Modernity*
309. Kelly H. Chong, *Deliverance and Submission: Evangelical Women and the Negotiation of Patriarchy in South Korea*
310. Rachel DiNitto, *Uchida Hyakken: A Critique of Modernity and Militarism in Prewar Japan*
311. Jeffrey Snyder-Reinke, *Dry Spells: State Rainmaking and Local Governance in Late Imperial China*
312. Jay Dautcher, *Down a Narrow Road: Identity and Masculinity in a Uyghur Community in Xinjiang China*
313. Xun Liu, *Daoist Modern: Innovation, Lay Practice, and the Community of Inner Alchemy in Republican Shanghai*
314. Jacob Eyferth, *Eating Rice from Bamboo Roots: The Social History of a Community of Handicraft Papermakers in Rural Sichuan, 1920–2000*
315. David Johnson, *Spectacle and Sacrifice: The Ritual Foundations of Village Life in North China*
316. James Robson, *Power of Place: The Religious Landscape of the Southern Sacred Peak (Nanyue* 南嶽*) in Medieval China*
317. Lori Watt, *When Empire Comes Home: Repatriation and Reintegration in Postwar Japan*
318. James Dorsey, *Critical Aesthetics: Kobayashi Hideo, Modernity, and Wartime Japan*

319. Christopher Bolton, *Sublime Voices: The Fictional Science and Scientific Fiction of Abe Kōbō*
320. Si-yen Fei, *Negotiating Urban Space: Urbanization and Late Ming Nanjing*
321. Christopher Gerteis, *Gender Struggles: Wage-Earning Women and Male-Dominated Unions in Postwar Japan*
322. Rebecca Nedostup, *Superstitious Regimes: Religion and the Politics of Chinese Modernity*
323. Lucien Bianco, *Wretched Rebels: Rural Disturbances on the Eve of the Chinese Revolution*
324. Cathryn H. Clayton, *Sovereignty at the Edge: Macau and the Question of Chineseness*
325. Micah S. Muscolino, *Fishing Wars and Environmental Change in Late Imperial and Modern China*
326. Robert I. Hellyer, *Defining Engagement: Japan and Global Contexts, 1750–1868*
327. Robert Ashmore, *The Transport of Reading: Text and Understanding in the World of Tao Qian (365–427)*
328. Mark A. Jones, *Children as Treasures: Childhood and the Middle Class in Early Twentieth Century Japan*
329. Miryam Sas, *Experimental Arts in Postwar Japan: Moments of Encounter, Engagement, and Imagined Return*
330. H. Mack Horton, *Traversing the Frontier: The* Man'yōshū *Account of a Japanese Mission to Silla in 736–737*
331. Dennis J. Frost, *Seeing Stars: Sports Celebrity, Identity, and Body Culture in Modern Japan*
332. Marnie S. Anderson, *A Place in Public: Women's Rights in Meiji Japan*
333. Peter Mauch, *Sailor Diplomat: Nomura Kichisaburō and the Japanese-American War*
334. Ethan Isaac Segal, *Coins, Trade, and the State: Economic Growth in Early Medieval Japan*
335. David B. Lurie, *Realms of Literacy: Early Japan and the History of Writing*
336. Lillian Lan-ying Tseng, *Picturing Heaven in Early China*
337. Jun Uchida, *Brokers of Empire: Japanese Settler Colonialism in Korea, 1876–1945*
338. Patricia L. Maclachlan, *The People's Post Office: The History and Politics of the Japanese Postal System, 1871–2010*
339. Michael Schiltz, *The Money Doctors from Japan: Finance, Imperialism, and the Building of the Yen Bloc, 1895–1937*
340. Daqing Yang, Jie Liu, Hiroshi Mitani, and Andrew Gordon, eds., *Toward a History beyond Borders: Contentious Issues in Sino-Japanese Relations*
341. Sonia Ryang, *Reading North Korea: An Ethnological Inquiry*
342. Shih-shan Susan Huang, *Picturing the True Form: Daoist Visual Culture in Traditional China*
343. Barbara Mittler, *A Continuous Revolution: Making Sense of Cultural Revolution Culture*
344. Hwansoo Ilmee Kim, *Empire of the Dharma: Korean and Japanese Buddhism, 1877–1912*
345. Satoru Saito, *Detective Fiction and the Rise of the Japanese Novel, 1880–1930*
346. Jung-Sun N. Han, *An Imperial Path to Modernity: Yoshino Sakuzō and a New Liberal Order in East Asia, 1905–1937*

347. Atsuko Hirai, *Government by Mourning: Death and Political Integration in Japan, 1603–1912*
348. Darryl E. Flaherty, *Public Law, Private Practice: Politics, Profit, and the Legal Profession in Nineteenth-Century Japan*
349. Jeffrey Paul Bayliss, *On the Margins of Empire: Buraku and Korean Identity in Prewar and Wartime Japan*
350. Barry Eichengreen, Dwight H. Perkins, and Kwanho Shin, *From Miracle to Maturity: The Growth of the Korean Economy*
351. Michel Mohr, *Buddhism, Unitarianism, and the Meiji Competition for Universality*
352. J. Keith Vincent, *Two-Timing Modernity: Homosocial Narrative in Modern Japanese Fiction*
354. Chong-Bum An and Barry Bosworth, *Income Inequality in Korea: An Analysis of Trends, Causes, and Answers*
355. Jamie L. Newhard, *Knowing the Amorous Man: A History of Scholarship on* Tales of Ise
356. Sho Konishi, *Anarchist Modernity: Cooperatism and Japanese-Russian Intellectual Relations in Modern Japan*
357. Christopher P. Hanscom, *The Real Modern: Literary Modernism and the Crisis of Representation in Colonial Korea*
358. Michael Wert, *Meiji Restoration Losers: Memory and Tokugawa Supporters in Modern Japan*
359. Garret P. S. Olberding, ed., *Facing the Monarch: Modes of Advice in the Early Chinese Court*
360. Xiaojue Wang, *Modernity with a Cold War Face: Reimagining the Nation in Chinese Literature Across the 1949 Divide*
361. David Spafford, *A Sense of Place: The Political Landscape in Late Medieval Japan*
362. Jongryn Mo and Barry Weingast, *Korean Political and Economic Development: Crisis, Security, and Economic Rebalancing*
363. Melek Ortabasi, *The Undiscovered Country: Text, Translation, and Modernity in the Work of Yanagita Kunio*
364. Hiraku Shimoda, *Lost and Found: Recovering Regional Identity in Imperial Japan*
365. Trent E. Maxey, *The "Greatest Problem": Religion and State Formation in Meiji Japan*
366. Gina Cogan, *The Princess Nun: Bunchi, Buddhist Reform, and Gender in Early Edo Japan*
367. Eric C. Han, *Rise of a Japanese Chinatown: Yokohama, 1894–1972*
368. Natasha Heller, *Illusory Abiding: The Cultural Construction of the Chan Monk Zhongfeng Mingben*
369. Paize Keulemans, *Sound Rising from the Paper: Nineteenth-Century Martial Arts Fiction and the Chinese Acoustic Imagination*
370. Simon James Bytheway, *Investing Japan: Foreign Capital, Monetary Standards, and Economic Development, 1859–2011*
371. Sukhee Lee, *Negotiated Power: The State, Elites, and Local Governance in Twelfth-Fourteenth China*

372. Foong Ping, *The Efficacious Landscape: On the Authorities of Painting at the Northern Song Court*
373. Catherine L. Phipps, *Empires on the Waterfront: Japan's Ports and Power, 1858–1899*
374. Sunyoung Park, *The Proletarian Wave: Literature and Leftist Culture in Colonial Korea, 1910–1945*
375. Barry Eichengreen, Wonhyuk Lim, Yung Chul Park, and Dwight H. Perkins, *The Korean Economy: From a Miraculous Past to a Sustainable Future*
376. Heather Blair, *Real and Imagined: The Peak of Gold in Heian Japan*
377. Emer O'Dwyer, *Significant Soil: Settler Colonialism and Japan's Urban Empire in Manchuria*
378. Martina Deuchler, *Under the Ancestors' Eyes: Kinship, Status, and Locality in Premodern Korea*
379. Joseph R. Dennis, *Writing, Publishing, and Reading Local Gazetteers in Imperial China, 1100–1700*
380. Catherine Vance Yeh, *The Chinese Political Novel: Migration of a World Genre*
381. Noell Wilson, *Defensive Positions: The Politics of Maritime Security in Tokugawa Japan*
382. Miri Nakamura, *Monstrous Bodies: The Rise of the Uncanny in Modern Japan*
383. Nara Dillon, *Radical Inequalities: China's Revolutionary Welfare State in Comparative Perspective*
384. Ma Zhao, *Runaway Wives, Urban Crimes, and Survival Tactics in Wartime Beijing, 1937-1949*
385. Mingwei Song, *Young China: National Rejuvenation and the* Bildungsroman, *1900-1959*
386. Christopher Bondy, *Voice, Silence, and Self: Negotiations of Buraku Identity in Contemporary Japan*
387. Seth Jacobowitz, *Writing Technology in Meiji Japan: A Media History of Modern Japanese Literature and Visual Culture*
388. Hilde De Weerdt, *Information, Territory, and Networks: The Crisis and Maintenance of Empire in Song China*
389. Elizabeth Kindall, *Geo-Narratives of a Filial Son: The Paintings and Travel Diaries of Huang Xiangjian (1609–1673)*
390. Matthew Fraleigh, *Plucking Chrysanthemums: Narushima Ryūhoku and Sinitic Literary Traditions in Modern Japan*
391. Hu Ying, *Burying Autumn: Poetry, Friendship, and Loss*
392. Mark E. Byington, *The Ancient State of Puyŏ in Northeast Asia: Archaeology and Historical Memory*
393. Timothy J. Van Compernolle, *Struggling Upward: Worldly Success and the Japanese Novel*
394. Heekyoung Cho, *Translation's Forgotten History: Russian Literature, Japanese Mediation, and the Formation of Modern Korean Literature*
395. Terry Kawashima, *Itineraries of Power: Texts and Traversals in Heian and Medieval Japan*
396. Anna Andreeva, *Assembling Shinto: Buddhist Approaches to Kami Worship in Medieval Japan*